TURN AROUND AND TAKE A BOW!

MY MUSICAL LIFE

TURN AROUND AND TAKE A BOW!

MY MUSICAL LIFE

Mike Dixon

Matador
Unit E2 Airfield Business Park,
Harrison Road, Market Harborough,
Leicestershire. LE16 7UL
Tel: 0116 2792299
Email: books@troubador.co.uk
Web: www.troubador.co.uk/matador
Twitter: @matadorbooks

PAPERBACK ISBN 978 1803132 495
HARDBACK ISBN 978 1803132 501

British Library Cataloguing in Publication Data.
A catalogue record for this book is available from the British Library.

Printed and bound by CPI Group (UK) Ltd, Croydon, CR0 4YY
Typeset in 11pt Minion Pro by Troubador Publishing Ltd, Leicester, UK

Matador is an imprint of Troubador Publishing Ltd

For Natalie, Lillie and Meg

Mike has conducted Royal Variety Performances, concerts with major stars including Dame Shirley Bassey, Sir Tom Jones, Lionel Richie and Queen, recording sessions at Abbey Road Studios, many West End Musicals and worked closely with Lord Lloyd-Webber, Leslie Bricusse, Tim Rice and Don Black.

This is his story.

A little peek behind the scenes, before the curtain opens, into the world of entertainment from a unique, hands-on perspective.

Thank you Colin Edmonds, David Sutcliffe and Patricia Turnbull for helping in the process of proofreading and tidying my writing. I am deeply indebted.

Cover photograph by Tom Sandars.

Anthony Cherry – you are a legend. End of!

CONTENTS

FOREWORD

by Anthony Cherry

Dear Reader,

What you hold in your hand is a remarkable book. Mike's career is not only a fascinating personal journey, but also a unique snapshot of one of the most creative and exciting periods of musical theatre, and concert music history, there's ever been.

Over many a long lunch, or rehearsal, or performance, I have urged Mike to write down his memories of working at the forefront of this industry. His book is by turns fascinating, instructive, funny, moving and awe inspiring. If you are interested in the way musical theatre works, or are a performer, or musician or conductor – or if you have just spent many happy hours listening, watching and applauding – this book is for you.

Allow me one memory of my own to show you Mike Dixon. In 2010 I produced a celebration of the music of Elvis Presley in London's Hyde Park, called *Elvis Forever*. The headliner was Tom

Jones, the cast included KT Tunstall, Michael Ball, Craig David, Tony Christie, Suzy Quattro, Mica Paris and more. Priscilla Presley came over to make a special appearance. Chris Evans presented and perhaps best of all, Elvis's own rhythm section, the TCB band, came to be the driving motor of the sixty piece BBC Concert Orchestra. As a finale, I had cheekily announced that Elvis himself would sing in Hyde Park! And he would, via the footage of his Las Vegas concert, and with our musicians playing with him live.

Technically, to pull this off, the rhythm section and the conductor all wear headphones to be able to hear a 'click track', keeping them in time with Elvis, and allowing Mike to keep the entire orchestra together with the vocal track too. Priscilla Presley had introduced Sir Tom Jones and after three amazing songs he left the stage to thunderous applause. Chris Evans strode onto the stage excitedly, "Thank you Priscilla! Thank you Tom! ... How can you top that!? ... There's only one way ... There's only one star ... We promised you he would sing in Hyde Park and he will ... Ladies and Gentlemen – ELVIS PRESLEY!" With the crowd frankly going bonkers, Mike cued the 'click track' to begin.

As the fans roared out and Elvis began to roll on the big screens the 'click track' – CUT .... Nothing! Elvis' drummer Ronnie Tutt pushed off his headphones. Keyboardist Glen Hardin, bass player Jerry Scheff and the legendary guitar player James Burton followed suit. Everyone looked to Mike, who instantaneously ripped out his earphones, while still watching the screen and raising his right hand. A split second later, gathering the orchestra with his left arm and watching Elvis breathe in, Mike gave the downbeat. The orchestra blasted out the opening fanfare, Elvis sang, "When no one else can understand me, when everything I do is wrong ..." and somehow, the tempo held, somehow Mike pulled the orchestra, backing singers, TCB band and 30,000 people together.

Perhaps I don't need to tell you how passionately we sang, "The Wonder of You". Perhaps you can imagine the lumps in the throat, the full hearts, the rolling tears. Perhaps you were there? What's certain is that in those moments we also saw all of Mike's years of experience, his musicianship, his craft, his personality and leadership. You'll learn more about all of that in the book you hold.

That's the wonder of you, Mike.

PROLOGUE

"We will sing hymn number one hundred and forty-seven – again!"

The booming voice of Doctor J. L. Cresswell, Headmaster of Devonport High School for Boys, echoed around the cavernous school hall while he hawkishly glared down at me. The reason he yelled was that six hundred eleven to eighteen year old boys had just laughed very loudly at the end of my somewhat risqué jazz arrangement of the last verse of *Morning has Broken*.

It was 1972, I was fifteen, playing piano for school assembly and, though the Cat Stevens version was all the rage, I had decided to play my own arrangement which involved a key change into the last verse littered with as many crunchy jazz chords as I could muster and the grand finale was a whole tone scale in octaves followed by a huge jazz chord flurry. There was a moment's silence and then the school erupted.

Hence the above instruction from 'Doc'...

What was I to do? Obviously I would have to play the hymn again but would I kowtow and play safe? I toyed with safety while I was playing the first two verses but as that final verse loomed I felt that I had no option but to play what I had written especially for that assembly.

So I did indeed play my last verse plus the ending! I was shaking as I played the key change then the jazz arrangement and finally the ending jazz flurry.

This time dead silence from the school, not a murmur, such was the fear that our Head instilled in all of us. What this did for me, though, was to raise my status in the school into the stratosphere. I became a hero instead of that strange sissy kid who does musical stuff. I was now the boy who stood up to 'Doc Cresswell'. I was suddenly 'cool' and it was my musical ability that had enabled me to get there.

My Music Teacher at Devonport High was Trefor Farrow. He was the epitome of 'cool' in desert boots and corduroy trousers. I think I saw him behind the Headmaster smirking, proudly…

ONE

LEARNING THE
RUDIMENTS

Plymouth in 1957 was very much a city still licking its wounds from the devastation wrought by the 1940/41 blitz. The reconstruction of the city centre – *A Plan for Plymouth* – masterminded by Sir Patrick Abercrombie, was well underway and yet outside that hallowed central area progress was pitifully slow. There were craters where houses had been near our flat in North Road and even in and around Ocean Street when we moved there in October 1958.

However, in North Road we were near the main Plymouth Railway Station and as a baby, sitting in my highchair, I loved watching the steam trains outside the rear window. We overlooked the turntable and I was transfixed. It must have been a great respite for my dear mum, Jean. The train drivers would wave and I was smitten by all the excitement, steam, noise and the smuts. I was, by all accounts, a happy, smiley and friendly child who constantly tried to engage people in conversation as soon as I was able. Very gregarious and full of bubbling energy.

My father, Tom, was working for Farleys Rusks when I was born in January 1957, having spent some time as a bus conductor after the war. When he was working at Farleys he became the Union Representative, effectively the Shop Steward, I suppose. During his tenure he managed to keep peace between management and workforce and all potential strikes were nipped in the bud very quickly because he had such inherent diplomacy skills and an all encompassing sense of right and wrong. I think those particular genes made their way to me, too, and they have served me well.

He spent most of his war years in the Middle East and told me stories about his motorcycle training for the Military Police in the desert that made me wince. Learning how to fall off the bike at 50mph. Heroic stuff.

Then at the end of the war he was a batman for some bigwig generals, the result of which was that there was no-one who could iron shirts, polish boots and generally keep things

1955 Mum & Dad's Wedding

spick and span better than him. After the war he became a bus conductor and had his head turned by a beautiful girl from St Budeaux called Jean Hellyer. Their romance blossomed and in 1955 they were wed.

Dad gave up smoking when I was born – apparently before that he would leave half smoked cigarettes in ash trays around the flat. Of course, I have no recollection of him smoking but unfortunately I followed in his footsteps and smoked myself. More of that later.

Dad had three siblings. Older brother, Fred and two younger sisters, Louie and Betty. They lived in Beaumont Road, in a council house that overlooked the River Plym and Laira rail depot. Dad returned from the war in 1947 and got home to find his mother very ill. Fred returned from his war in Burma a while later and once Mary knew her two boys were safe and sound she was able to gently slide away, she gave up her fight and basically had a stroke and died. Dad's father, Alfred, had worked in Dublin early in the 1920s firstly as a prison officer and then later as a bus conductor. He had met Mary Ellen Murphy whilst on the buses and they married in 1921 and moved back to his home, Plymouth. Fred, Tom and Louie were born in quick succession and they all went back to Dublin where Alfred again worked on the buses.

They lived in Clontarf, on the outskirts and somehow Alfred found out that an informant had passed on to the IRA that he had been a prison officer and that therefore he was on their hit-list. He came home and told Mary Ellen that he had to get out of the country right away. Mary Ellen took Fred and Louie to the docks and then onward to Plymouth. Alfred took Tom, who was not a well child, suffering from convulsions at this time, to the docks.

Alfred couldn't get on the ferry at that point and, because he was being followed and he feared for young Tom's safety, he asked an old lady beside the ferry entrance to look after Tom for a short while whilst he lost the people 'tailing' him. Alfred went careering off through and over the dock sheds and somehow managed to dodge them. There were shots fired but no-one was hurt and, in major haste, Alfred got back to the dock and the old lady, grabbed toddler Tom and jumped onto the boat as it was leaving.

They all arrived safely in Plymouth and the story of the 'little old lady' on the docks has become a little bit of Dixon folklore.

Jean had wanted to be a teacher. She was bright and got into Stoke Damerel High School for girls where she thrived and blossomed. Her father, a strict authoritarian who liked using 'the belt', had a son and a set of twins with a first wife who sadly died in childbirth. He then married Gwendoline and together they had two daughters. Jean in 1933 and Doris in 1935. The children from his first marriage were orphaned out. It was not unusual at this time – to us it seems horrific – but then it was almost normal. Jean didn't know about her half brother and sisters until she was ten. Harry, Kay and Ethel.

Harry played upright bass in a jazz band and by the time I knew him he was writing articles for Gramophone magazine and books all about Stereo Sound – he also helped to pay for my piano lessons. I rather liked his choice of cars. From a *Humber Super Snipe* to a *Riley 4/Sixty-Eight* with an *Austin A30* van in between, but the great thing about that *Super Snipe* was that you could hide away in the footwells in the back, the car was huge, especially if you were around 4 or 5! When Harry died in 1974 it was such a tragedy and far too soon and I always owe him a great debt of gratitude for helping me so early on. I would have loved to have had him as guest of honour at one of my concerts.

Once Jean knew about her step siblings she made sure that they stayed in her life and her loyalty and commitment to family has continued through the generations. Family would regularly come and stay. Uncle Harry with wife Megan and children Jane and Paul, then another time just with Jane and her boyfriend David, or Mum's Auntie Louie and family, then cousin Martin and new wife. You get the picture – somehow Mum and Dad would fit everyone in to be able to stay at 29, Ocean Street. It was as if we were living in a Tardis at times! Much later, in the early noughties, a mysterious new cousin called Sylvia found Mum and Dad. She was the daughter of Mum's half sister, Kay, and had been adopted. After her adoptive parents died Sylvia wanted to trace her birth mother. The search eventually led Sylvia to 'new' Auntie Jean and Uncle Tom and consequently Sylvia and her husband Steve were welcomed with wide open arms and even wider open hearts. That was a direct result of the loyalty and commitment to family that was embedded in Mum's DNA.

*

1958 Mum, Dad & Me

Mummy Jean and Daddy Tom – I called them as a toddler. Those early years went by quite simply and peacefully. I was happy and content with a loving and strong family around me. My sister Jackie arrived when I was four and a half and I was particularly pleased because she made her entrance into the world along with a red tractor that was just for me. What a lucky boy!

Various relations had pianos in their houses and I always found myself drawn to these extraordinary looking pieces of furniture with amazing white and black bits that I could just about reach and guess what? Those white and black bits made mesmerising sounds when you did manage to reach up and touch them. I loved making a noise and found that I could make up little tunes – well at least I thought they were tunes, anyway.

In Ocean Street the walls outside the two-up, three-down terraced houses were a perfect height for taking your Matchbox or Corgi cars out for a spin. The iron railings had long since been taken away for use in the war effort leaving bare granite. The gaps for house entrances meant that lots of incredible jumps had to be made with the toy cars. Some didn't survive… I tended to look after my things and I do still have a collection of some of those old toys, miraculously, including my original Corgi James Bond Aston Martin DB5! I don't think that one was ever taken outside. That was when my appreciation of and fascination with cars started. I think that if you had asked me around this time, "What do you want to be when you grow up?" I would have said without hesitation, "A racing driver!" I loved my toy cars so much.

That fascination with cars has stayed and I am the proud owner of an Alfa Romeo Spider, now twenty years old, and I am also a member of Goodwood Road Racing Club and the Goodwood Supporters Association and I rank my yearly visits to both the Goodwood Revival and the Members' Meeting as halcyon days each year and, yes, I do dress up for the Revival.

Uncle Fred (Dad's elder brother) lived with his wife Pat and their family fairly close by in Renown Street before moving to nearby Wolseley Road. Their children Sue and Andy were ten and eight years older than me but Elaine, Neil and Les were much closer in age and there was one occasion when I got into a little trouble with them. They were on one of their *Swallows and Amazons* type expeditions around and about and I was out the front of the house playing, I was around four. You could play just outside the house back in 1961. I joined in with them and thought that just looking in through the front porch and whispering that I was going on an adventure was enough to let Mum know. We went over the main road at the bottom of Ocean Street and

1960 The Dixons

into the wilds of Camels Head, where it felt like we were in a phantasmagorical forest, and continued on to the footpath that ran beside the railway over the creek, Shaky Bridge. Hugely exciting, especially when the train to Cornwall was wheezing its way over and the bridge was literally shaking, but all the time I had this nagging feeling that being this far from home wasn't quite right. Eventually I plucked up enough courage to say that I really thought I should go back and reluctantly they walked back with me and deposited me outside the house. As you can imagine Mum was beside herself with worry and not best pleased and I learnt pretty swiftly that running off without *really* letting her know was not a good idea and further adventures were somewhat curtailed.

Mum and Dad had missed their footing on the ladder of buying their own property because Dad's wages from Farleys were just under the threshold needed, so the house in Ocean Street was privately rented. I grew up with a bath in the kitchen and an outside loo. Oh, the glories of a privy outside and with no heating in mid winter! It wasn't until I was eighteen and about to go to Music College that a proper bathroom and inside loo were installed. Whatever you grow up with seems normal to you, doesn't it, so truthfully it was entirely fine and we got on with it. Saturday, early evening, was filling in the football results on Dad's Pools sheet followed by *Doctor Who*, then bath night and the fablon coated work surface beside the kitchen sink was lifted up and the bath filled. The heady days of a daily shower were a long way off!

On walks out with mum I was, apparently, quite a gregarious child greeting everyone on the way to the shops and asking how they were. The Corner Shop ruled and on each of the streets that made up our area of Keyham – Ocean Street, Renown

Street, Victory Street, Fleet Street and Admiralty Street – were a plethora of shops. Mostly grocery stores but there were two butchers, Mr Meager and Mr Dyer, a Post Office, newsagent, hairdressers, hardware store and even a haberdashery! Fifty yards up the road from our house was Mrs Rogers' shop where I was able to get a Lucky Bag of random sweets for three old pence or 3d. Further up the road was Petherbridge's where mum would get most of her groceries and you could buy biscuits by weight and take them home in a brown paper bag which Mr Petherbridge would twizzle to close – and make quite a show of it, too.

As well as all the shops there were churches: an Anglican Church – St Thomas the Apostle between the top of Ocean Street and Renown Street – a Roman Catholic Church, primary school and convent – Church of the Holy Redeemer which was just up the road from where we lived – and a Methodist church – Keyham Methodist Church – on Admiralty Street. Mum and Dad were members of St Thomas's and Dad became a sidesman and eventually a Church Warden.

Dad's predecessor as Church Warden was a kindly older man called Mr George Burnard who lived with his wife just down the road from the front door of the church in Renown Street. As a child I was fascinated by his collection of photographs of old Plymouth before and after the Second World War and in particular the photographs that showed the creation of Royal Parade in the rubble left by the blitz. Abercrombie's plan in the making.

Sunday morning was up and at 'em to get to the nine o'clock service with all the exciting bells and smells that a 'high church'/anglo-catholic service could muster. There was a sense of 'theatre' in the service, with the Servers and the Vicar dressed up in their cassocks and surplices and all the paraphernalia of the smoking thurible with the incense. There was also at the back of the church an organ gallery which intrigued me and I loved the sound that that wonderful instrument made but with no idea how!

Anything musical seemed to hold a fascination over me and I was soon to find out that music would permeate every part of my life in extraordinary ways.

TWO

TIME FOR SCHOOL

Mr Parish was the captivating and rather charismatic headmaster of Drake Primary School. A wiry haired man who played classical music records as we entered the hall for school assembly. One of the recurring pieces was *The Hebrides Overture* by Mendelssohn, such an evocative piece and so full of the sound of the sea. It captivated me and remains one of my favourite pieces, so much so that in 2003 I jumped at the chance of conducting it when asked if there was something I would like to include in a *Friday Night Is Music Night* for BBC Radio 2. That was a long way off from my time at Drake Primary, though.

As well as enjoying singing in the choir at age six I was presented with the opportunity to play the recorder. For most of my friends it was very much a trial – and for their parents – but I loved the instrument. I even seemed to make sense of the basic rudiments of musical notation and lapped up all that was presented to me. The red book entitled *The School Recorder Book*

1 was delved into and the green *Book 2* as well, and it did seem to come very naturally to me without much tension and angst.

I actually can't remember learning to read music, I suppose because it was at the same time as I was learning to read and write English. We don't remember that process, do we? It just *happens.* Well, all those musical hieroglyphs became very much second nature to me and it wasn't long before I was asked to play the occasional solo in school concerts and assemblies.

Mr Parish one day, quietly, asked me if we had a piano. I replied that we didn't and he then proceeded to tell me that he had decided to replace his old piano at home. He said that he would make a little competition at school to see if anyone really merited having it. He also said that I shouldn't worry as it would most probably be me who won. Essentially dear Mr Parish was telling me that he was going to GIVE me a piano – extraordinary! The 'competition' was writing an essay, five of us entered, and by some 'miracle' I won and I was given said piano. Mum and Dad were thrilled on my behalf and after a month it was delivered to our house and I took possession of it.

It sat quite well in the dining room that was now my bedroom as I had grown out of sharing upstairs with my sister Jackie, and piano lessons were booked with Mrs Mitchell, a rather stern short lady with a hump, who lived down the road from us. The lessons were 2/6d (12 ½p) a week and Mrs Mitchell had a rather annoying habit of rapping my knuckles with a ruler if I got things wrong.

As I write this I am reminded of the musty smell in her piano room – anyone who has an old piano will know the smell I am talking about – and there was some old drapery hanging from the top of the piano down to the music stand that seemed to focus the smell when you sat at the keyboard. Not the most convivial of environments but somehow I persevered. *Jibbidy-F and A-C-E* and *Sugar and Spice* were the starter books, closely followed by a simple book of the songs in *The Sound Of Music*. Only after that could I move onto something more classical – so Beethoven's *Moonlight Sonata* came next. Quite a juxtaposition of music really, more shades of the eclectic mix of music that was to come my way in later life!

Practice was always a problem. Mrs Mitchell would mark where I was supposed to reach each week and most of the time I would ignore that and either just 'play' at home (improvise or pick out music by ear) or sight read hymn books, instead of doing my homework. Basically, I seemed to be able to give her the impression that I had practiced when really I had spent my time at the piano exploring and, I suppose, developing other musical skills that would come in handy later on, in other words I 'got away with it'. Sometimes it didn't work, though, and my attempts at pretending that I had practiced rather backfired and I would be duly reprimanded, though the aforementioned ruler on the knuckles was not very nice. I am vividly reminded of those misdemeanours and find myself cringing at the memory when I hear *The Sound of Music* sometimes. Gradually, however, the piano became my ally and I found myself spending hours playing and exploring, losing myself in music and lapping up all the sonic possibilities that my straight strung Hocking piano could muster.

We didn't have a record player at Ocean Street until I received one on my tenth birthday so the wonders of LPs and 78s were limited to visits to my grandparents, where they had a radiogram, and my Auntie Doris and Uncle John, where they had a rather fancy record player that could stack LPs. The radiogram at Mum's parents house was an extraordinary bit of furniture that seemed magical to my eyes and ears. It was a VHF wireless (radio) as well as a record player so sometimes I heard reruns of *The Goon Show*, which sparked all sorts of attempts at impersonating *Bluebottle* or *Eccles*, or I listened to *Sparky's Magic Piano* or *Bimbo, Bimbo, Where You Gonna Go-ye-o* by Jim Reeves, both of which I practically knew by heart.

If I was at Auntie Doris's house then the LPs that were played, you could say, piqued my interest in Musical Theatre and probably were responsible for that part of my career subsequently. I would listen to *Salad Days* by Julian Slade or *South Pacific*, with Richard Rogers' soaring, brilliant and evocative score, dancing around the living room transported to magical places like *Bali Hai* and when the flying saucer appeared in *Salad Days* I would dash around like a whirling dervish! We would always spend Christmas Day with them, and after my cousins, Julie and Angela, were born another abiding memory is, each year, all of us glued to the TV watching the *Morecambe and Wise Christmas Special*. There was generally a competition to see whether Jean or Doris would laugh themselves to tears first! Ultimately I think it was a draw…

*

Drake Primary School was built in the late 1950s and is a three story utilitarian design, big windows, with three class rooms per floor. There were two playgrounds on two levels, one for the juniors and one for the infants. Adjacent to the junior playground was the School Hall and in between the hall and the main school building was a corridor with cloakrooms, the dinner hall and a couple of infant classrooms. It was a pretty straightforward walk to school through Ocean Street to Admiralty Street – there were criss-cross joining roads on each third of all the streets – and then a walk over the pedestrian bridge above the train line, down to Keyham Station and then left either along Saltash Road or along the back lane until you got to Johnston Terrace and the front entrance to the school. The whole walk took about ten minutes, a bit longer on the days that you managed to time walking over the bridge as a train went by!

Most days I would go home for lunch – or dinner as we called it – and get myself back to school for the afternoon. On one fateful day I was wearing a new black school blazer with Drake's Drum as the emblem on the pocket and as I walked over the railway footbridge it started to rain. I really didn't want to get my new blazer wet so I started running the rest of the way. I ran off the bridge and straight over Admiralty Street where I narrowly escaped being run over by a big red number eleven bus – a Leyland Titan PD2, actually – with the driver's cab separate from the body of the vehicle.

The driver screeched to a halt and proceeded to jump out of the cab and run after me. "You stupid boy, wait till I get my hands on you!" he shouted and I felt like I was running for my life. The criss-cross road adjacent to Admiralty Street was in front of me with the back lane just a little up the hill, so I ducked into the lane and hid behind one of the dustbins, holding my breath and hoping upon hope that he wouldn't see me. After a couple of minutes – which seemed like an hour – he turned tail and walked back to his stationary bus, muttering under his breath.

I ran the rest of the way home extra carefully and with tears streaming down my face. How stupid had I been to not look for traffic, it really had been quite a close shave. When I got in Mum was understandably concerned as to why I was crying and I felt that I couldn't possibly tell her the truth so I blurted out that I was upset because I didn't want to get my lovely new blazer wet. This little fib kept bugging me for years and when I was eleven on a walk on holiday in Cornwall I finally plucked up the courage to tell Mum and Dad the truth. Their reaction was, of course, perfect and the guilt that had been sitting with me about the whole story and the lie for five years was gently and soothingly taken away.

The lower playground and I had a rather close encounter when I was six. Running games of 'it' were in and I was hurtling around during morning break when very suddenly my two front teeth and the playground tarmac made very swift contact after I tripped over someone's rather large Clarks' school shoes. It was allegedly an accident, and Mrs Beard my class teacher was in agreement as she 'there, thered' me but I was never really sure. At the time I couldn't tell as I was rushed home and then Mum took me to Freedom Fields Hospital by bus with a rather large gap in my gums and a nasty gash through my top lip where one of my two front milk teeth had tried to make a hasty exit when confronted with the aforementioned playground. A couple of stitches later I was back at school and the aftermath was that I was able to sing *All I Want For Christmas is My Two Front Teeth* for a few years until my adult teeth finally started to appear.

Around this time I had a red scooter and a Batman outfit – including the cape, well mainly the cape, in truth – and my friend Stephen Eke and I enjoyed many hours riding our scooters down the hill from the top of Ocean Street to the bottom. Stephen was a little shorter than me and was the perfect Robin. He was quite good at the '*Holy mackerel, Batman!*' sort of expletives. We were the Caped Crusaders of Keyham for a time, well at least until *The Monkees* came along! Another friend, Helen G, lived fairly close in Renown Street and sometimes we would walk together to school. Helen was my first 'crush' with her blonde pigtails. At this time Drake Primary had made the bold step of installing a swimming pool in the lower playground.

It was a rather Heath Robinson affair, built on top of the playground with four foot prefabricated sides, but it did have some benefits! We would get changed fairly close by, near the stairwell of the main building and one day I suddenly noticed that Helen's towel had ridden up a little too far, well, far enough for me to see the difference between boys and girls, at least. An unexpected part of my education, certainly, and as exciting as the couple of times a year or so later when confronted with the opportunity to '*show you mine, if you show me yours*' with a couple of the other girls in my year. A natural curiosity and a bit of a rite of passage. All very innocent and without threat or fear, just natural inquisitiveness, really.

Although music was the most important thing to me I did also find myself involved in all the plays and end of term shenanigans that went on including, one year, a version of *The Emperor's New Clothes* where I was playing the Emperor. To my horror I was expected to play the part where he is given the invisible clothes, wearing a pair of navy blue tights and nothing else! I can still feel the shame of it, but somehow the little show worked and my embarrassment evaporated quickly as the audience applauded our efforts.

*

There was one blight in those early years which I have since discovered has coloured my life and has left me with a long lasting unpleasant residue. As a very young boy I had really enjoyed going to see Mum's parents, my Grandma and Grandad. The radiogram and its musical delights were so intoxicating and such fun but when I got a little older things started to change. It started when I was ten and old enough to get the twenty seven bus out to Kings Road, Higher St Budeaux all by myself. I would take a Birds Eye Chicken Pie with me for my lunch and to begin with all was well. Grandad had a little sideline in conjuring tricks and was actually rather good, having been a member of the Plymouth Magic Circle for a while.

So I would be encouraged to pop upstairs while the chicken pie was cooking to watch and even to learn some of the tricks. He taught me the disappearing half a crown trick (palming the coin) and a couple of simple card tricks and I was hooked. Unfortunately Grandad also wanted me to play some other games and these I didn't find enticing or interesting in any way whatsoever. Each week, I would find ways to extricate myself from the awful situation and very gradually the 'other' games were phased out.

The most frightening part is that as a ten year old boy you feel helpless, there is a malevolence hanging over you and you feel that not a single person can help you. He actually warned me never to tell anyone, the guilt that was therefore engendered meant that I didn't utter a word of what happened to a living soul until I was eighteen. I wish that I had found the courage to tell Mum and Dad but I couldn't. You see part of the abuser's power over you is making you feel that no-one would believe you and that it is entirely your own fault.

Apart from leaving me with the emotional scars it also left me with quite a lot of sexual confusion some of which I didn't even begin to address until I was in therapy during my forties. When I was working at the Dominion Theatre on *Grease* and *We Will Rock You* I found that I couldn't use the loo on the first floor because the smell of the bleach being used took me right back to being upstairs with him. The damage caused by this kind of abuse is horrendous and permeates all aspects of your life subsequently and I certainly empathise with anyone who has gone through anything similar, you are not alone.

The other disturbing part of this story is that as an adult I talked with some of my younger relations on the Hellyer side of the family and, though I was the only one to be actually abused, they acknowledged that they never liked getting too close to him, that there was something 'creepy' about him and sitting on his lap was to be avoided at all costs.

He died in 1982 and I did visit him in hospital towards the end but I still felt nervous being close to him. I even played the organ for his funeral – perhaps that was a good thing as it meant that I felt I was working, rather than a family member 'grieving'. Although it is hard to feel sorry for him, I do, now, understand that he must have been a sick man and I am mostly sad for him for the hurt and pain he caused. It was a very difficult time and the ramifications of his actions have lasted in one form or another all my life.

*

Meanwhile school life continued apace and somehow I was able to compartmentalise enough to focus on music, school work and fun with my friends. My musical prowess was increasing leaps and bounds and by the time I came up to my Eleven Plus exam Mr Parish suggested that I should look into trying to get into Exeter Cathedral School as my treble singing voice was, in his opinion, good enough.

I had sung various solos in School Christmas Concerts and missed out on singing the first verse of *Once In Royal David's City* only because I had a nasty cold and lost my voice – a major sadness at the time – so becoming a Choral Scholar was an exciting possibility. Sadly the cost was prohibitive, given Mum and Dad's circumstances, so we looked at the other options.

The first was to gain a scholarship into Plymouth College, the local Private school and the second was getting a good enough pass to go to the local Grammar school, Devonport High School for Boys. One of my friends at Drake Primary, Philip Shute, had gone to DHS the previous academic year and peer pressure prevailed – I wanted to go to the school where my pal had gone, nowhere else. I worked hard at the verbal reasoning tests that were the backbone of the Eleven Plus examination in 1968 and I was offered both the scholarship to Plymouth College and a place at DHS. Naturally I chose Devonport High School. Actually, as you will find out, it was probably one of the best decisions of my life because of one extraordinarily talented teacher!

THREE

CHURCH MUSIC, GUITARS & GIRLS

The Organ Loft at St Thomas's Church was a particularly special place. To get to it you had to unlock the secret door in the side porch of the church, climb the stone spiral stairs and then open the wooden latched door. Inside was an ante room that was a treasure trove of faded, old, dog eared organ music, hundreds of hymn books and all the gubbins that made the organ work, the electric bellows and the on/off switch. It was like being in a version of Aladdin's cave, if you were me. Very exciting indeed. It also became a secret place for a few romantic trysts – the art of romance for a teenager! The only other door in the little room took you into the organ loft itself and on your left was the organ console, ahead of you was a mezzanine containing all the pipes and in front of all those pipes were the pews where the occasional choir of St Thomas's sat. To sit at the console and experiment with all the organ stops – attempt to get all the cobwebs of the innards fully blown away – was one of those musical highlights in my young life. It was thrilling to get the organ full throated and raw and to be so close to that sound. That thirteen year old boy felt like he was Keith Emerson playing The Royal Festival Hall organ in *The Three Fates* from the eponymous debut album by *Emerson, Lake and Palmer* which had come out that very year. Even if, in reality, it was only a two manual (Great and Swell) and it had quite a small range of sounds – Diapasons, Flutes, Vox Humana, Cornopean – it did at least have both a 16ft Bourdon and 16ft Diapason in the pedals and 8, 4 and 2ft stops plus a 'mixture' on the Great manual so you could thunder away to your heart's content. More sonic possibilities for me to explore, I was lapping it up.

I had started playing the organ just after joining Devonport High School. It was a terrific addition to my musical development and I started playing occasionally for Sunday services pretty quickly afterwards. Playing for services actually became a very good initial training for being a Musical Director, as it happens, because you have to pay attention to listen for cues and accompany the singing, you also have to quickly learn to extemporise if there is a bit of a hiatus, or extra music is needed at the end of a hymn to cover the fact that the 'collection' is not quite completed. All in all, good experience.

When I had arrived at Devonport High in September 1968 – sparkling, in a brand new uniform, green blazer with long trousers for the first time, and a brown leather attaché case with space for my packed lunch plus the ridiculous school cap – I was placed in form 1w. My neighbour, Tim Thornton, was also wearing long trousers for the first time and he and I forged a friendship on that day that has lasted right up to the present. Tim was the son of the very first Dockyard chaplain who was also the vicar of St Aubyn's church in Devonport and he didn't exactly follow in his father's footsteps as much as completely refashion them, because dear Tim ended up as The Archbishop of Canterbury's right hand man, The Bishop at Lambeth. His dry wit and cheeky smile evident even then on that first day, sitting in class with form teacher John Bowden in front of us.

We were known as 'scruffs', all of us slightly tremulous first year boys. At any time expecting the onslaught of the initiation ceremonies that had been threatened, though I am pleased to say that nothing untoward happened to me! We had to wear the stupid school cap anytime we were in uniform outside the school grounds for the first two years of our time there. As you can imagine, we found as many ways as possible to evade that rule and bulging blazer pockets were hastily emptied and the cap thrown on the head if you saw any sign of a prefect or teacher on the journey to and from school.

Form teacher, Mr Bowden – *JB* as we called him – was a clever, witty man, in his late twenties at this point but he also became somewhat of a support to me when I found out that he was the regular organist at Plymouth's mother church, St Andrew's. He took us for English and he certainly was influential in my love of the language. At the end of my first year his comments on my school report are worth repeating if only to point out that his understanding of the human psyche was pretty spot on: *He is a bright, interesting pupil who suffers from garrulity and an overmastering desire to be the centre of attraction. When he has learnt a greater measure of self-control he will do very well.* I'm not sure I ever did learn that greater measure of self-control…

Trefor Farrow, *Tref*, was the music teacher and it wasn't long before he noticed that I had a good level of proficiency in reading music when we had class singing. I became a member of the choir and soon found that I was being asked to sing alto to bolster up the sound as I could read the part, leaving those less capable to sing treble, which was mostly the tune. It didn't take long before I was asked to join the school Madrigal Group, which I suppose was the inner sanctum of musical talent at the school. That led me, at thirteen, onto my first 'broadcast'…

1970 was a big year in Plymouth, it was the 350th Anniversary of the Pilgrim Fathers setting off to the 'New World' in The Mayflower and there were multifarious events to celebrate the fact. One such event was a Radio 4, 'God Slot' show which was to be broadcast from St Andrew's Church in September, it was called *Soundings by Swann* and featured Donald Swann, of *Flanders and Swann* fame, and Barry Wilsher a well established actor who had played one of the lead roles in an early series of *Doctor Who* called *The Faceless Ones*. Donald Swann was pretty much a household name, everybody knew *The Gas-Man Cometh* and *The Hippopotamus Song,* and with his partner Michael Flanders' erudite, half spoken, half sung style complemented by Swann's reedy tone and brilliantine piano playing, their duets were infamous.

Tref announced to the Madrigal Group one day that we had been asked to be part of that event and that a few of us were to work with a small group of pupils from Devonport High School for Girls, we were to form a little choir and we would perform with Donald Swann. John Bowden, also featured as choral accompanist on the mighty *Rushworth and Dreaper* organ of St Andrew's. As you can imagine there was much excitement, but it was mostly about the fact that we were going to work with a group of girls! In an all boys school the pent up testosterone that sits constantly under the plimsoll line can at any point erupt, so to hear that we were going to work with 'girls' was such a thrilling statement, full of pubescent longing and hope.

Actually, it did end up being a pretty exciting time, we had to rehearse at their school, which happened to be a good three miles away and the four girls chosen were not only talented but also bright and sassy. There were no shenanigans, even though we were hoping for some. Rather, the event itself became the focus and between us all we made a pretty good job of it. I sang my duet, *I Lie Down With God* with John Pope accompanied by Donald Swann and we all sang together with Barry Wilsher narrating, in an original piece especially composed by Mr Swann called *The Story Of Bontzye Schweig*. Tref, who had coached us all and was essentially Musical Director of the event, was very pleased with us and it certainly gave me a taste of professional musical life. Donald Swann was very gracious, supportive and complementary to us all and a real delight to work with.

In fact, in 1985 I had the chance to thank him when I was at the recording of Denis Quilley's *This Is Your Life* at the London Palladium where I was Associate Musical Director of *La Cage Aux Folles* and where Denis was playing one of the two lead characters, Georges. I saw Donald Swann over the other side of the stage, who was there as a special guest, and after the recording I thanked him and was able to tell him that the conductor of the show he had just watched had his first taste of professional music making fifteen years earlier with him in St Andrew's Church, Plymouth. Bless him, I am not sure whether he really remembered but he certainly pretended well. Following the radio show two fundamental truths hit home. Firstly, rehearsals generally meant that dreaded PE/Games could be avoided and secondly, that musical ventures frequently involved working with those creatures of the opposite sex. It was a win win situation!

1970 and Mayflower 350 also presented another unforgettable experience. Each August Bank Holiday Devonport Dockyard and the Royal Naval Barracks opened their doors to the general public for *Navy Days*. A real 'Boys Own' weekend when we were able to clamber over warships, cruisers, aircraft carriers and submarines, watch helicopters, hovercraft and even the Field

Gun Crew at really close quarters. Dad had taken me most years since I was old enough and it was a real annual highlight. In 1970 HMS Ark Royal was in port and open for the weekend. We got on board at exactly the right moment, as it turned out, and after walking through the belly of the carrier to the hangars and the aircraft lifts, where the Phantoms and Buccaneers would be taken to the flight deck, Dad and I were taken heavenward instead and found ourselves up top on the river side of the deck. There was an almighty roar and suddenly Concorde prototype 002, piloted by chief test pilot Brian Trubshaw, came into view, with its snoop nose down, giving us a slow one hundred and fifty metre fly past along the line of the River Tamar towards the open waters of The Sound. It wasn't on the schedule, it's not even mentioned as a possibility in the Navy Days programme but it really happened and there are no superlatives that can convey just how futuristic it felt and amazing it was to witness the event.

1970 With guitar

Life at school progressed, my academic prowess was pretty average on the whole and I generally found myself around the middle of the class for everything except music or anything associated with music. I started well with languages and even quite enjoyed my first two years having to learn Latin, however I had to choose between Latin and Music for my third year and, naturally, I chose Music. Everything seemed to be pointing me in that direction and I even took my 'O' Level Music a year early. I also did a fair amount of public speaking and writing and had a couple of pieces published. Admittedly only in DHS publications, but my poem *20th Century Skitzoid* (sic) *Man* written when in Lower 6a, made it into Henry Whitfeld's tome about Devonport High School called *A Torch in Flame* published in 1987.

I performed a fair bit, including playing *First Voice* in Dylan Thomas's *Under Milk Wood – To begin at the beginning: It is spring, moonless night in the small town, starless and bible-black* – but I also found myself cast in a couple of theatrical ventures which I didn't enjoy as much. *The Thwarting of Baron Bolligrew* by Robert Bolt, in which I played Sir Graceless Strongbody and *All The King's Men* by Richard Rodney Bennet in which I played Colonel Massey, who was the Commander of the Roundheads. The second half of that event was a performance of the play, *The Jackdaw of Rheims,* adapted by our drama teacher, Mr Clayton, and I was much happier helping to create the music that underpinned the production with a couple of my schoolmates. I appeared in many concerts at school, however, including a *Monty Python* style comedy gig that, looking back, must have been absolutely excruciating to watch and a concert where a little group made up of six of us promising musicians recreated some mediaeval music including a version of *Gaudete* that had been made popular that year by the rock/folk fusion band, *Steeleye Span.*

After all that I waited until my final year in the Sixth Form before I trod the boards again and this time it was a big joint venture with Stoke Damerel High School for Girls. Gilbert and Sullivan's *Trial by Jury* at Plymouth's Athenaeum Theatre and I was playing the Defendant. My leading lady, from the sixth form of Stoke Damerel, Cheryl Hearder, was really rather good and she and I had a gentle romance while we were working together on the project. It was still win win!

Devonport High was originally built as a Naval Hospital and comprised four three story granite buildings joined together by a colonnade of forty-eight or so arches which overlooked the main games field. At the end of the colonnade was a further building which housed the school offices, including the dreaded Doc Cresswell's Study, the School Hall, Gym and in the basement, close to the changing rooms, was the room that became like a second home to me, Tref's Music Room. It was a place of refuge and at the back of the classroom was a separate small room next to the music cupboard which eventually almost became my own study – I was there so much. By the time I got to the episode of *Morning Has Broken* recounted in the Prologue I was one of a handful of chaps who were constantly in and out, plotting exciting musical ventures and rehearsing for upcoming concerts. Just above the Music Room was the under-stage store room where bits of old stage sets, curtains and exotic subversive magazines like *Oz* could be found, if you knew where to look. We used the room to rehearse as well and as Tref was encouraging us to open our musical horizons, it became a good place to listen to *Pink Floyd* or *King Crimson* and especially my favourite, *Emerson, Lake and Palmer.* This highlights one of the most inspirational aspects of my time at DHS. The fact that I had chosen to go there, coupled with the fact that there was a young, bright, hugely talented and charismatic music teacher who would mix and match Randy Newman with Richard Strauss, or The Beatles with Maurice Ravel and who actively encouraged us to listen to as varied an amount of music as we could, wasn't stuffy or disparaging of modern music, meant that my musical education was as eclectic as possible.

Tref also introduced me to the Plymouth Youth Orchestra. He was the conductor and generally there was no need to use a piano player, so as I had a good working knowledge of the recorder he suggested that I take up playing the oboe because the fingerings were almost identical. There was, however, the matter of the double reed that you have to blow through to generate the sound. Imagine trying to control blowing through two very tough blades of grass and making that sound consistent and pleasant. Oboe reeds are like that. I did make the grade to play in the orchestra but only just and I mostly sat in the Oboe 2 or Oboe 3 chair. To compare the sound I made with that of a duck would be unkind to the duck however, but truthfully, it was a means to an end.

We also had a couple of amazing day trips to London by charabanc and train. The first was to see the opera *The Marriage of Figaro* at the newly renamed *English National Opera* at the London Colosseum, a vast auditorium compared to anywhere in Plymouth, and we had the treat of a backstage tour where the sheer size and complexity of it all was mind boggling. The second was to visit *The Royal Albert Hall*, again simply enormous, and to watch a performance of William Walton's *Belshazzar's Feast* which combined the full forces of the orchestra with a huge choir and soloist in a thrilling and tantalising oratorio that had the hairs on the back of my neck standing up and positively dancing with joy! The journeys homewards were also quite hair raising as under cover of darkness some gentle and fairly innocent fumbling was experienced in the back of the coach which made for a rather memorable end to the days!

It wasn't long before I became friends with some of the top echelon of the orchestra. It is true they were mostly girls, but as I explained before, music became a great common bond and on the whole I prefer them, anyway. Nicola Vincent, oboe, Christine Yiend, flute, and my first proper girlfriend, Karon Pearce, clarinet, along with Chris Prior, clarinet, and Robert Stokes, cello, formed *The Plymouth Youth Orchestra Sextet* and we performed for such salubrious audiences as the Mount Tamar Townswomen's Guild with my Auntie Doris playing the role of June Holland in the one act play, *Shepherd's Pie* by Mabel Constanduras – pretty heady stuff for a fourteen year old!

When I visited Karon's house we would spend a lot of time in her parent's dining room where there was a fairly decent piano and a very posh *Bang and Olufson* record player, my first experience of really good quality sound equipment. I heard the album *Jesus Christ Superstar* in that very room and I can still picture the psychedelic yellow and purple LP cover sitting beside the record deck in the corner.

Plymouth Youth Orchestra also helped me to feel just how much teamwork and togetherness plays such an important part in the creation of performance. Tref was the perfect man at the helm and a few years after I had joined with my 'quacking' oboe he suggested that I play a piece on the piano with the orchestra. So, I studied a piece by Gordon Jacob called *Concertino for Piano and String Orchestra* and in the concert at the end of the summer term, 1975, I played it and even got a mention in the Plymouth Evening Herald review the next day. I had also ditched the oboe a couple of years earlier and replaced it, as far as being able to join in with the orchestra is concerned, by playing percussion. The big plus about this was that I was able to audition for The

Devon Youth Orchestra. There were far too many brilliant blowers and scrapers for my oboe skills to enable me to join, so percussion could be my way in.

I managed to convince the powers that be that I was good enough, achieved my aim and was able to go to a fortnight long course which was held at Rolle College in Exmouth. The legendary percussion player, Sir James 'Jimmy' Blades was a guest tutor. I was so excited to meet him as he had also been famously teaching the drummer of *Emerson Lake and Palmer*, Carl Palmer. He so lived up to expectations and was like a warm, smiling pixie as he talked about his career and gave me a few pointers that really helped me to get by in this new environment. Being amongst the best of the best in Devon was exhilarating to say the least and though I was there as a percussionist I made my way, when main rehearsals were finished, as a piano player accompanying as many people as I could. The principal oboe, Isobel 'Ibby' Ward, played like an angel and we performed Poulenc's *Oboe Sonata* together, but I also made friends for life in that group of people. Karen White was principal flautist and had an extraordinary facility – she was also a good enough pianist to get into the Royal College of Music – and then there was Philip White (no relation) who was lead trumpet player. He ended up at The Royal Academy of Music and after a distinguished career there has now retired to continue his life as a composer.

The conductor of The Devon Youth Orchestra was a Mr R Bolsover. Just as at school we had some glorious names for masters, like *Emod* the DOME shaped French teacher, and *Blobbin*, the chemistry teacher called Mr Gibson who simply said at just about every lesson – well boys, you put a 'blob in this test tube and another blob in the other one' – so it was with Mr Bolsover. His name backwards, *Revoslob*, was much more satisfying and that name is etched in my memory for ever as at the end of my three year course at Trinity College of Music in 1978, it was to him, as County Music Advisor, that I had to prove my musical worth to secure my fourth year grant. I duly went to audition and he uttered the priceless words that he thought I would never make it in the music industry but he would, nevertheless, give me the grant. I'm still not sure why he had to put that caveat before telling me I had got the money but it lives with me forever. Thank you Mr Bolsover – oh, and by the way, I did do a little bit in the music industry!

*

All this time I was also caught up with a lot of Church music. From the organ loft at St Thomas's I progressed to bigger and more exciting things at the next door parish of St Mark's Church, Ford. The vicar of St Thomas's, Rev. Michael Courtenay and his elegant wife, Catherine, were very supportive but music was never that high on the agenda. By this time Dad was getting close to being a Churchwarden, Mum was Brown Owl for the Brownie troop and Michael Courtenay was very much a down to earth simplifier of all things ecclesiastical. He pushed through the making of a concrete altar to be placed in the middle of the sanctuary instead of against the wall at the back of the church. This was so that the celebrant would be facing the congregation, very much the new trend of the sixties. There were a lot of men in the parish helping on the day the new altar had its wooden support frame taken away and the marble top from the previous one was lifted into place. Father Michael was right in the middle of the fray, leading the troop. There was much huffing and puffing and one of the men almost lost his thumb, but once it was in place it did look very modern and progressive. He was a great leader but sadly not musical so as I had already started going to a youth club based at St Mark's, and I had found out that the vicar, Rev. Stuart King, was a musician himself, I started to move between the two parishes.

At St Mark's there was a proper choir, with cassocks and surplices, plus choir stalls at the front of the church and a full time organist, Ray Tipper. Father Stuart conducted choir practice and was a very good choral trainer. He could play the piano beautifully but he also sang with a rich high baritone voice and frequently took a solo if needed. He was a large man, rather overweight, as he liked the finer things in life, but very warm and jocular with a quick wit. He became a great friend and actually helped me financially by paying for my organ lessons. I have much to thank him for – a second patron, if you like, after my first, Uncle Harry.

Stuart had a curate, he was young, exciting and hailed from New Orleans. Rev. Thaddeus Birchard was his name and he created a youth group at St Mark's, called *Agapé*, the Greek word that came to be used to represent Christian love. We would meet at his house at the end of Ronald Terrace, near St Levan Road and by this time I had also started to play a bit of guitar and could strum along moderately proficiently. I had started playing it very occasionally at St Thomas's but here at *Agapé* with this group of interesting teenagers it really helped to define me. We would have regular singalongs at the end of meetings and occasionally ideas would develop that we would then use in the forthcoming Sunday service. Jill Dickinson was one of the leading lights in this and we bounced off each other well. She was a major ally and we had similar musical tastes.

In 1973 Thaddeus left St Mark's and in my summer holidays that year and the year after, I joined him in Poplar, where he was now vicar, for a summer school with local kids. He ran a two week course and I was one of the team – sometimes being a Pied Piper with my guitar. Again I was realising how I could use my musical skills in a positive way and it was good education.

Being a member of *Agapé* also pushed the boundaries of my education in other ways. I succumbed to peer pressure and began to smoke. It was quite easy really, and I funded my craving by saving up my bus fare and walking to and from Devonport High each day. I learnt how to 'roll my own' and even discovered the pleasures of liquorice papers. The weird thing about smoking is that you know it is bad for you and you want to stop, but somehow that insistence to continue overrides all your sensibilities. Almost as soon as I started to smoke I started to try to give up, something I didn't finally achieve until 1999!

Agapé also helped me discover rather more about girls and how they work. After meetings various liaisons were formed on the way home and the couple of weekend retreats that we had were actually little havens of education. Shall we say the innocent fumbling of my early teens was gently superseded. Discoveries made and questions answered but always within safe boundaries and somehow it was OK, because virginity was still intact.

At this point in my life, through those teenage years, I considered myself to be very much a Christian. I believed, I was confirmed and I had a prayer life. I also started thinking that I may have a vocation to be a priest so I was pretty much wrapped up in it all.

There was quite an Ecumenical movement going on in the early seventies and The St Levan Group of Churches (The three Anglican churches in the area plus the Methodist Church, Baptist Church, Presbyterian and Congregational Churches) played host to a mission with all sorts of interesting visitors and leaders taking special services and seminars. There were some amazing Nuns from the East End of London, a Franciscan monk who spoke in tongues and was a healer, and a stunning American singing group called the Fishermen, who sang *a capella* beautifully but also extemporised together in full harmony, magically and with breathtaking originality.

This idea of *vocation* in me had to be explored and I even had a meeting with the Diocesan Director of Ordinands, Canon Rice, in 1974. We talked about how I could make sense of this calling I seemed to have and yet keep my musical education intact and the conclusion we reached was that I could go to music college and if, after that, I still felt that I wanted to join the priesthood then I could go to Theological College but only for a two year course, not three. Anyway all this very quickly became academic as music ultimately seduced me and I gradually realised that, for me, at least, Christianity was not the nirvana I thought it was as a teenager. I questioned my faith constantly from then on, as many do, but it wasn't until very recently that I was able to acknowledge what my own personal belief system really is, and whether Christianity takes any part.

My conclusion is simply put in my personal *Credo* here:

> *I believe there is no higher force for good or evil than the power of Man.*
> *There is no heaven and hell.*
> *There is no afterlife, except in the memories of those who continue to live.*
>
> *We are stronger when we are simply 'kind' to one another. To 'be kind' is akin to the Judaeo-Christian message, 'love thy neighbour as thyself'. A simple maxim to live by, but one that has great and positive ramifications when adhered too. Our moral compass is informed and carries weight if we try to 'be kind' in all things.*

A Belief System should never be denigrated – everyone's faith is sacrosanct to them. However, healthy discussion about belief should be encouraged and welcomed. Even among Fundamentalists. (Maybe especially!)

There are universal natural laws which encompass evolution and time and I further believe that it is extremely likely that there are other civilisations amongst the stars. We will probably never see them but to dream about them and to hope is good.

MD Jan 2020

But back to the seventies, and in early 1972 just after *Godspell* came to London two things happened. I went to see the show (and saw most of the original cast, Jeremy Irons, David Essex, Marti Webb, Gay Soper and Mandy More and was also extremely interested in the band on stage and most particularly the piano playing Musical Director) and I played and sang *Prepare Ye* as an opening to the main Sunday Eucharist. *Godspell* and *Jesus Christ Superstar*, two vastly different takes on that story of Jesus, truly opened my eyes as to one of the musical tangents I could take and how varied that could be.

After *Salad Days* and *South Pacific* had piqued the interest of the eight year old me, here were the shows that set the teenager aflame with future possibilities.

Looking back at those teenage years highlights just how much of my musical tastes and strengths were moulded by the great teaching from Tref at school and from Stuart King at St Mark's. If I had to decide on my *Desert Island Discs* right now I can guarantee that most of them would come from this time. From *The Shadow of Your Smile*, played in a mellow jazz style by

Stuart, to Ravel's *Piano Concerto in G*, which I studied for 'A' Level music, by way of Michael Tippet's *Concerto for Double String Orchestra* and Gabriel Grovlez' *Petites Litanies de Jésus* or *Popular Song* by William Walton, all these pieces and many more besides, invoke a response from me that is more than just a happy memory. They have touched my soul.

When I listened to the second movement of Tippet's *Double Concerto* for the first time, I was in that study at the back of the Music Room and I was reading about the blitz in Plymouth. Before the piece ended I found myself in tears and I remember the feeling of desolation that went through me, so strongly, even now. At Plymouth Youth Orchestra we performed Walton's *Popular Song* from *Façade* and of course, at the end of the great *Morecambe and Wise with André Previn, Grieg Piano Concerto* sketch Previn plays a snippet of it with such elan. Previn was a hero and his regular BBC shows with the London Symphony Orchestra were another of my musical highlights, what a brilliant man. I was introduced to so much great music at that time, my musical brain was like a sponge and I am so grateful to Tref and Stuart for helping me soak it all up, making sure that I was open to all styles and to really guide me on my musical journey.

In July 2005 Tref retired. I had a call from his then wife, Lesley, asking if I would mind being one of the main guests at his retirement party. I was so pleased to be able to publicly thank him. He inspired me in so many ways and meeting him after such a long time was an occasion where all the years just evaporated away and suddenly I was that ambitious and cheeky eighteen year old again. Tref was exactly the same and though he has retired from school he continues to be a leading light in the musical scene in Plymouth. Great teachers are extra special and I am very lucky to have been taught by one.

2005 With Teacher Tref Farrow at his retirement

Whilst in my last year at Devonport High, headmaster, Doc Cresswell, sadly died. We'd had a fairly rocky relationship, as illustrated in the Prologue, and I was also the glowing recipient of the cane (three thwacks only) in my second year after a mix up with our old Religious Studies teacher, Holy Joe, plus I did have a few Headmaster detentions over the years. So it would be disingenuous of me to say I was sorry to see him go, however, the lot of an itinerant musician brings boundless possibilities and I ended up playing, composing and singing at his Memorial Service held in the Plymouth Guildhall in 1974. The experience of performing at the same venue where I had witnessed my first Classical Music concert, watching the Bournemouth Symphony Orchestra perform, and my first Jazz concert, watching the Stan Tracy Quartet, was too much of an opportunity to miss and I am very glad that I did.

I had started composing from the age of fourteen, nothing terribly brilliant but good enough to get friends to play along with me, the school madrigal group to sing and for me to explore all the musical ideas I was being fed. Whilst playing that organ at St Thomas's I wrote a few pieces to show off its range. I still have the manuscript of one of them and I can see how fixated I was with the overall sound, there were big broad strokes of dissonance juxtaposed with soft, gentle, plaintive and sweet harmonies. I never really mastered the pedals but I could at least get by and this piece does have a little section that is solely for the feet to play.

When I left school in July 1975 I went off to Rolle College for that Devon Youth Orchestra course knowing that I was about to start an even bigger musical journey. After the whole 'vocation' affair I had decided that music college was for me, but which one? I thought that it would be either The Royal Academy of Music, Trinity College of Music or Guildhall, so I started the audition process in 1974. I had a good audition for The Royal Academy and was interviewed by a legend of piano accompaniment, Geoffrey Parsons, but I was only put on the reserve list, though offered a place later. Then came Trinity, it was smaller, was based around the corner from Wigmore Street in Mandeville Place and it just felt right for me. I got in and also, as it happens, was offered a full unconditional grant. In other words my place was not beholden to how good, or bad, my 'A' Level grades were going to be. Naturally I ditched even going to the Guildhall audition and swooped on the opportunity that was offered to me by Trinity and accepted with due haste!

However, before I write about my time at Trinity there is a very special place filled with special people that I need to explore…

FOUR

TREYARNON

It's August 1957 and a young man is standing under the awning of a Post Office in the little village of St Merryn trying to shield his beautiful young wife and their seven month old baby, wrapped up tight in his Silver Cross pram, from the rain as it comes down in stair rods. Nothing is open, it's a Sunday. They managed to get to the Post Office from Plymouth, by train to Padstow and then a taxi to St Merryn, but their destination is a little known campsite on the North Cornish coast called Trethias and on that campsite is a cream, egg shaped caravan called *Nick's Own* with their friends, Jean and Eric Thorne, waiting for them. The problem is that the taxi driver didn't know where Trethias was and simply dropped them at the closest village which as it turns out is around three miles, through windy, narrow Cornish roads, from their goal. No phone close by and seemingly no hope of getting any help until the Cornish summer stops throwing water at them and becomes more benign, when suddenly a travelling salesman in a smart, black car pulls up and asks where they are headed. Quite by chance he knows exactly where Trethias is and gets them to hop into the car and fifteen minutes later they are in the fields of Trethias atop the cliffs in between Treyarnon Bay and Porthcothan. He drops them off – I must dash – he says, and as quickly as he appeared, he disappears down the track in the middle of those fields and away.

Dad always referred to him as their Guardian Angel and was sad that they hadn't had the opportunity to thank him properly for his gracious intervention and rescue on that day. The man didn't even tell them his name, he really was our very own Good Samaritan and this was how our annual pilgrimage to what has become my spiritual home began. Treyarnon Bay and Trethias campsite have been part of my life ever since, with many important consequences.

For the next three years the journey to Trethias was still by train except that on arrival in Padstow the destination of the taxi ride was now known, thank goodness. My first memory, which must be from summer 1960, is the view of the little iron bridge that the train crosses just before arriving at Padstow station. In my mind's eye there are clouds of steam, and the sound of the gentle *da-dum da-dum* as the wheels roll over the rail clips.

In 1963 dear Lord Beeching and his rail axe were in full swing and the Padstow branch line was no more. Fortunately, by then, we were no longer beholden to British Railways because we had wheels. Well, when I say wheels, I mean that Uncle John (Mum's sister's husband) very kindly used to bring us down in his little black *Austin A35*. All of us on board, plus luggage and provisions for two weeks. I used to sit on Dad's lap in the passenger seat and Mum and sister Jackie would be in the back sitting on towels and bedding with the carrycot. Uncle John would drive us to the little cream van and then, after a quick cuppa, off he would go, back to Plymouth. I was allowed to operate the indicator switch, which was situated on the middle of the dashboard, as I got older, a major treat! It must have been quite some three dimensional jigsaw fitting everything into the car and if you listened carefully I'm sure MDR 487 let out a little sigh as we all got out.

1965 Nicks Own – The Caravan at Trethias

1973 Dixons outside Stolls' blue Caravan
with Austin A35 'MDR 487'

The caravan, which belonged to John and Betty Stolls who were friends of Mum and Dad from Plymouth, was a veritable treasure trove of *Heath Robinson* cleverness. A sofa and a table that turned into beds, gas lamps, secret cupboards and there was a smell, no, an aroma that instantly conjured up 'holiday' when you walked through the door. Jackie and I were much more interested in what was outside, though. From the campsite it was a ten minute walk down the hill, past two fields and a few houses to the final bit of path hewn out of the blue stone and peppered with sand that took you directly onto the beach before the steps were built.

Soft, golden sand with little rock pools either side when the tide was out and the rolling waves of the Atlantic sea to your left and to the right were the sand dunes. Hills and secret paths that could easily double as a desert island where you might meet Robinson Crusoe or some aliens from *Doctor Who*. The beach and environs were limitless in their possibilities. Of course there wasn't just the beach, because it was only a stone's throw from the little caravan to cliff walks and vistas that are breathtaking. Turning left out of the field instead of straight on down towards the beach and you were above Fox Cove with its submarine like rock in the middle. Further walking over the bouncy, wiry grass and there were the other coves, Warren, Pepper and Wine, with its seemingly huge stack rock standing like a mystic guardian at the cove's entrance. In between each of the coves a finger thin promontory containing the remnants of iron age settlements, undulations and secret little nooks and crannies that were begging to be explored. Along with the sound of the waves crashing and the seagulls gulla-gulla-ing, every so often you could hear a skylark up in the heavens or see a kestrel hovering like a majestic, ancient, grandmaster about to pounce. Very occasionally a few sleek cormorants would fly quickly across the opening of a cove, so close to the surface of the water that they might disappear underneath the white horses at any moment.

Through most of the sixties and just into the seventies the air was frequently filled with loud rumblings as the Shackleton aeroplanes made their regular maritime patrol sorties. The Shackleton was a development of the Lancaster bomber from WWII and even though those four Merlin engines which crackled and roared on the wings of the *Lanc* had been replaced by four Rolls Royce Griffon engines they still created a mighty sound as they flew by. The Nimrod, based on the Comet, replaced the Shackleton in the early seventies and flew much higher so we heard it less, however there was one other aircraft noise that regularly assailed our senses and that was the sonic boom of Concorde on its daily trip to and from New York. Not too loud as we were a good few miles from where it dropped out or achieved supersonic speed but still very exciting and terribly 'space-age'.

Trevose Head lighthouse also entertained us on a regular basis with the use of its foghorn, made famous by Sir Malcolm Arnold, who lived for a time in Primrose Cottage near Trethias farmhouse, in his piece, *The Padstow Lifeboat*, composed in 1967. Dotted through it he had the French horns impersonating the D that boomed out whenever there was a hint of fog or mist. Actually the real foghorn note was somewhere between a C and a D but for musicality Arnold made it a D. Quite authentic it sounds too. Now, of course, GPS has enabled the foghorn to be silenced but the lighthouse itself still lights up every evening and gives an almost eerie pulsating glow though in 1995 that glow was changed from red to white when the lighthouse became fully automated.

There was one other particularly evocative smell – bacon! Walking with Dad out on the cliffs to search for mushrooms while Mum cooked the bacon in the morning was very special because, just as you got closer to the caravan field, there was this salty aroma fizzing in your nostrils. The mere thought sends the taste buds into a frenzy, even now.

But actually, more important than all those beautiful sights, sounds and smells is the simple fact that the longest lasting friendships were started down there.

1974 Treyarnon folk on the beach

In 1963 a family pitched their tent beside us. Mum, Dad and four children. The Family Patient: Margaret, Derrick, Anne, David, Joy and Peter. That year there was torrential rain and, to help keep their tent from being washed away, Dad helped Derrick dig a trench around it. Bonds were formed. They were from Kingston-on-Thames, which sounded a million miles away, but that meant the family lived really close to London which was tantalising to six year old me. They were musical and fun and we would meet up on the beach where Margaret would create the most intricate sand castles, like mini helter-skelters, with little grooves cut in and out so that you could send little rubber balls careering around, down and through them, and, of course, we would all play together in the caravan field. Daughters, Anne and Joy and now grand-daughter Jo have continued the tradition with more and more elaborate sand sculptures. If you see a school of lifelike sand dolphins on the beach it is very likely that the Patient family were responsible.

Family Chandler, who own and run Trethias, rather cannily have only ever had caravans nestling on the perimeter, never in the centre or bunched up. The park has three fields, the first, as you come in through the gate, called *Doodel*, which is now populated by static caravans, then straight ahead there is *Cliff* field which comprises a mixture of statics down the near side and pitches for tents or trailer caravans along the top and far side, then the field we were in, *Gull* field which has seven statics and the rest of the edge of the field is for tourers. Back in the early sixties things were pretty basic with no shower, toilet or washing facilities. At various points in each of the fields were standpipes with taps where we would go to collect our water or stick our head under to wash our hair. A little elsan chemical toilet completed the 'mod-cons'. A couple of toilet blocks were built in the mid sixties, closely followed by a shower block a couple of years later, which also had a phone box and washing machine, spin dryer and mangle. Those buildings, though now thoroughly refurbished, remain today.

Gerry and Betty Chandler ran the park in a simple, no nonsense way. The Trethias homestead and farmhouse was a half mile down the private road that you had to travel along to get to the park and Betty kept a little shop selling basic provisions with vegetables available from Mrs Grey opposite the farm. The farmhouse was also important to me as a teenager because it housed the only piano that I could get my hands on when I was there. Gerry and Betty very kindly let me practice when I was getting ready for my Grade Six and Grade Eight Associated Board Examinations which were pre-requisite qualifications to enable me to take 'A' Level Music and to get into Music College.

Betty was also the keeper of 'The List'. Now this was a sacred document because if you wanted to own a permanent plot and have your own static caravan your name had to be at the top of it. There are various rumours about how the list was kept but most favour a particularly safe and secure method, keeping the names together in an old biscuit tin, on butter paper! Mum and Dad put their names down in the late sixties and they got their own plot in 1987. I put my name down in 1971 and my name finally came up in 1996. The current waiting time is around forty years! When Gerry retired, his son, David, took over and now David's son, Leroy is heir apparent, running things together until David retires.

Along with the Patients there were, and still are, many families who are regulars and who we formed bonds with as children. We rented *Nick's Own* from the Stolls, as did the Thornes, so we only ever met together down there on the day we arrived or the day we left but that was at least some time to play with Nick and Cathy Stolls or Andrew and Mary Thorne. Lindsey Reid, née Norman, and her sister, Sue were a little older and very occasionally babysat for Jackie and me on the rare occasions Mum and Dad went to the Tredrea pub. (Known as the Ted Ray for those of a certain age.)

In Trethias folklore there are names that always figure when reminiscing about those simple holidays; the Pelhams, Pitts, Dellars, Bullys, Tipples, Holingsheads, Faircloughs, Jacksons, Hansfords, Smiths et al. There were little tribes of children who were able to play all sorts of games in the wide open fields and who, as they got older, went further afield and ventured to Constantine Bay, Booby's Bay and the lighthouse at Trevose Head, not forgetting the southern cliff walk towards Porthcothan Bay. Gangs that, as they got older still, progressed to evening parties in each other's caravans, or barbecues on the beach with campfires and sizzling sausages! Sometimes the barbecues were just family affairs but there were also plenty of times when larger groups would congregate around an open fire.

One year when I was in my teens and gently strumming my guitar during one of these events we were suddenly assailed by a group of streaking young men from the other side of the beach screaming and gesticulating wildly. There was mayhem for a few seconds until my Dad and a couple of the other Dads grabbed frying pans and whacked a couple of the chaps very sharply on their backsides. There was more screaming and gesticulating as they scarpered back whence they came nursing quite sore nether regions but it was a source of much mirth and merriment for all of us teenagers!

By the time I was around ten Dad had bought Uncle John's little *Austin A35* and the Stolls had upgraded their caravan to a two tone blue one which now stood in *Doodel* field in the corner just past the gap between fields. We could travel further afield easily and even have excursions to Padstow. I could bring my guitar and I had my own little bedroom in the new caravan. The friendships we started always managed to miraculously continue where they had left off the previous year – without communication in between, no mobiles back then, of course – and there was always a massive tingle of excitement and expectation as the holiday got closer. The fact that so many families should really be called Trethias Dynasties now, with all the generations that have come down, is testament to the influence that this special place has had over us all.

When Mum and Dad took over their spot just below the shower block in 1987 and had their very own caravan it was as if they had taken possession of an ancestral home and when, a couple of years later, a brand new 28x10ft van took the place of the battered one they had inherited it was as if that ancestral home had just had a first class upgrade. They were also the first to be fully plumbed in with working shower and toilet. Swish! Gas lamps were now electric and the little condenser box that used to sit under the van keeping the milk cool was now a fully functional electric fridge.

There were also other treasures that used to sit under the van or in the shed – the wooden surf boards or body boards – and every year we would get them out and how exciting it was to be back in the sea, trying to keep our heads above water, riding in on the waves. Marine ply, strong, heavy and, if you mistimed a wave, they would give you a nasty whack in the stomach.

We were always being reminded about the dangers of the water. With awful regularity people would be drowned in the gully between Trethias Island and the mainland down on the left of the beach, not heeding the warnings about the currents or they would be washed off the rocks between the coves whilst fishing. Rescue helicopter crews and lifeguards, frequently refining and rehearsing their drill, were the unsung heroes putting their lives on the line to save someone underestimating the tide or simply thinking that they knew best.

One year there was a major alert up at Trethias with the coastguards and police roaring through the fields and out onto the cliff with blaring sirens on their Land Rovers, followed, naturally, by a good few of us teenagers. When we reached the edge of Warren Cove we saw what looked like a cream dummy below, one hundred feet down on the sand, almost embedded in the seaweed. Slowly it dawned on us that this was, in fact, a body, and shortly after we were gently ushered away so that the police could haul the remains up the cliffs. The realisation was chilling and was made even more personal to us on the park when it was eventually announced that it had been a fisherman who regularly stayed in one of the caravans and who had been reported missing some two weeks earlier. If someone is washed off the rocks between the coves normally the tides take the body northwards up the coast to a place called Stinking Cove, so it was very unusual that this particular body had stayed in close vicinity for so long. It was unsettling for us all but it also reinforced our understanding of just how dangerous the coastal waters are, and how careful we must be to heed those warnings and follow the advice of the lifeguards.

In May 1969 a small tanker was being taken for scrap at the end of its working life in fairly inclement weather. At the time the *SS Hemsley I* was the oldest registered British steamship and the captain rather misjudged his position in the fog, after losing power and steam, and radioed in that they had foundered at The Lizard when actually they were stuck over one hundred nautical miles away on the rocks at the end of Fox Cove. Fortunately the crew were mostly able to clamber up the one hundred foot cliffs and all were saved, but the ship was lost. Over the following couple of years the rusting hulk was broken up and dragged to the top of the cliff by a little crane and the Stolls' original caravan, our little haven, *Nick's Own*, was used as a rest hut by the reclaimers. An ignominious end for that very special little cream egg. At low tide there are still some parts of the shipwreck visible, but the lumps are so barnacled and rusted that picking them out is quite a challenge.

My first wife, Susie, came down a few times over our years together but she was never really a caravan lover. She did try, though. Then as soon as I had got together with my second wife, Jo, we made an excursion down to meet Mum and Dad. Her daughter, Lillie, (who I effectively adopted in 1993) was four and a half and was completely enthralled with the place. Chasing seagulls in her little yellow dress and loving the idea that a dragon lived nearby. (There is a set of books written by Rosemary Manning about this dragon and its home between Treyarnon and Constantine and the first book, *Green Smoke*, was our night time reading.) Lillie got the Treyarnon bug just as her sister Meg did a few years later after she was born in 1996. Another Treyarnon dynasty in the making?

Natalie Turnbull began her Trethias sojourns just after she was born in 1965. Patricia, her Mum, was best friends with Mary Pelham and Natalie was destined to grow up with rather more brothers and sisters than she actually had, in that Lucy, Harriet and Henry plus real brother, Jonathan, made a fantastic extended family. The Pelhams and the Turnbulls would come down and stay in the Pelham's caravan for weeks on end. Mary and Patricia would pack all the kids in a little green mini van and drive them down from Northwood, while Rodney and Colin, the Dads, would appear occasionally, work permitting. I knew the Pelhams very well as a kid, but I was a few years older so I didn't play with them all. I don't think that the Dixon two weeks ever coincided with Natalie's visit during those sixties and seventies but the Turnbull name was nevertheless familiar.

So Natalie was steeped in the folklore of Trethias and, like me, has visited the place for the whole of her life. In the eighties, apparently, Natalie, Lucy and Harriet watched my sister, Jackie, get to know this nice young man, Paul Gill, who came down to the site each year. They were teenagers then, but their relationship blossomed and they married – a proper Trethias couple. Jackie and Paul took over Mum and Dad's caravan and kept it going until they very sadly had to give up after Paul decided he wanted to get some special attention and have a quadruple heart bypass followed by a stroke. Life can be so very cruel and it was such a difficult decision to make, but it was just too much for them to continue.

*

In 1996 when I finally got offered my permanent plot the first space that I was shown was down in *Cliff* field and as it was quite a way from where I had spent my time down there as a lad I asked David if I could defer and wait for the next one to come up. Lo and behold, that second space offered in 1997 was, in fact, the plot that Eric and Jean Thorne had been given around the same time that my Mum and Dad got theirs. It had one of the most spectacular views out onto Trevose Head at the top of *Doodel* field right by the opening to *Gull* field and close to where the Stolls had ended up, but more important than all that, it was right beside the Pelhams. I took possession in 1998 and we took Lillie and Meg down as soon as we could.

The following year turned out to be incredibly significant because I was down there again, but just with Lillie and Meg because Jo and I were in the middle of our split. I had told her that, for my own sanity, I had to call a halt to our marriage and naturally that caused much heartache, soul-searching and pain. The news was not public in any way, though. Lucy Pelham, now Davies, was next door and Natalie was staying with her friend Claire Macgregor a couple of vans along. By this time I did know Natalie, she and I had ended up sitting next to one another playing a musical game at a party in Rojano's restaurant, Padstow, when she was down with her boyfriend and I was there with Jo, but in 1999 she was single. This particular week we seemed to spend quite a lot of time together, chatting and playing 'bit-bat' out on the field and though my break up with Jo was settled between us, as I said, no one else knew, consequently Natalie and I were simply very friendly. Then everything changed because one day Lucy quietly asked me a very simple question. "Mike, do you know any nice men who would be suitable for Natalie?" My response was quick, to the point and has had wonderful, long lasting consequences. "Well," I said, "how about me!" And I then explained to Lucy that Jo and I were splitting up but that we hadn't made the news public, yet, and that I really rather liked Natalie but couldn't do anything about it until things had settled down.

Nothing was said to Natalie, naturally, but Lucy gave me her work number and six weeks later I was standing on Chiswick Railway Station and with trepidation and a welling up of excitement I phoned her at the office in Mars HQ, Slough. I asked the lady on the switchboard if I could speak to Natalie Turnbull and told her that my name was Mike Dixon. "Oh, hello Mike," Natalie said, matter of factly, "what do you want, then?" – it turned out that there was another Mike Dixon working in the Mars Salesforce and she naturally assumed it was him calling – I was taken aback but I said, "It's Mike from Treyarnon…" Apparently she hesitated, went a bright puce colour but quickly recovered her composure to continue talking to me after she realised she had mixed me up with the other chap. We chatted for a short while, happily, and agreed to meet at a little restaurant in Charlotte Street, London and the rest, as they say, is history.

Now, though, it is time to gently spool back to 1975 and follow my musical journey taking me from Plymouth to London…

FIVE

TRINITY COLLEGE OF MUSIC

Campbell Philip Dysart Simpson and I met on the very first day at Mandeville Place in September 1975. We were among a group of freshers being escorted around the majestic old building that perched between Manchester Square and Wigmore Street in the heart of London. Lillie Langtry had apparently 'entertained' the Prince of Wales, later Edward VII, in the room that we knew as the Principal's office, back in 1878 or so. The building had pedigree. Campbell and I hit it off immediately; he was tall, urbane with a massively quick wit and a devil may care attitude to authority that appealed to my burgeoning anarchic tendencies. We had been placed together simply because we were both First Study pianists on the Graduate course and we had a lot of classes in common. During the induction we had walked from Mandeville Place northwards along Marylebone High Street to the rehearsal rooms, Dinely Studios in Blandford Street, by way of Hinde Street Church and the huge lower ground room there, where College Choir rehearsed. The most important landmark, though, we had to wait a few hours before we could explore. The Angel pub, on the corner of Thayer Street and the High Street was THE watering hole for Trinity students and over the next four years it is fair to say that I spent an awful amount of time in its smoke filled bar. That first term there was one record that we continually played on the Jukebox in the corner. It had proper musical credence and was extremely good value as it lasted at least two more minutes than most of the other offerings onboard. *Bohemian Rhapsody* was number one for pretty much the whole of my first term at Trinity College of Music and I loved it. Little did I know how important that record would become personally for me in my career.

So here I was at Trinity and after the amazing time in the summer holidays with my friends at the Devon Youth Orchestra I was definitely ready for exciting new musical adventures.

Treyarnon played its part, too. The Patients, on hearing that I was going to go to Music College in London suggested that I stay with them for a term or two, or at least until I found my feet and so I bowled up to One Tree Cottage with my red trunk full to the brim after saying farewell to Mum and Dad on Plymouth Railway Station a couple of days before that first day of term. Margaret and Derrick made me feel very welcome and it was the perfect place, though the journey to Trinity on the 65 bus to Richmond followed by the tube to Bond Street station did take this young lad from Plymouth a couple of days to get used to! Anne was already well into her time as a medical student but David was pretty much contemporary with me so he was also starting a new journey, based at home and studying at Charing Cross Hospital and we exchanged social notes frequently.

My smoking habit was in full swing and I experimented with a few brands during those early weeks at college. There was a bit of a poncy tobacconist between the main building and Dinely's and I eventually settled on Du Maurier in their distinctive red packaging and flip opening box. Of course it wasn't in any way cool but the tenuous excuse I have is that this was 1975. By the time I left college the red packet had been replaced by a desert scene and Camel became my brand until I finally stopped in 1999.

1975 Outside The Angel Pub, Marylebone

It was so freeing being away from home like this. I was suddenly in an environment with more freedom and opportunities than I had ever had before. I was in a college with like minded people, people whose central motivation was music and people who were hugely talented. It was a real nirvana for me.

In my second week Campbell told me that there was a party on the Saturday evening and that we had been invited. There was a rather lovely second year singer who I had noticed round and about and I plucked up courage to ask her to the party. To my utter astonishment she said yes. I had already mentioned to the Patients that I had been invited to a party and it was in Clapham and that I may not make it home to Kingston so all was well, there. It was just as well I did because when I met her at Bond Street tube that evening she was wearing a rather special *Laura Ashley* flowery black velvet dress with a slit up the side and it was very obvious that she was wearing the full works underneath. Goodness me – let's say that my induction to college life was completed that night.

In the morning she was singing in the professional eight piece choir in St George's Hanover Square so I bowled along with her before making my way back to Kingston, and for a few weeks we were quite the item. She shared a little first floor flat in north west London so we sometimes continued our liaisons there and sometimes even in one of the rehearsal rooms in Dinely's! Then the bombshell. She told me that the guy she was going to marry was turning up so we would have to cool things off for a bit. I was devastated, I had no idea she was engaged and I certainly wasn't going to be just a pleasant diversion for her, so we parted ways. Campbell immediately cottoned on and very soon after some loquacious coaching I was back to normal and ready to continue enjoying all the facets of college life once again. By the time that first Christmas and New Year came along I was more than back to normal and took Campbell up on his invitation to join him at his parent's place in Hythe for the New Year.

After a fabulous Christmas with my family I made my way by train to Hythe. So here I was on New Year's Eve sitting in the Simpson parental living room with a healthy livener in hand, before going out into the sprawling and bustling metropolis that was Hythe town centre. Very gradually and stealthily the most appalling aroma came from the corner of the room where Campbell's Dad was sitting reading the Telegraph and started to fill our nostrils. Campbell exclaimed, "Father, you've farted!" to which his father retorted without missing a beat, "Of course I have, you don't think I smell like that normally, do you?" Now, you have to imagine a cut glass accent as you read this, after all there is proper lineage in his family.

Later that evening we did indeed explore the sights and sounds that Hythe had to offer and after a very pleasant couple of hours in one pub we found ourselves having a snowball fight outside another one, and it was just after midnight. The snow had started just after we reached town and it was coming down now in quite a flurry. We discovered that it was quite easy to make said snowball bigger and bigger if you just keep compacting it. The ball that we ended up throwing at each other seemed to develop a life of its own and suddenly there was an almighty crash as it went over my shoulder and through the plate glass window at the front of the pub. Campbell and I tried to scarper up the hill towards his home but the snow caused us to falter somewhat, with three steps forward and two steps back. I think it was the snow but it may have been the 'couple' of drinks that we had consumed.

Anyway after ten minutes of trying to get up the hill, with me losing my glasses on the way, the crisp night air suddenly flashed blue as a police Range Rover appeared as if from nowhere. Our, not so slick, endeavours at escape were useless. We stopped when the officers called to us and when asked, "Have we been playing snowballs, boys?" our reply was very firmly in the negative. The boys in blue were not taken aback by our denial as they simply said, "Well, well, well, it must have been two other chaps wearing *Trinity College of Music* sweatshirts, mustn't it? Now what are the chances of that? In Hythe. On New Year's Eve?" Silence.

I'm afraid it was a fair cop and we were taken back down to the pub where we apologised profusely to the landlord and landlady and promised to pay what was necessary to cover the cost of replacing the glass. The police were feeling very lenient on that early New

Year's morn and we were let off with a caution. I am sorry to say that 'mister and missus landlord' never received a penny from us, it was a promise we never kept. Hopefully their insurance paid out!

Campbell was, and still is, one of the most extraordinary piano players I know. An amazing technical facility, memory and ability to extemporise, seamlessly sliding from Billy Mayerl to Scott Joplin by way of Chopin, Liszt and Burt Bacharach. All of the above used on a regular basis in the Commodore Club or similar on any of the Cunard flagships over the last twenty five years or so. More important than any of that though is that he must be the only person at music college to have ever done his thesis on *The Piano Playing of Mrs Mills*. He is a legend.

Back to college and one of the reasons that I will always be thankful to Trinity was that I had a quite extraordinary select group of teachers. Starting with the man I spent most time with, my piano teacher, Tony Lindsay. A slight, elvish character with a dour northern wit, he and I hit it off immediately. He will always be very special to me, I always felt that he 'got' me. He was also one of the very few people in my life who always called me Michael rather than Mike. I like that. I felt supported and encouraged in all my musical endeavours with him.

He had been one of the legendary pianist Arturo Benedetti Michelangeli's very special pupils and stayed in Bolzano on one of his unique piano courses around 1960. When Tony was teaching me he was in a very fine piano duo with his partner Simon Young. He very quickly realised that I was never going to be a concert pianist, but I was a really rather good sight reader and accompanist and he encouraged me to get as much playing as I could by accompanying as many people as possible.

Instrumentalists and singers were always needing someone to accompany them so I made it my business to try and do as much of it as possible. One of the people I played for in that first year was a really talented clarinettist called Christine Parkin. She had a beautiful tone and fabulous musicality and I worked on the *Dance Preludes* by Lutoslawski for the *Dame Ruth Railton Prize for Woodwind* with her. Challenging but hugely satisfying music that really worked for us. With me playing the evocative piano accompaniment she won the prize in her second year, much to the chagrin of the older woodwind pupils. That meant, though, that at College Prize-giving in 1977 we would play the pieces in the concert that precedes the awards, and the venue – The Wigmore Hall. This was to be the first of three concerts playing in that fabulous building. The following year it was with flautist Neil McLaren playing Fauré's *Fantaisie* and in my final year, 1979, it was with the gorgeous soprano Veronica Veysey and we performed *L'invitation au Voyage* by Duparc and Poulenc's *La Petite Servante*. It was such a privilege to play there and I still get goosebumps remembering those concerts.

1979 Veronica Veysey, me & Tony Lindsay – Wigmore Hall

I played with many singers over my four years at Trinity but very early on found myself playing Brahms *Four Serious Songs* and Elgar's *Sea Pictures* with an extraordinary contralto called Lucy Coleby. We were playing in the Lecture Theatre of Trinity where the concert grand was a nine foot Bösendorfer with the extra notes at the bottom covered by a little black flap, still one of my favourite pianos. It was one of the regular Wednesday afternoon concerts in front of our peers and some invited guests. One of the special guests was a lady in her eighties, Gladys Puttick, who had been one of the most innovative and forward thinking teachers of her generation. A veritable 'Nadia Boulanger' of Trinity and highly revered. In her youth she had seen Brahms play and I was somewhat stunned when she quietly came over to me after the concert and whispered that my playing was like hearing Brahms himself at the piano. Antony Lindsay standing beside me beamed with pride, his elegant coaching and patient advice had paid off. Lucy developed into a fine contralto and has had a successful operatic career in Germany. I loved playing with her and a short while after the concert we recorded the songs in the recently opened Berwick Street Studios where she had managed to get a late recording session booked. Actually she was having an affair with one of the 'high-ups' in the Vice Squad (The Sweeney) and he funded her, so being in a recording studio right next to Soho was quite apt, really. Sadly the results of that session have long since disappeared but I remember we didn't leave the studio until 3am!

Elizabeth 'Libby' Hawes was one of the best voice teachers at college and I learnt a lot sitting in her classes playing through lieder and French Songs with the many and varied singers that were on her roster. Veronica Veysey and I became a respectable duo and not only performed at Miss Hawes' private soirées in her elegant Georgian house in between Chalk Farm and

Swiss Cottage, but also in the more prestigious of the college competitions. The reason that we performed at the Wigmore Hall in 1979 was because we had won the *Dorothy Hawes French Song Prize*. One of the few prizes where the award is not just about the soloist but actually about both performers. There was an added bonus that year as we were put into an inter college song competition and though we didn't win, we did get a professional recording session as a runners-up prize. The session was at the Bishopsgate Institute and the piano I was to play was Dame Myra Hess's old piano that she had bequeathed to the Institute, her Rosewood Model D Steinway Grand dating from 1927. Probably the finest piano I have ever played. Happily that recording still exists and Veronica and I played a mixture of songs, from Debussy's *Fantoches* to Brahms' *Wie Melodien* by way of a couple of Ralph Vaughan Williams' songs and even some Lully. It was a glorious time full of the joy of simple music making and it also helped my understanding of the singer's psyche which has, of course, given me such valuable base knowledge in my subsequent career.

The other teachers who have had a lasting impression on me are Felicity Young and James Gaddarn. Felicity Young took over from Gladys Puttick when she retired and was already established when I arrived. General musicianship, keyboard skills and musical history were all brought to vivid life by Felicity. A very prim, twin set and pearls kind of lady, always carrying her little handbag under one arm. With her clipped way of speaking, it was as if there wasn't enough time to give us all the information she needed to impart, but what pearls of wisdom they were.

College choir was taken by the legendary James Gaddarn. In his earlier career he had been an assistant to Sir Malcolm Sargent and at his behest was choral director of the Royal Choral Society.

Mr Gaddarn was not known for his clarity of beat, rather he was known for his great musicality, wit and understanding of text. He almost led the choir by osmosis. In my first year I was very much in awe – though I did at least on a couple of occasions make myself quite conspicuous by wearing a little hint of make-up, well if it was good enough for David Bowie – but Gaddarn's innate musicality won through and sometime in the second year I became one of a small and select group of people who accompanied the choir for those rehearsals. Wrestling with piano reductions of Walton's *Belshazzar's Feast,* Bach's *Mass in B minor,* Tippett's *A Child of our Time,* Vaughan Williams' *Donna Nobis Pacem* with Pippa Dames Longworth and John Hancorn as soloists and even Britten's *War Requiem,* I would always try to pop in the odd musical quote to illustrate his instructions. Sometimes a little too facetiously. He would sigh and look down his nose at me, witheringly, so I gradually learnt to play to the crowd a little less. Ultimately my association with James Gaddarn took me outside college as in my final year I would travel with him in his weed infested, slightly dilapidated 1950s *Bentley R Type* over the Westway and on to Ealing where I played for his rehearsals with The Ealing Choral Society. I won the *Alan J Kirby Choral Conducting Prize* in that final year, nothing particularly strange in that except that I never did any choral conducting while I was at college. It turned out that I won the prize because James Gaddarn thought it would be a good way of saying thank you for playing for college choir. He was a true original and I am so grateful that I spent time with him in such a positive way.

When I say I didn't do any choral conducting, that wasn't strictly true because in 1977 the college orchestra was performing Holst's *The Planets* in The Royal Albert Hall for a special charity concert and the ladies of the choir were needed to sing the ethereal chorus at the end of *Neptune.* In the score Holst asks that the choir be hidden and, of course, the RAH has a gallery at the very top of the building so it is the absolutely perfect place to hide them from view. The very last bar is to be repeated until the sound of the voices is 'lost in the distance' and it was decided that the choir would gently walk backwards into the corridor outside as the door gently closed over. Now there is one slight problem when you are up there; if you can't be seen by the audience then you can't see the conductor, so I was asked to stand with them and 'relay the beat'. In the very place where only a few years before the fourteen year old me had watched *Belshazzar's Feast* in awe, now I was actually performing myself, even if it was in complete anonymity!

Not all the teachers at college inspired me and I had the composing stuffing taken out of me by my harmony and counterpoint teacher, so much so that it wasn't until after college that I started writing again. I can't even recall his name, but he was very young and louche with piercing eyes and his negativity and criticism was devastating. Most of the time the musical energy of the people in the building had an infectious and inspiring reaction, this was the only time the opposite was true.

I started college with organ as my second study and my organ teacher, Geoffrey Hanson, very soon realised that I was not going to be the next George Thalben-Ball and we parted company at the end of the first year, though I did enjoy playing the large 1957 Walker organ at St Mark's Church, Regents Park where I had my lessons. I then spent a couple of terms with a charming lady called Valda Aveling and studied harpsichord before I was able to change to piano and piano accompaniment as my principal studies with dear Antony Lindsay teaching me both. Under his tutelage I won the *Lilian Florence Smith Prize for Piano Accompaniment* in my final year.

This was the height of the 'permissive society' and before the monstrous spectre of AIDS had started its evil journey so it was at Trinity that I first met 'openly' gay people. Some wonderful friends, like ex trolly-dolly oboe player, Marc James, composer David Crisp and my wonderful teacher, Tony Lindsay. But there were also some not so wonderful attempted liaisons when slightly older gay men harassed and tried to push themselves onto me. Not something I want to dwell on given my childhood experiences, but a form of abuse, and like so many, sorry to say, never reported.

*

Staying in Kingston with the Patients was the best springboard into living in London that I could have wished for but after two terms of trekking into Bond Street each day I was eager to move on, so I packed my trusty red trunk and moved to a flat in Camden Town.

58, St Augustine's Road became my home for the next four years. A group of five friends had hatched this plan to find somewhere and between us we found a rather tatty three bedroom ground and first floor apartment in an absolutely fantastic location. Three bedrooms, three boys and three girls. We had to decide how to make that work, so I proposed that, to begin with, I share with one of the girls. I was very happy in female company and this seemed a good solution. Helen Clow was supposed to be part of the six but she had to postpone for a term or two so a Canadian girl called Linda Scanlon took her place and that was who I shared with until Helen arrived. Downstairs in between the sitting room and kitchen was Mark Lowther with Alexis Affonso, upstairs, in the back bedroom, myself with Linda and next door Barbara Boothman and Siân Jones. Over the years, of course, the personnel changed significantly and for my last year there I had the downstairs bedroom all to myself. So, here I was, very much in the metropolis now, and instead of a journey that took me ninety plus minutes, I could easily get to college in thirty to forty-five.

St Augustines Road became quite the party house and I loved being there. Campbell was one of our regular visitors, frequently making use of the sofa or floor depending on the volume of noxious substances that had been partaken. I think it would be fair to say that the boys at 58 were not the most housetrained and there were persistent house meetings to try to change that, generally led by Barbara. To no avail, I'm afraid. We were very much chaps of our generation and looking back I wish I had been better.

Hazel Shaw was a pretty good fiddle player and I found her in a Dinely's rehearsal room playing the Mendelssohn *Violin Concerto* one day and asked if she would like me to accompany her. It wasn't long before we became an item and our happy relationship lasted for nine months. Hazel even came down to Treyarnon, so it must have been serious! She was a little shy and demure but somehow things clicked very well for us. Her flat was about twenty minutes away from No. 58, in Caledonian Road. The walk past derelict warehouses and a couple of old pubs was not for the faint hearted, as I discovered late one evening, after Hazel, her flat mates and I had spent a few hours telling ghost stories. On the journey home I found myself looking this way and that, starting at any sudden noise and, mercifully, eventually arrived at St Augustines Road. I was now sharing a room with Helen who was fast asleep when I arrived. Carefully I started to get ready for bed, my imagination still running wild. The window in the room was floor to ceiling with a very smooth double sash casement when, all of a sudden, I thought I could hear something scratching on the wide cil outside. We were on the first floor, it couldn't be anything. Nonsense. I looked away. No, there it was again. Helen's bed was closer to the window, I was standing at the foot of my bed looking directly at the curtains and I found myself transfixed as, through a chink in the curtains, I could see the window moving very slowly. I tried to whisper to Helen to wake up, no good, my throat had tightened with fear. The window continued to rise and then suddenly with a 'swish' the curtains swept to one side and there was Campbell, his eyes popping, crawling into the room. "Wotcher, Mike," he said, "any chance I could doss on your sofa for the night?" Well, the air was suddenly quite blue, Helen woke up not best pleased, and the 'ghostly' apparition eventually stayed downstairs on the couch.

In my second year I was on the Student Association as part of the social activities team. The Christmas party this year was going to be in a little club on the edge of Soho. A huge number of the students were there, it was a big event. Suddenly at around 11pm the party came to an abrupt halt when the police rushed in and informed us that there was a suspected IRA bomb in nearby Oxford Street and we had to evacuate. This was the time when a bomb scare was all too commonplace so, although there was an element of fear, most people simply got on with following the cordon put in place by the police, who directed us to Charing Cross Road and away from Oxford Street.

Hazel, her two flatmates Sarah and Jo, and I made our way back to their flat. When we got there we immediately put the radio on to see if there was any further news. It was unnerving and sobering to hear that from around midnight there were a number of small devices going off along the length of Oxford Street, no-one injured, but very dangerous nevertheless. The next day at college one of our friends, John Tobin, calmly let us know that he had dodged the cordon the night before because he wanted to get to his flat near Wigmore Street which would have taken him hours if he had followed the diversion. Basically he had quietly ambled along the length of Oxford Street just minutes before the bombs went off. A very lucky escape.

I was hugely fortunate to get a full grant for my whole time at Trinity but usually around halfway through term things started to get a little tight, financially. A couple of the older piano players at college told me about an interesting and potentially entertaining way of adding to the term coffers. Around the corner on Marylebone Lane was the London College of Dance and Drama and pianists were always needed for ballet classes and the like. So I turned up and offered my services.

I ended up playing quite frequently and thoroughly enjoyed myself. Extemporisation and understanding how the classes worked came to me quite easily. Of course it helped that one of the teachers, Jill Henderson, took me under her wing and really was very clear in her musical instructions before any given exercise and I learnt very quickly how a ballet class was structured and what types of music were needed for the various disciplines within.

I also played music that was contemporary and that people knew. For example, *Pliés*, which is usually one of the first sections of class, sits really well when accompanied by *Cavatina* from *The Deer Hunter* which was very popular at the time. It was a good challenge for me to find something that would fit really well with the movement, it was also really satisfying seeing how the girls in class responded to the motivation of having music they knew. There was also one wonderful coincidence about Jill, which I only found out much later. Her sister is Mary Pelham, so she knew all about Treyarnon and just maybe that explained the 'simpatico' that we felt when I played for her classes.

Jill was also responsible for the one and only time that I graced the boards as a dancer. Well, when I say dancer what I mean is that for one performance they were some men short for a particular routine and I was asked to fill in and lift one of the students into a 'fish' position. All very tasteful, darkly lit and I got away with it! However, all this dance experience was more grist to the mill for my theatre career later on, plus on top of it all, I got paid for it!

The other rather useful little job that I occasionally did was play in one of the local pubs. The Prince Alfred in Marylebone Lane – now a café called Caffé Caldesi – was quite a good boozer and literally round the corner from our favourite haunt, The Angel. It was never my favourite thing having to cope with a lot of rather drunk requests but it helped pay some bills and was good experience.

Flat mate Mark Lowther played the organ at nearby St Paul's church and I occasionally helped out. There was also a very good AmDram company there and I quite enjoyed getting involved. Mark and I occasionally played duets, including an absolute cracker that I have only recently re-found the music for. It was called *Les Clochettes* by a little known French composer called Durand de Grau. Very exaggerated, silly and fun. Alongside that duet we were also known to perform *Come Into the Garden Maud* with me flexing my Victorian melodramatic vocal prowess, or not, depending on your point of view! As a group we even performed little playlets and I rather fell for my leading lady, Mary, after we had played opposite each other in *The Red Barn*. She lived quite close in Camden Mews and, as she was rather older than me, I seemed to find myself a little over embroiled too quickly in a 'grown up' relationship. Eventually I had to call a halt, it was very sad but for my sanity it had to stop.

All of this took place in front of a rather complicated backdrop. It was my Graduation year, and I was President of the Student's Association. During my tenure we did manage to get funding to enable my successor into the post, Robert Richardson, to have a sabbatical year, so mine was the last year of combining final year studies with being President. I have found in my life that if you are very busy, adding more to do and getting busier actually helps you to get everything done – if you want something done ask a busy person, I suppose.

One of the duties I had to perform as President was to look after our guest adjudicator during and after the *Student's Association Chamber Music Prize*. In my year it was the composer Sir Lennox Berkeley, and sitting in a restaurant after the event I had the extraordinary experience of hearing him talk about his composition lessons with Nadia Boulanger and then what it was like to meet and work with Maurice Ravel. To be so close, one hand shake away, if you like, from people who influenced the whole of music in the twentieth century, this was touching history itself. I still get a buzz working out those connections. I can get back to Mozart in five handshakes, because of Gladys Puttick and the Brahms story, a bit like *Six Degrees of Separation* but historically, my version is *Five Handshakes of Separation*.

Here's the path:

Gladys **Puttick** to **Brahms,** who was taught by Eduard **Marxsen**, who was taught by Ignaz **Von Seyfried** who was taught by **Mozart**, voila!

So my life was incredibly full and yet somehow I managed to survive that third year and even got my GTCL qualification at the end of it. (GTCL was the BMus equivalent at the time)

My licentiate examination, LTCL, taken the year before and a prerequisite of reaching the GTCL, was a little touch and go, however. My examiner was the famous pianist, John Bingham, and after managing quite successfully to get through my prepared pieces he asked me to play some scales. Now, scales have never been high on my list, maybe they should have been, but I was always keen to get onto the 'real' music, so I never practiced them. John asked me to play C♯ harmonic minor in apposition. There was a pause while I computed what that meant and then I tried, but I couldn't even work out how to play it one handed, let alone two hands going in opposite directions which is what I was supposed to do. Anyway, after my third attempt he politely asked me if we should 'move on', fortunately the next part of the exam was sight reading which I sailed through. The marks he gave me are a perfect illustration of my technical prowess:

Scales – 3/10

Sight Reading – 14/15

So my overall result of 75/100 ended up being quite respectable in the circumstances.

Phil White, from Devon Youth Orchestra, had gone to the Royal Academy of Music and we made sure that a couple of times each term we would meet up and keep our friendship going. He was focusing on composition and doing very well. In just the way that Trinity suited me, the RAM suited him well and he thrived there. I was quite envious of the Academy's Student Union – with a bar and a café – but Trinity was so much smaller those kind of facilities were impossible to contemplate. In my year as President we were able to increase our space by about thirty per cent, however. We were moved to a bespoke area in the basement and had some new amenities specially built. Still no bar, but at least there was acknowledgment that the Student's Association existed for the benefit of all the students and our Board of Governors and Principal, Myers Foggin, ceased thinking that we were merely a nuisance.

During all the madness of my third year I also joined Harold Clarke's Wind Ensemble, NOT on the oboe, I hasten to add, that part of my musical life was firmly under lock and key. No, I was asked to play the piano for Martinu's *La Revue de Cuisine* with the crème de la crème of his players. It was a special concert for the Bedford Park Festival in Chiswick. Harold wrote a review where he said, '...in which Michael Dixon gave a very fine impersonation of a 1920s jazz pianist.' I was very happy with that.

Being at Trinity gave me such a rich and varied experience both in my musical and social life. Chris Bracewell, a bearded hippy in a sports jacket, who had been at Trinity a few years before me, was the organist at Hinde Street Church, where we had our choir rehearsals and the like. He formed many ad hoc vocal and orchestral ensembles and we performed 'scratch' Messiahs, and Mozart Requiems, fairly frequently in the church. He was also a GREAT party giver and lived on the church premises. So after any one of these performances we would all traipse upstairs to his apartment with at least one bottle of something alcoholic and proceed to stay up merry making for as long as we could. There were many nights of sleeping on the floor, climbing over comatose and sometimes not so comatose(!) bodies.

Such brilliantly mad times, with Campbell very often taking centre stage with yet another hilarious story of his antics. His mode of transport in the latter years at Trinity was an old off-white *Austin A55* van with the words *Van Ordinaire* emblazoned down the sides. I even literally shared driving the thing one evening around Parliament Square, we were both a touch on the tipsy side...oh, and I hadn't even taken my driving test!

There was also an incident where we purloined a pal's *Citroen Dyane* to get us from Marylebone to a party in Chiswick. It was quite an accommodating car – there were twelve of us on board! I was in the passenger seat with three people on my lap, seven in the back and Campbell had managed to wind himself into the canvas roof – so with our driver, twelve. There were quite a few horrible scraping noises as we turned corners but basically the trip across London went without a hitch until we were stopped by the Old Bill in the Goldhawk Road. Three people scarpered into the bushes in the ensuing melée but the cops were still somewhat flabbergasted that nine people got out...

At the end of the third year I was also thinking about how to finance myself so I applied for a job as a répétiteur at The Royal Ballet – having had so much experience playing for class at the London College of Dance and Drama it seemed like a good idea. To my surprise after the audition I was offered a position but it occurred to me that playing for class for the next ten years or so and then, possibly, getting the chance to conduct the orchestra if I was very lucky, was not the route that I wanted to follow.

My friend, Bill Worrell who was a year above me, took me along to watch him 'dep' on piano and keyboards on the show I had listened to in Karon's back room only a few years before, *Jesus Christ Superstar*. It was such an eyeopener being onstage with him, one side Keyboard Heaven, the other Guitar Hell and in the pit all the legit players and the cast mingling all around. I loved being there, it was thrilling, but when Bill said, "When do you want to start 'depping', then?" my sense of self preservation kicked in and I declared that it was far too soon for me to contemplate, I didn't have the wherewithal or the confidence to do it. It was too early. So after all that and my completely bonkers third year I decided that I would concentrate on my playing and do a post-grad year, staying on at Trinity where I knew that I would have great people to work with. Along with

James Gaddarn and the Ealing Choral Society I also played piano for rehearsals of The John Bate Choir in Richmond, continued playing at The London College of Dance and Drama and also for rehearsals of Fulham Music Theatre.

It seemed that St Cecilia and her musical acolytes were pushing me in a theatrical direction...

SIX

CAREERING INTO A CAREER

Fulham Music Theatre (Formerly Fulham Light Operatic Society) was one of those slightly dotty, old fashioned AmDrams with a few really talented performers and quite a few keen but not so talented.

They were ALL fun to be with though, and under the baton of the *Joyce Grenfell-esque* Musical Director Stella Hornby they didn't sound half bad. Towards the end of the first term of my fourth year I started working with them and ended up being Musical Director for their annual pantomime at Fulham Town Hall. It was great fun and it has to be said that the Principal Boy, Audrey, in her thigh length boots turned quite a few heads, including mine!

After the fun and frolic of *Dick Whittington* the next show was Sondheim's *A Funny Thing Happened on the Way to the Forum* which was followed by Cole Porter's *Kiss Me Kate* and then Sandy Wilson's *The Boyfriend*. Hugh Halliday was a staff director/producer at English National Opera and had previously been the drummer in a band called *Unit 4 + 2,* whose number one hit was *Concrete and Clay* in 1965. He was the new Director/Choreographer for the group and on *Funny Thing* and we hit it off together immediately. He was cheeky, fun and made everyone feel good in rehearsals. A supportive director.

1978 Playing for Fulham Music Theatre

On top of working on *Funny Thing* with him in early 1979, he was choreographer for the revival of the musical *The Canterbury Tales* which opened in the Shaftesbury Theatre in April 1979 and he asked me to be his dance accompanist. Here I was, second term of my fourth year and I was working on a West End show. Two of the dancers, Kim Mendez and Leonie Palette, were very kind to this new boy and I loved how they seemed to radiate show business all the time. It was a revelation.

The Musical Director was a smart, camp and witty man called Denys Rawson, who took a shine to me and asked if I would be interested in playing in the pit. I was flattered but decided that it would be better to finish my fourth year, so I declined. I learnt a little about the temperament of actors while working on that show, though.

The movement rehearsals had finished on one particular day and instead of going for a drink with the dancers I stayed at the theatre to watch the actors rehearsing on stage. The director, Martin Starkie, was in full flow and the Prioress, a highly respected actress called Anna Sharkie, found something he said somewhat at odds with how she felt about her character, shall we say. There was a little hiatus on stage as she walked into the wings, screamed some expletives very loudly, threw her script across to the other wing and finally sashayed back onto stage and in a very pronounced stage whisper said that she was now ready to carry on! A proper learning curve.

Later in the year, and just a few months after I left Trinity, Hugh asked me to work with him again. This time it was for a TV musical drama called *Witches!* based on the story of the Pendle Witches, written by Jeremy James Taylor for Granada Television. Again he was choreographer and he wanted me to play for rehearsals. What's particularly amazing about this, though, was that because I was playing for the dance rehearsals I was asked by production to play piano for the recording sessions which were to be at ...Abbey Road! I was officially contracted by the fixer, George Hamer and I bowled up to the studios in early November 1979 for two sessions starting at 10am and I was shown into Studio 3. The hallowed vaults of Abbey Road! To say that I was excited would be a bit of an understatement. I was also somewhat unsure of protocol and my sense of excitement was well tempered by the nervous energy swirling around inside me.

George was the go-to studio orchestral contractor and the small band that he had booked was full of the top players of the time. Hal Fisher on drums, Frank Ricotti on percussion, Kenny

Baker on trumpet, Don Lusher on trombone, just some of the musical icons that were there.

Then I met the bass player, Pete Morgan. I immediately recognised him because Pete was the regular bass player on *Parkinson* with Harry Stoneham's band and I had also seen him in the legendary Dudley Moore's jazz trio, another of his regular gigs. He was such a gentle man and he immediately sussed that I was a new boy and put me at my ease. In the breaks, when we all walked downstairs to the canteen, he made sure that I was looked after and sat with me.

It was my first time in this most famous of studios and I am so fortunate that there have been many, many visits since.

Around the same time as I started playing for Fulham Music Theatre, Campbell asked me if I would like to share some other work with him. He was accompanying pupils for a singing teacher, called Ian Adam, and Ian needed some fresh blood. When Campbell introduced me, in Ian's little terraced house in Ovington Street behind Harrods, I knew that we would get on. He was sparkling, very smiley, hugely camp and more than a little suggestive, but all of that was tempered by his soft Scottish accent and once I got behind his little grand piano to work with him and witness his teaching skill I saw first hand the mastery and consummate talent that he had. Ian was THE singing teacher in London at that time. So many big West End actors came to him for coaching. He knew how to get the very best out of people as he flattered, cajoled and chastised with equal measure but with charm at all times. The first twenty minutes of each lesson was Ian and the pupil's time alone. He would warm their voices while downstairs in the chintzy basement we would warm the teapot, eat the biscuits and chew the cud.

My work at Trinity stood me in good stead in accompanying the actors as they made their way through the musical theatre rep, because sometimes Ian would suggest something classical and, of course, that was right up my street. The people on his books were so diverse. From established West End lovies, like Gay Soper and Stephanie Lawrence, to famous actors needing very quickly to try their hand at singing to secure a TV or movie role, like Terence Stamp or Dinsdale Landen. A highlight for me was *Pan's People* dancer Cherry Gillespie turning up. As gorgeous in real life as she was on *Top of the Pops*.

Ian let me come and go as other work dictated. I remained on his roster of piano players, along with Campbell and the now sadly lamented Martin Smith – a hugely talented pianist, composer, actor and singer who was one of the vast tranche of performers that we lost to AIDS through the eighties and nineties – and I stayed on Ian's roster until the mid eighties. I still use some of the vocal exercises and techniques that I learnt from Ian now.

The actor and director Richard Franklin (Captain Yates in *Doctor Who*) was another of the pupils on Ian's books and in November 1979, just after those first Abbey Road sessions, Richard asked me if I would be interested in being Musical Director for a pantomime he was directing over Christmas. The show was to be in New Brighton, just across the Mersey from Liverpool, and rehearsals would be one week in a little church hall in Pimlico. The timing was perfect for all the other commitments I was juggling and I said yes, please. This version of *Dick Whittington* was effectively the start of my professional career in theatre and dear Richard was the instigator.

I was introduced to the producer Barrie Stacey in his office at the very top of one of the dingy buildings in Denmark Street and my comment of, "This office looks like the perfect fairy grotto!" to which he replied, "Ooh, daughter, I think we'll get along!" endeared him to me immediately. A few weeks later I was in rehearsals for the show with a fabulously mixed bunch of people. It was a baptism of fire. Barrie was not the most generous of producers but he did get shows on and gave work to a great many people – even if, generally in a Barrie Stacey production, the sets wobbled a bit.

We had one week to get the show ready, one week to put not just the songs together and arranged but absolutely everything. Steve Poulter, the stage manager worked like a dervish and also had to play the Sultan – don't ask. He and I seemed to have the same (filthy) sense of humour and got on instantly.

I was told that I had a huge band – me and a drummer – but I also had to play the theatre organ for at least one number, it was part of the Floral Pavilion, New Brighton contract with Barrie. So I quickly put together a dance routine that featured *The Muppets Theme* and *The Charleston* and that seemed to placate them. The Dame, Chris Shaw, was a larger than life Drag-Act, known as *Diamond Lil*, but for our production he tamed it all down to play Sarah the Cook very effectively. His voice was actually astonishing – a big booming baritone – but more of that shortly.

After our week of rehearsal it was off to New Brighton on the Sunday. All of us in one coach on the train to Liverpool. We used it to good effect though, as with Steve P at my side, we did a full *a capella* run through whilst on board, much to the amusement of the other passengers. They even applauded at the end of the company numbers!

The theatre was a huge barn of a place, all on one level, seating around a thousand screaming kids and their teachers or family. Two shows a day after our Monday dress and tech rehearsal and we were off! Thursdays was boiled-sweets-thrown-at-the-stage matinee and the challenge for us in the pit was dodging them, but generally the atmosphere was electric and the audience loved the show. I was in my element.

There was a little restaurant round the corner from the theatre called The Mexicana and it stayed open for all of us 'turns' from the theatre. Alf and Lil ran it and basically it was a drinking club with chilli con carne thrown in. It was our little haven and was home to many mad escapades – including one very drunken eve when Steve, his assistant Colin Small and myself decided to do a 'Sisters' routine, stark naked with a little bow tied delicately around our nether regions, through the whole place. There were normal punters eating as we ran through, I'm sure they must have nearly choked on their chilli!

Helen, from No. 58, came to visit me just after Christmas for a few days, she thought her 'little brother' as she called me, may be a bit homesick. Well, I introduced her to Steve. She wasn't very enamoured at first but, miracle of miracles, a bond was made and they have been happily together ever since.

We ran for four weeks and in the penultimate week Chris, the Dame, asked me if I would like to go on a little tour with him as his personal Musical Director. As I said before, he did sing rather well and I was pretty much open for new adventures so I agreed. The 'Tour' was in fact two weeks of going round the working mens clubs of South Wales, Manchester and Liverpool. In the two weeks between the end of the panto and the start of the tour I needed to buy a keyboard to take round with me. So in quick time my Rhodes Suitcase 88 was fully purchased and I was ready. Though I am not sure lugging around that electric piano was ultimately very good for me, it was not the lightest piece of equipment!

Each venue had its own resident band, usually an organist, bass player and drummer, so I had to gently coral these leviathans of musicianship into coping with Chris's slightly dogeared charts. To be fair, though, a couple of the clubs had pretty good players and I really enjoyed the 'seat of the pants' aspect of the gig. A good learning curve too, as in each venue it was a 'talk through' the music, there was never time for a proper rehearsal.

If I thought panto was a 'baptism of fire' then this two week tour was the full on 'burning bush'! However, to witness Chris at the end of his set, dressed as Mae West in a red rhinestone, figure hugging dress and matching sequinned hat, scarf and cape, singing *The Holy City* in full 'cod' operatic style, getting a standing ovation from The Rover Club clientele in Cardiff is a particularly spectacular and peculiar musical memory for me.

My first tiny forage into the BBC came just afterwards when contralto, Alex Denman, who was one of the talented Fulham Music Theatre members, asked me to accompany her for a BBC audition. It was to sing a song by Martin Smith and the audition was at BBC rehearsal rooms in Park Royal, now long since gone. At that time the rehearsal rooms were bustling and when we got to the main room there were a row of little music studios where the two BBC accompanists, Paul Maguire and David Firman, were waiting for their next 'victim'. As we walked down the corridor I could hear one of them practicing the piano accompaniment of the Lutoslawski *Dance Preludes* that I had played at the Wigmore Hall just a couple of years before. I knocked on the door, Paul introduced himself, and I explained that I knew the pieces pretty well. We had a brilliant conversation and I just loved the serendipity of so many bits of my recent musical past colliding in that room. Both David and Paul became allies that day. I was very lucky. Sadly Alex wasn't so lucky, she sang Martin's song really well but she didn't get the part she was auditioning for, however she did go on to have a very good operatic career.

Over the next couple of months in early 1980 things just seemed to slot into place and one job led to another. Barrie Stacey needed someone to cover as Musical Director for a little tour of *Hans Christian Andersen* that he had out on the road. Robert Meadmore, Michael Kirk and gorgeous ballerina Ursula Hageli, from the

Northern Ballet, were the principals and I had an absolute ball working with them. Robert with his mellifluous vocal prowess, Michael, his acerbic wit and 'Urkie' with her astonishing *développé*. Far too much fun and frolic – I think we partied solidly the whole six weeks. That job segued straight into a charity concert for the pianist Russ Conway where I was playing for a young male singer.

We were in Hastings, the concert had gone very well and afterwards we were taken to a little club. My singer friend knew the owner so we got in for next to nothing. Quietly sitting at the bar I suddenly realised that the two chaps next to us were starting to take the Mickey. "Oi, fairy, who's your girlfriend?" That sort of thing. (I should point out at this point that my dress back then was a little flamboyant, big check jacket, wide flares and blue polkadot necktie hanging down.) We tried to ignore the jibes coming from my left but eventually I snapped and turned to them with, "Why don't you just f*** off and leave us alone!"

The next thing I knew was that I was lying next to the adjacent pillar with blood pouring out of my right eyebrow and a very sore head. One of these 'gentlemen' had whacked me with his bottle of beer. My pal made an attempt to retaliate but all was taken out of our hands as the bouncers took these two chaps away and taught them the error of their ways outside. Being friends with the owner had some benefits.

I was not in the best state but two girls who had been dancing together on the little dance floor on the upper level immediately came over and offered to take me to hospital. So off the four of us went in their car. A little while later, stitched and eye-patched up, we went back to my friend's house where I was going to stay overnight anyway. I will simply say that we all had a very good time and the following day the girls drove me back to London after a little stop off at their flat in Brighton where I played their piano in the corridor while they had a bath together. They were the first openly bisexual couple that I had met. Even though I had an eyepatch covering what was now a huge black eye, you could say I had an eyeopening experience and my memory of it all is in two dimensions not three!

*

While I was working on *Hans Andersen* Michael Kirk suggested that I could move into his little flat in Hammersmith. St Augustine's Road had been a fantastic place to be and for the last couple of years I had been in my own room downstairs – no more sharing – but it felt like the right time to go. So Westcroft Square and brilliantly funny evenings with Michael and his flatmate, Penny, were the new order of the day. Michael is the only man I know who can say that his rear end was used to advertise women's jeans, by the way. The Wrangler adverts that were around at the time featured his bottom. Honestly!

He also was a regular performer at *The Aba Daba Musical Hall*, which was based in a pub near Kings Cross called the Pindar of Wakefield, and I went along with him one evening to meet their regular pianist and Musical Director, David Wykes. Well, a week later I played my first gig with them and I continued on and off, as other commitments would allow, until 1984. Michael was one of the regulars along with people like Shaun Curry, Geoffrey Robinson and the tantalising Colette Kelly. The shows run by Aline Waites and Robin Hunter were similar in style to the BBC's *The Good Old Days*. Yet another style of playing to add to my musical armoury and I loved it.

A rather seedy producer called Malcolm Knight had contacted me. Would I be interested in being Musical Director for a National Tour of the musical *Hair*? Naturally I jumped at the chance and after some hasty auditions and a couple of pre production meetings there I was, booked. I also needed to put together a four piece rock band for the show and the bass player,

Mike Tomich, all long hair and American cars, was proposed by the producer. Mike suggested Keith Hall on drums, as they both played together for a band called *Pickettywitch* and we found a terrific guitar player called Steve Crook. Sorted.

So there I was in July at the Churchill Theatre Bromley for the first day of rehearsals. Janie Chappel and Steven Slater along with Michael Bruce, Susie McKenna, John Goldsmith and Jo Ward-Bevan were the leads and the rest of the cast was brilliantly diverse. Susie was playing Chrissie, who sings *I Met a Boy Called Frank Mills*, she was someone I hadn't auditioned, but her talent just shone through. It wasn't the best ever production of *Hair* but it was certainly energetic and played with conviction. At twenty-three I was very young to be Musical Director but I just got on with it, really didn't think anything of it, the hubris of youth, I suppose. The show was very much developed during those rehearsals, I rearranged sections on the fly as we needed them. The ensemble made a pretty good sound together and musically I certainly felt we were working well. Our 'Hud' was played by a man called Honeyboy Keith Williams, notoriously well endowed, by all accounts!

Henry Metcalfe choreographed and the aforementioned Malcolm Knight directed. Once the band joined me on stage and we got the show into dress rehearsals it was really rocking along. By this time I had added to my Rhodes piano various effects pedals and a small Korg synthesiser so I was most definitely in my 'Keith Emerson' or 'Rick Wakeman' phase. I even had a black cape with silver embroidery which I wore for the band playout. Over the course of the tour our 'moment' evolved into quite a tour de force for the four of us, which naturally we loved!

During rehearsals I got more than a little besotted with Susie. She was living not far from Hammersmith and she offered to drive me to and from rehearsals in her little Fiat. I confided in my drummer, Keith, quite early on and he, in no uncertain terms, told me to let her know how I felt. So I did.

By the time we left Bromley and really started the tour it would be fair to say that Susie and I were an item. Along with Jo Ward-Bevan, John Goldsmith and sound operator Peter Miller we formed quite a little band of brothers and tried to secure digs together. When the tour reached my home town of Plymouth, I was able to introduce Mum & Dad to Susie but it felt too soon for us to stay together in their house, so John shared with me.

John was playing Woof, the sad, openly gay character with the family friendly song entitled *Sodomy*. A gentle soul and one of the warmest and kindest people you could meet, who ended up looking after all the crowd movement and choreography on *Top of the Pops* – he stayed there for years. Mum wasn't too sure about having an openly gay man staying with us, but by the end of the two weeks they were joined at the hip, doing the ironing together, gossiping and giggling. My folks loved him. They also really took to Susie even though the first time they saw her was on stage and, as this was *Hair*, at the end of Act One she was completely naked!

There are so many stories about this tour, but one of my all time favourites was when we performed our first show in Bradford, at the Alhambra. On these weekly and two weekly tours generally the Monday is 'get-in' day, when the set, sound and lighting is put up and then on the Tuesday there is a spacing call for the cast, because every stage size is different, and that incorporates a sound call with the band as well. There is never a complete run through so the new crew of the host theatre, who behind the scenes make the show work technically, have to rely on the DSM (Deputy Stage Manager) calling all the cues on headsets and cue lights. Consequently the show that evening is the crew's first show.

On this particular night everything went well until the end of Act One. Now what was supposed to happen was that at the end of the song *Where Do I Go?*, which follows on from *Hare Krishna*, on the very last chord all the cast drop their Kaftans and stand proudly naked on stage, legs apart and arms out to the audience.

As I cut the chord off – blackout – and the cast gather their Kaftans from around their feet and off stage they scarper. That is what was supposed to happen but unfortunately the lighting operator must have been so transfixed by them all standing in the buff that half a second after the blackout the lights suddenly and surprisingly snapped back on again. What this meant was that our entire cast were caught in the very unflattering position of bending over, grabbing their clothes and hare tailing it off into the wings. The applause was somewhat drowned out by the screams and yelps of our boys and girls interrupted in this most embarrassing of ways. However what the audience saw is nothing compared to the vision that was presented to the four of us in the band at the BACK of the stage. I will leave that to your imagination!

Later in the tour we played the Harlow Playhouse and Susie's Aunt Edna, 'Aunty Ned', came along as it was the closest venue to her home in Stonebridge Park. She was diminutive in size but, with a very pronounced North London accent littered with expletives, she was not diminutive in her opinions. Susie asked her if she enjoyed the show and she replied, without blinking an eye, "Oh, I loved it, Susie and Mike, bloody loved it, but I tell you what, if that black boy came at me with that thing I'd run a f***in' mile!" Honeyboy's reputation very neatly observed by dear Aunty Ned!

Hair also presented some interesting conundrums because of the nature of the piece. Here we were at the start of the eighties looking back at the US history of only twelve years before and, at times, perhaps a little too realistically. Basil Soper, the company manager, called me into his office one day and asked if I had noticed anything strange on stage, any smell that might have been a little unusual? By this time in my life I had smoked a little bit of pot and experienced magic mushrooms but I wasn't very versed in the field, shall we say. In Act Two there is a whole 'trippy' section where cannabis and other drugs are seen to be used and herbal cigarettes were substituted, naturally, for the show. One of our cast members was basically taking the realism too far and actually smoking a joint on stage every show and after I had also witnessed it, unfortunately, he had to be sacked from the tour. Method acting taken a little too far!

Playing that show for four months was the closest I ever came to actually being in a rock band. We melded together really well and I learnt so much from Keith, Mike and Steve. It was genuinely exciting playing that score and those songs with them every night, we had laughs and a few barneys, but that is part of the rite of passage, isn't it? We even came to call ourselves *Dixon and the Dickheads!* A moniker that stuck and has been used over the years for a few of my theatre show bands.

Towards the end of the tour Susie and I decided that it would be a good idea to see if we could find a little flat to rent once the tour was over and we found a perfect basement flat in Stoke Newington. 29, Dynevor Road, nice and close to the High Street. I even had my piano brought up from Plymouth, though the old boy who lived above us was not the most generous of neighbours – or perhaps he was just a critic, I'll never know.

Hair finished on Dec 6th we moved in on Dec 7th and on the morning of Dec 9th we heard the devastating news of John Lennon's murder and I can still feel the horror and shock as I write this. It was our generation's 'Kennedy moment', if you like, and I will always remember where I was and that reaction.

Over Christmas and into the following February *The Dickheads* had a little *Godspell* moment. We were asked as a band, and with me as Musical Director, to play a new version of the show, first at the Northcott Theatre in Exeter and then at Nottingham Playhouse. It was a joint production directed by Crispin Thomas and Richard Digby Day and choreographed by Jenny Arnold. A challenge for Keith and Mike, particularly, as on this show there were special new orchestrations by Terry Davies which didn't always do what you would expect. Fortunately there was only one time that I had to intervene and stop Keith from throwing his sticks at Terry, mostly they were very definitely and defiantly thrown to the floor. Anyway by the time we had finished Band Calls we were pretty much sorted and peace reigned. The cast included Jonathan Kiley, Jennifer Caron Hall, Chris Villiers, Brian Parr, Kate West, Carola Stewart, Beverly Klein and Reece Dinsdale. It was very different in style to the original I had seen in London only a few years before but here I was doing the job that had fascinated that young me. Steve Crook and I shared the vocals for *On The Willows*, the haunting song traditionally sung by the band as the Jesus character goes to the garden of Gethsemane, which was a bit of a first and I really rather enjoyed it.

1980 Dixon & the Dickheads –
Steve Crook, Keith Hall and Mike Tomich – Godspell
(Keen eyed will have noticed Steve and Mike have swapped guitars)

When Godspell finished I was able to slot back into working with Ian Adam, Fulham Music Theatre and Aba Daba again while Susie went off for a season of two weekly rep in Swansea.

Barrie Stacey called me in April and told me he was going to put on a Beatles show in London. "Daughter, would you like to be Musical Director for me?" he said. You can most definitely imagine my reply was in the affirmative! I think I was, indeed, careering into a career.

SEVEN

THE WEST END

Theatres are a bit like churches, the audience sit looking towards the front, the actors put on costumes just like the priest and servers with their cassocks and surplices, some are bastions of great architecture, the music is cued in at specific times and both supply succour and sustenance for the soul. If our regional theatres are the Parish Churches and Abbeys then the hallowed West End is where the Cathedrals are, and no theatre is more revered and cathedral like than the London Palladium. The mention of its name conjures up images of Garland, Sammy Davis Jnr, Sinatra, Danny Kaye, Bing Crosby, Chaplin, Laurel and Hardy, Morecambe and Wise, Bruce Forsyth, Bassey – all the greatest entertainers of the 20th Century – and it is where two of the most career defining moments happened for me. *La Cage aux Folles* and *Joseph and the Amazing Technicolor Dreamcoat*. 1986-87 and 1991-93.

But first I had to 'pay my dues'.

I was so excited to be Musical Director and arranger of my very first West End show and after I agreed my contract with Barrie it was all systems go. It was a revue type show using the words and music of the Beatles and it was called *With a Little Help From My Friends* to open at The Duke of York's Theatre on 31st July 1981. The director Geoffrey Ferris would go on to be Associate director of *Phantom of the Opera* and the script came out of an idea by Barrie and Terry Francis.

Rehearsals started at the end of June and obviously we had to cast it well before that. Jacqui Reddin, Janet Shaw, Paul Burton, Steve Devereux and Michael Heath – a young and strong cast with great vocal potential and of course it was a perfect vehicle to get *The Dickheads* back together again. So I set about starting to arrange the songs and tried to make the piece hang together as a whole. Although I had arranged *Hair,* my experience of writing drum parts was pretty scant so a couple of days before band calls, in a panic, I called Keith. He came round to the flat when rehearsals had finished and, after working through the night, by 6am we had completed them and I knew a LOT more! My first 'all-nighter', and not my last!

The process of 'putting a show together' is complicated and even for this small scale piece it needed so much time and energy from everyone involved. But this was my West End debut as a Musical Director and I was just twenty-four – it was so exciting. My lovely dancer friends from *Canterbury Tales*, Kim and Leonie, had most definitely whetted my appetite two years earlier.

Once we got into the theatre everything ramped up by another gear and there were technical rehearsals, sound checks, lighting and finally the Dress Rehearsal. We were all having a fabulous time. The cast were giving it 'large' and we were so looking forward to our first show with an audience. Four previews to tidy up any loose ends and tighten it and then the Opening Night.

That first preview sailed along and although it wasn't a full house we got a fairly good reaction. So far so good. Then the second preview, there were loads of empty seats. Nevertheless, a good applause and we were still hopeful. The remaining two previews, the same. Then the official Opening Night with the party and all that fun and frolic inevitably followed by the 'reviews'.

All our expectations were very suddenly dashed. The reviews were disastrous and the inescapable consequence was that not only did the audiences dwindle even more, but to add salt to the wound, the management had to put the final notice up at the stage door. Normally the final notice would mean that you have two weeks left to play on your contract, but this one simply said that we would get the two weeks money and that at the end of the first full weeks of playing we would close. Including previews, twelve performances in total.

We were all devastated. It was such a kick in the teeth, after all that hard work getting the show on. It seemed so unfair. There is no recompense, all the work is lost and everyone's job just evaporates. In hindsight I do know that the show wasn't particularly good but when you are involved so closely with the creation of something like this it is very difficult to have some objectivity and at twenty-four I think mine was in short supply! Our producers had hoped that a little wedding over at St Paul's might bring tourists to the door of the theatre but sadly the Royal Wedding of Prince Charles and Lady Diana Spencer generated absolutely nothing for us, and, quite frankly why should it have? Notwithstanding all that, it hurt, my goodness it hurt.

Whenever I now hear of a show having to close suddenly, I am plunged back to that time in that theatre and I feel really sick to the stomach for all the people involved. This one, though, was the start of me 'paying my dues' and during the eighties I experienced similar heartache on quite a few occasions.

My doldrums were lifted a little when Richard Digby Day, director of Nottingham Playhouse, asked if I would be interested in writing the music for a production of *A Midsummer Night's Dream*. It was a great diversion for the autumn and especially interesting in that it starred the gold medal winning ice skater, John Curry, as Puck. I asked my guitarist from the *Dickheads*, Steve Crook, to join me and we wrote a little score that was very much in a 'pop rock' style and we performed it together for each performance.

For Christmas 1981 Barrie Stacey asked me to go to Liverpool for *Snow White and the sev…* I'm afraid I can't actually finish the title of the show as on a few of the performances there were only four real actors playing the dwarfs, the other three were cutouts – honestly! Susie was with me on this one, as dance captain and she also played a friend of Snow White, oh, and Doc! We opened in a very cold and desolate Royal Court Theatre, Liverpool. It was usually used as a Rock Concert venue at this time and having a little panto playing morning and afternoon was too much for the house staff. One day we turned up for the morning show and the theatre was locked. After some hasty negotiations between Barrie and the theatre managers everything was cleared out and we finished our short Christmas season in Widnes Town Hall where, just like in the Floral Pavilion a couple of years before, I had to play the theatre organ to fulfil the contract. Never again!

There is one 'review' that I do have to relate here, though. It is still my all time favourite. The theatre reviewer from the Liverpool Echo simply wrote, 'The worst thing about this pantomime is that the seats are facing the wrong way.' Think about it…ouch, ouch and ouch!

After the heady start to my career I was starting to get to the real nitty gritty and it was hard. The early part of 1982 presented a really interesting diversion, though. Bill Kenwright needed a Musical Director for his tour of *Joseph and the Amazing Technicolor Dreamcoat* for just two weeks. Jess Conrad – the evergreen pop star from the late fifties and sixties was starring as Joseph. So far so good. But the venue was Belfast's Opera House and this was the height of the troubles. I didn't tell my folks where I was going until I returned. Mum would have been too worried.

I was able to offer the drum chair to Keith Hall from the *Dickheads* and off we went after a couple of band calls at Sadler's Wells. There were checkpoints everywhere over there but we were well looked after. The most interesting part of this two week sojourn was that the choir of kids I had to work with came from two different schools. One Catholic and one Protestant. They had to appear at rehearsals and the show separately and their teachers (and the Catholic nuns) tried their damnedest to keep them apart. I loved the fact that when they were with me I was able to mix them up and they ALL got on really well. So sad that as soon as the curtain came down they were back to their sectarian factions. I heard from one of the kids a few months later and she told me how grateful she was to have had the opportunity to do the show but the thing she was most grateful for was the chance to mix with the other side. I was touched by that.

When I returned from Belfast I started to feel that I needed a mentor, someone older and wiser who could guide me in the business. The closest I had previously come had not gone well. Ray Cook was THE Musical Director of the seventies and eighties. I had watched him conduct the original West End production of *Sweeney Todd* and I just happened to bump into him one day on the steps of Drury Lane Theatre. I tried to ask him if I could have a chat about the business and explained that I was hoping to follow in his footsteps. Well, before I had even finished I am sorry to say that he blanked me. I was completely ignored. It felt very strange and hurtful. Maybe I wasn't forthright enough or maybe he was having his own issues to deal with, whatever it was I vowed there and then that if I ever got into a position where people might wish to ask advice from me I would always try my best to help. Now, of course in these days of email and social media, I still try to adhere to that and I always reply.

In the meantime the rep theatre director's grapevine must have been working overtime as I received a call from Michael Winter who was running York Theatre Royal and he needed a Musical Director for his forthcoming production of *A Funny Thing Happened on the Way to the Forum*. It would keep me away from the West End but at least it was work, so I agreed. The following week Michael called again and told me that a guy called David Firman was going to re-orchestrate the show and would I please go and meet him. The same David Firman that I had met briefly at the BBC! This was providence indeed.

York proved to be yet more great training in the dark arts of Musical Direction. David's musical ability exceeded anything that I had come across before. A dry humour mixed with innate talent, ears that could hear a pin drop on Mars and great theatrical nous. The orchestrations for the show were beautiful and our cast, which included the great Barry James, who I had seen in *Superstar* as King Herod, appreciated the invention. Barry was playing Hysterium to Jonathan Owens' Pseudolus, a double act as good as Jack Gilford and Zero Mostel in the movie.

Michael Winter asked me to stay on and write music for their next production, Tom Stoppard's *Jumpers* and then I was supposed to work on *No, No Nanette* with him. Fate had other ideas.

Firman was orchestrating and supervising the music for a brand new piece written by Alan Price and Trevor Peacock and directed by Braham Murray based on the Daily Mirror strip cartoon *Andy Capp*. The show was set to open at The Royal Exchange Theatre Manchester and, if it was successful, on to the West End. Tom Courtenay was the eponymous lead with Alan playing piano as the narrator and commentator on proceedings. David asked me to come on board to be Musical Director for rehearsals but that was all because Alan's band was booked to play the show. So far so good, this meant that I could go off and do *No, No, Nanette* straight after the show opened.

About three weeks into rehearsals Alan, Braham and David took me aside and asked if I would be Musical Director for the show as no-one in Alan's band had any experience of working with actors and they were worried. Well, after a hasty grovelling phone call to Michael Winter I was released from *Nanette* and there I was, Musical Director proper of *Andy Capp*.

The Royal Exchange Theatre is akin to a super large Lunar Module deposited in the centre of a corn exchange by NASA. In the round and with all seven hundred seats no more than ten metres from the stage. This was my first of two visits. (The second, in 1987, was for the interesting Woody Allen revue *The Bluebird of Unhappiness* with Haydn Gwynne, John Bennett, Pam Ferris, Teddy Kempner, Trevor Peacock and Derek Griffiths.) Andy Capp, though, was a revelation. David's skill in crafting Alan Price's very singable tunes into theatrical moments, plus the whole experience of being involved in the ground up building of the show, was awe inspiring.

The supporting cast, including Val McLane, Judith Barker, John Bardon, Vivienne Ross, Trevor Cooper and Nicky Croydon, were engaged and full of invention. For me working with a full range of ages and also with Tom, a proper star-name, was more of that theatrical education that I was craving. When we heard that the show would indeed transfer to London my decision to get out of *Nanette* was vindicated. We were to open at the Aldwych Theatre. The show had to be re-worked for a proscenium arch and the band was extended to include another woodwind player, trumpet player and trombone doubling euphonium. David's idea was to give us a palette of sounds that included a Northern brass band.

We rehearsed the new version of the show at the Shaftesbury Theatre, remember the script throwing incident from *Canterbury Tales* was on that very stage! We had all of two weeks to 'convert' the show from the round and on the first day things were so slow – it is a tricky process – that, after the choreographer Sue Lefton had managed to get three minutes of the company number *It's Better to be in Simple Harmony* re-choreographed in two hours, David and I sat in the aisle patiently working out that we only needed another fourteen weeks at that rate to complete the job! Of course, it was eventually done and once again I was Musical Director of a fully fledged West End show.

Because this show ran for a respectable five months at the Aldwych, various other beneficial events happened. A star studded opening night gala and party at the Savoy, a cast album recording, SWET Awards (now known as The Oliviers) and *Pebble Mill at One* television recordings plus, for me, the icing on the cake was being asked to join Alan and his band for a 'one night only' TV show recorded at Newcastle City Hall with his Animals sometimes nemesis, Eric Burdon.

It was a different experience working with Alan in this way. This was his natural habitat and he ruled the roost. In the theatre he was really part of the team and we had a really good working relationship but this was different. He had asked me to be there and to experience what it was like so I basically sat in with his band gently playing electric piano and 'gurning' every time a camera came close but it was a bona fide rock gig and I have a video copy of it, to boot!

Tom Courtenay and Val McLane as Andy and Flo were a handful but I managed to hone my diplomacy skills a little and we had good times. Tom with John Bardon as best mate Chalky sang a brilliant going-home-from-the-pub-after-a-skinful song called *Good Ol' Legs* which highlighted just how smart and funny Trevor Peacock's lyrics were attached to Alan's music.

Rather than being in the pit the band were set stage right just by the edge of the stage and cascading upwards slightly into a box, where Russell, our drummer, was neatly perspex screened off. We used headphones as we played which enabled us to allegedly hear each other and the actors better. Most of the time this worked a treat but all this radio-microphone technology was still in its infancy and occasionally for a few seconds the cast would be drowned out in our ears by the strains of Bonnie Langford or Tim Curry singing *Pirates of Penzance* at the Theatre Royal Drury Lane or a passing mini cab reporting that he had a 'POB' or being told where his next pick up was. I think we even got *Cats* one night from the New London! Fortunately this only happened about once every three or four shows and after a while we actually got used to it.

I also experienced the musicians' 'dep' system for the first time. To begin with I was quite worried about the concept, where a player can substitute another player so that they can either work elsewhere or take time off, but actually if it is policed carefully and the original player or owner of the 'chair' realises that it is their name in the programme and takes care of business, then it can be quite a breath of fresh air. Obviously like any system it is open to abuse and nowadays the better 'fixers' in the West End make sure that a) you are not presented with more than a specified number of first time deps and b) you are made aware beforehand who your band will be each night. Generally any change of player in the rhythm section – drums, guitar, bass guitar, keyboards – will feel like the engine in your car has suddenly changed and you have to perhaps alter your clutch technique to make it work as efficiently, but the standard of musicianship is so high that you very quickly get used to it. I have always worked on the basis that players want to play the best they can, so if a new dep is on it is better to encourage and help them through any tricky corners rather than ignore and shout at them after the show, which I fear is not uncommon. It took me a little while to get used to the system but ultimately I found it exhilarating as it brings new interpretations to the piece and stops the repetition becoming tedious. At all times you have to protect the actors and make sure that nothing will phase them and at all times you have to remember that the audience is watching the show for the first time. For me the benefits outweigh the disadvantages.

Way back when I had my rehearsal time on *Canterbury Tales*, Kim and Leonie introduced me to a new restaurant in Bedford Street called Joe Allen. The original was on West 46th Street in New York but this was a really good sister venue suited for the West End. Red and white check tablecloths and the famous burger not on the menu – you just had to know it was always available. Jammed full of theatrical paraphernalia, posters and pictures it was pretty much always full and very busy. When it shut up for the night at around midnight there was another much less salubrious place, opposite the Cambridge Theatre's stage door on Shelton Street, called Macready's which stayed open until at least three. A glorified drinking club where 'thesps' and 'musos' could hang out. There was also a little central courtyard garden where the smell of cigarettes was usually flavoured with cannabis. I loved going to both places and still go to Joe's but sadly Macready's is long gone.

Andy Capp closed in February 1983 and I had a very interesting interlude straight afterwards. Two ex Trinity friends were involved in a revue called simply *"i"* which was to open at the Piccadilly Theatre in March. Robert Purvis had written some of the music and Roger Ward was Musical Director. I went in as keyboard player and to be assistant to Roger. Kate Young and Andy Lynwood played two other keyboards and we started band calls slightly mesmerised. The show was under rehearsed, and quick changes were happening right beside us with various members of the cast screaming and shouting that the costume they had been given was cutting their fingers. The sequin effect was in fact cut glass! It was mayhem. The show managed to limp along and basically closed before it even opened. We just about finished a dress rehearsal on 16th March and on Sat 19th March that was it! The show went on with a different team a couple of months later simply called *"y"* – quite apt really! Andy went on to play keyboards in many West End productions and set up his own recording studio, but Kate, dear Kate…

Well, at this point she was brand spanking new and just down from Scotland, a composer and potential Musical Director material. Clever, funny, naturally talented, and with a vivacious personality, she endeared herself to all of us in the band. So after the debacle of *"i"* when I needed someone to 'dep' on *Cinders* I asked her to come in. I had just arranged a song by Howard Goodall for Wayne Sleep's *A Dash of Christmas* and after introducing Kate to Howard, he asked her to be Musical Director on the show. Brilliant! Kate went on to work with Howard on the musical he wrote with Melvyn Bragg called *The Hired Man* and she took over from me as Musical Director for *Joseph* in 1993. She was a real trailblazer and one of the first female Musical

Directors in the West End – if not THE first. There was so much sexism and misogyny amongst fellow musicians yet somehow she brushed it off and let her innate musicality and charm shine through. She had a terrific career but also had a major battle with the demon drink and finally cancer got her in 2020, such a great loss.

Back to 1983 and after the fiasco of "*i*" the hope of gaining meaningful employment yet again was foremost on my mind. David's copyist on *Andy Capp* was a woodwind player called Dick Ihnatowicz and he was about to work on a new show transferring from the legendary King's Head Theatre to the tiny Fortune Theatre. Mike Reed was arranger and Musical Director but he needed to leave the show the week after it opened at the Fortune so that he could go and conduct *Singin' in the Rain* at the Palladium and Dick recommended me as a potential take over. Mike met and auditioned me in the Ballet Room underneath the stage at Drury Lane. He put his fiendishly difficult arrangement of a piece called the *18th Century Drag* in front of me and I attempted to get through it. He obviously approved and *Mr Cinders* was my next West End adventure.

Mr Cinders was the antithesis of *Andy Capp*. A piece originally written for Binnie Hale and Bobby Howes, performed at the Adelphi in 1928 and the lion's share of the songs were written by a wonderful 'Godfrey' like character called Vivian Ellis. Vivian was famous for writing *Bless the Bride* and particularly well known for the theme to Paul Temple, *Coronation Scot*, which was used for the radio series from 1949 to 1968. The most famous song in *Mr Cinders* is *Spread a Little Happiness* which had only recently been made famous by Sting and in our production Denis Lawson and Christina Matthews sang it. It is one of my all time favourite songs and I will play it still at the drop of a hat.

Mike Reed very quickly became a mentor and friend. His musicality is simply magnificent and his arrangements for *Cinders* were classic, quirky and so clever. At The King's Head the show was arranged for just two pianos. Mike and the brilliant Lesley Hayes. Lesley was everybody's favourite audition pianist for years and years. For the transfer to The Fortune, which was such a small house with four hundred and thirty seats, Mike upped the ante and added a cello and a soprano sax who doubled clarinet and flute. We had Myrtle Bruce-Mitford on cello and Dick on the woodwind chair, with Lesley on 'tac' piano and Wurlitzer – it was joyful to play.

Because the show was so bijou and in a small house it remains the only show that I have ever done with NO sound system. Not a microphone or loudspeaker in sight. I played a very nice Yamaha grand and we simply balanced naturally all together. I was right in front of the cast in the tiny pit and if I couldn't hear them then neither could the audience. During the course of the run of five hundred and twenty-seven shows we had a few changes of personnel on stage. Lonnie Donegan took over from Denis and then Lionel Blair replaced Lonnie. However my favourite 'gals' in Dressing Room No.6 remained constant! Janthea Brigden, Julie Ann Blythen and Stephanie Lunn. When I left the show a couple of months before it closed to work on *Six For Gold* – a new musical by Mike and his writing partner Warner Brown at the King's Head – the 'gals' presented me with a beautiful glass inscribed 'To Michael, love No.6', makes me smile just thinking about it. They were definitely my favourites!

Vivian, who died in 1996, was eighty in 1983 and wrote *Please Mr Cinders* especially for our production. He was a grand old gentleman of the theatre and a joy to be around. It was Dan Crawford, the anglophile New Yorker from Hackensack, New Jersey, who created the King's Head Theatre out of the old back room come boxing gym in Islington, who brought Vivian and

Cinders out of retirement. Dan was a man with great ambition and a visionary in theatrical terms. This was the first of many associations.

We recorded the album for *Cinders* in Angel Studios. Norman Newell produced it but he was concerned that the four piece band would be too small a sound for the recording. There was a frantic day of scribbling in Mike's house a couple of days before the sessions when Mike and Dick, with a little bit of help from me, hurriedly expanded the band to a six piece by adding double bass and percussion. Actually, it was a really good idea. The arrangements kept their quirky twenties feel and simply sounded fuller with the extra players. The show was nominated for various awards and again we had to record a section for transmission on the SWET Awards (Society of West End Theatres) television show. There is also a very young looking Dixon playing piano for Lonnie Donegan on a Gloria Hunniford show for ITV somewhere in the archives!

I was with *Cinders* for well over a year and it enabled Susie and I to buy a house and move from Stoke Newington to South Tottenham. 5, Gorleston Road was a small terraced house in a quiet little road where after a hasty loft conversion I was able to set up my first very basic home studio. Getting that Rhodes piano up the loft ladder was not for the faint hearted!

Six for Gold took me to the summer, and the rest of 1984 was a complete mixture of events ranging from auditioning hundreds of people around the country for a Granada TV show called *The Fame Game* (comics auditioning stand up at 9am has to be the hardest gig of all, mind you the couple who auditioned with her singing and him cutting her dress off to reveal that she was wearing full stockings and suspenders underneath really did take the biscuit – they didn't get past that first audition, you will not be surprised to learn!), playing keyboards on a Bobby Crush album entitled *First Love* which was produced by Mike Reed, playing tambourine as an extra on a feature film called *John and Yoko – A Love Story*, where I was standing beside the *Give Peace a Chance* love-in bed, ghosting an especially difficult piano part in a song called *Seasons of Love*, arranged by David Firman for *Victoria Wood – As Seen on TV* Episode 1 (transmitted in January 1985) and finally Christmas, it was back to Old Time Music Hall for a season of *Mrs Cole's Music Hall* at Sonning.

*

The new year of 1985 brought with it an idea from Dan Crawford and Observer Theatre critic Robert Cushman to put on a show about the lyricist E.Y. Harburg. The man who wrote the lyrics for *Wizard of Oz*, *Finian's Rainbow* and a whole raft of great standards, including *It's Only a Paper Moon*, *April in Paris* and *Brother Can You Spare a Dime?* The first part of the process was to spend a couple of days working with Robert and playing through as many of the songs as we could find and a very happy time ensued with Imelda Staunton singing them through with me.

Once the long list was reduced to a shortlist of around forty-five or so we were ready to start casting for the show at the King's Head. My friend from panto, Steve Poulter, was stage manager for us with the legendary 'Mother', David Grant, as company manager and we were off.

The linchpin of the show needed to be someone who could absolutely *be* E.Y. 'Yip' Harburg and between Dan and Robert a plan was hatched to see if the American actor Jack Gilford would be interested. Jack was the original Hysterium in *A Funny Thing Happened on the Way to the Forum*, played opposite Jack Lemmon in *Save the Tiger* (Oscar nomination) and the original Herr Schultz in *Cabaret* on Broadway. His impish charm and twinkle mixed with his Yiddish roots and his own personal history of persecution in the McCarthy era meant that he was the perfect choice. He agreed and, with his wife Madeline, made his way to the less than salubrious rehearsal room and teeny 100 seat King's Head Theatre from New York. The cast we finally fixed on was a fantastic mix of experience, talent and youth. Simon Russell Beale's first West End show along with Mandy More, who had just played Johanna in *Sweeney Todd* at Drury Lane, Isabelle Lucas, Michael Cantwell and Barbara Rosenblat.

1985 Look to the Rainbow – Jack Gilford & Barbara Rosenblat

I had free rein to let my imagination go wild on the musical arrangements and that was completely liberating. Dan's exuberance for all things musical theatre was infectious and even when the coal ran out for the fire in the rehearsal room we all carried on pushing to get the show ready, we just wrapped up a little warmer.

Unlike *With a Little Help From My Friends* this show received fantastic notices when it opened at the beginning of March. So much so that an immediate transfer to the West End was brokered by Dan with Peter Baldwin and Louis Benjamin of Stoll Moss Theatres. We were moving to the Apollo Theatre on Shaftesbury Avenue!

Beyond excited – this was a show that I had put my personal musical mark on and when the next conversation was about making the band bigger for the West End and who should orchestrate it, I really felt exhilarated. Dear Jack and Madeline had become firm friends in that short space of time and Jack gently piped up with, "We know Luther Henderson really well. I'm sure that he would be interested." Luther was the man who made *Ain't Misbehavin'*, the show about Fats Waller, work. He was the orchestrator and piano playing Musical Director on Broadway whose first job after leaving the Juilliard was orchestrating Duke Ellington's *Beggar's Holiday* with Billy Strayhorn for Broadway in 1946. For me he was the most perfect person for the job. All those *Handshakes of Separation* would be working overtime for me if he was able to do it.

So on the final Saturday of our run at the King's Head there he was. A beautiful black man in a kaftan top wearing beads with the most generous of smiles and infectious of laughs. We met after the show and went out with Jack, Madeline and Dan for dinner. He was so magnanimous in his praise for the show and in particular what I had done with the piano, bass and vocal arrangements. I literally was up there somewhere on a cloud. He agreed to do the job and that very evening in between courses we settled on a line up for our expanded band. It was to be Musical Director/Piano, Piano/Electric piano, Double bass, Percussion, Violin, Cello, Trumpet, Trombone and two multi woodwind players. Ten pieces in all. His closing gambit as we parted was classic. "Whatever happens, Mike, no hitting!" Such a statement from the most gentle of men.

Effectively we had done our out of town try out and next was the real thing. Along with the bigger band the cast was slightly extended with the addition of all rounder John Chester and singer Andrea Levine. Dear John was one of the first people I knew to succumb to the awful plague that was decimating our gay friends at that time, and it was only a few years after we finished the show that I heard he had died. Such a talent, a great dancer and singer. Choreographer Dennis Grimaldi also asked if we could extend a couple of numbers and Paper Moon was a 'tap' tour de force for John with Mandy More. My dour but twinkly Scottish assistant, Robert Scott, ended up playing solo piano on stage for a couple of numbers and the band itself was perched on a raised platform at the back of the stage with me facing them from my Yamaha grand. This was still very much a Musical Director at the piano job but there were a few occasions where I needed to stand and wave my arms about, I wouldn't call it 'conducting' yet, but it was moving towards it.

I would always pop into Jack's dressing room before and after the show – it's a good 'taking care of business' thing to do – and my *Handshakes of Separation* were given more credence because Jack and Madeline had a pretty starry set of guests visiting. Two of the highlights were Larry Hagman and 'Skitch' Henderson. Larry was the arch baddy JR in *Dallas* but his pedigree was extraordinary, being the son of Broadway legend Mary Martin. It was Bing Crosby who gave Skitch his name because he was always *a-skitchin'* music in the routining rehearsals at MGM. He played and routined songs for Judy Garland in *The Wizard of Oz* and went on to be the Music Director of the New York Pops Orchestra.

Luther's orchestrations were perfect and the band loved playing them, ally that with the fact that the actors were loving singing the vocal arrangements and you can imagine there was a lot of positive energy and hope in the Apollo Theatre. The notices were also really good and we were poised for a good run. So we thought.

Dame Audience had other ideas. A show centred around a clever, witty, Yiddish writer with an interesting story proved not be everyone's cup of tea and, after the initial flurry of theatre cognoscenti, by week three we were starting to worry. The audiences were looking pretty thin. At week four the producers called the dreaded meeting with us all and the two week notice went up.

Following this awful news the cast and band had a separate meeting after which David 'Mother' Grant and I went to the producers with a keep-the-show-running plan. We would all work for nothing for the next two weeks and the money saved in wages could be used to fund advertising and keep the show on. Well, that's what we all naïvely thought. The producers regretfully declined our offer pointing out that the money saved would only be a drop in the ocean compared to the money needed, so sadly the official letter of notice had to stand. This was such devastating news. It felt like déjà vu, but this time it just didn't feel fair, just or right. More 'paying my dues' but a lot more people suddenly finding themselves without a job. On top of everything I was just a couple of weeks away from marrying Susie! Timing.

It took a while to recover from this body blow and dear Dan Crawford helped considerably by asking me to look after the wonderfully eccentric singer Bertice Reading. She was playing a short season at the King's Head and Mike Reed was playing for a couple of shows but someone was needed for the rest. John Etheridge from Soft Machine was Musical Director on guitar and Marc Megiddo on double bass. It ended up being a great diversion and following the King's Head we had a few shows in the Ritz Hotel, then a couple of days in Puerto Banús on the Costa del Sol and finishing off with a season at the Stork Room, one of those interesting clubs in the West End with a somewhat chequered history.

Bertice always got ready upstairs in the club and I was tasked with going to get her. Her dressing room was literally beside the ladies powder room where all the 'hostesses' would hang out in between shifts. It was eye opening, to say the least, but mostly it revealed to me how completely normal the girls were. I quite enjoyed my little chats with them, while waiting for Bertice to finish her make-up. I also did a couple of particularly fun TV shows with Bertice. A *Wogan Show* at BBC Theatre, Shepherd's Bush, and a little feature on *Pebble Mill at One*, both with John and Marc. Bertice's blend of wry humour and knock 'em down vocal prowess mixed with her cool Pennsylvanian drawl was captivating. She'd been discovered by Bill 'Bojangles' Robinson – more *Handshakes of Separation* for me!

Susie's association with Pantoland had started a couple of years before and this coming Christmas her friend and mentor Kenneth Alan Taylor had become Artistic Director at Nottingham Playhouse – a move from Oldham Coliseum. Susie was his favourite Principal Boy and he asked me to join in the fun. So *Mother Goose* it was for Christmas 1985. We did actually have a complete ball and apart from the usual all nighter to get the parts done for the band it was a breath of fresh air and brilliant to be able to spend Christmas working together.

David Firman and Michael Reed are two very different characters and I was so grateful that after my wish that I needed a mentor, here I was with two of the best Musical Directors in the business. Their influence on me was strong and their friendship, constant.

The next part of my journey was to involve David again, but this time it would challenge me and broaden my musical ability exponentially. He was going to be Musical Director for the biggest new show of 1986, *La Cage aux Folles*. It was to play at The London Palladium and he asked me to be his assistant. That meant that I would work with him on all rehearsals, play piano in the orchestra and at least once a week conduct the show. I was going to conduct at the Palladium! I also got the title Musical Associate and off we went.

The show had recently opened to huge acclaim on Broadway with George Hearn as Albin and Gene Barry as Georges and it had won six Tonys. For the London version George Hearn would reprise his role and Denis Quilley would take the role of Georges. There was a wonderful synergy here. Both men had played Sweeney Todd and both were at the top of their game. There was a great generosity in how they both worked and their stage relationship was utterly believable. The show had a cast of thirty-six or so and a band of twenty-eight. An interesting little bit of trivia – our version had one more player than on Broadway. On Broadway the oboe part was incorporated in one of the woodwind chairs – so that one player played saxophone, clarinet, flute AND oboe plus cor anglais. In London that was not an option so a separate part was created for Nicki Woods to play.

Jerry Herman's score was a joy to work on and I managed to bag one of the best seats to witness the show's recreation. Arthur Laurents, who had written the book for both *West Side Story* and *Gypsy*, was director and I was in the room playing piano for all his rehearsals. Not just the big full company calls, but all the scene work. He was very much 'old' Broadway royalty and ruled the roost in a very authoritarian way, which is very much of that tradition. Yet more *Handshakes of Separation,* though, and a huge privilege to witness greatness firsthand.

When we had our first music run through in the rehearsal room I was playing piano, David conducting and everyone was waiting with bated breath to hear George sing the show's biggest song, *I Am What I Am* for the first time. Just before he sings those first words – completely a capella – there is an emotional build up and a furious ripping off of his wig then a pause. I swear that pause went on for hours. It was astonishing. Such control from George and then in a whisper, that had all the gravitas of Laurence Olivier's Hamlet, out it came. *I...Am...What...I...Am...I...Am...My...Own...Special... Creation.* Gradually the accompaniment joins and the number takes on a life of its own, giving George all the heart and truth that he needs to continue his emotional journey in the story. It was a complete WOW moment, the cast all stood and applauded wildly. The thing is that this was only a rehearsal. George maintained that honesty and truth every single time he performed it on stage as well. A true leviathan of the theatre.

The Cagelles were a wonderful mixture of West End male and female dancer/singers but we also had a couple of specialist Can-Can guys, Buz Butler and Stephen Lubmann, who could jump-splits for days. All in all it was such a talented and stellar company. I was in seventh heaven.

The orchestra that was booked by leading West End fixers, Chick and Allen, was full of the very best players, naturally. I was reunited with bass player Pete Morgan from that first session I played at Abbey Road, and along with Bobby Armstrong on kit, we made a pretty good rhythm section. Nicki Woods sat in the extra woodwind chair and played oboe and cor anglais absolutely beautifully. Under David's baton the twenty-eight pieces soared. Don Pippin's vocal arrangements and Jim Tyler's orchestrations were stupendous and then in week two of the run it was my turn to stand in front of the full cast and orchestra and conduct my first show. No rehearsal, just some very good advice and tuition from David and off I went. I suppose this really was a dream come true but for that very first time to say that I was nervous would be understating the truth somewhat. The whole matinee show that Wednesday went through in a complete blur.

I do remember various smiling faces in the pit willing me on and the cast just went for it with me. You know the old conductor joke – written message on score says, 'Wave your arms around and when the music stops *turn around and take a bow!*' – well it did sort of feel like that. I had 'got away with it' as we all say. Of course I was somewhat elated and, after seeing the principals to make sure they were happy, I went off with David and a couple of band members for supper before the evening show. The Italian 'greasy-spoon', Anella's, opposite the stage door was a favourite haunt and while we were sitting there sax player Johnny Franci said to me, "Great job Mike, great job, but tell me, how did you subdivide the beat at the beginning of *Mascara* into thirty-two like that?" I was perplexed. Yes, the beginning of the song is very slow and I know I got the tempo about right, but what did he mean? He demonstrated for me and lifted his right arm, feigned a very slow four beat with a nervous shake of the hand, and the penny dropped. It was the nerves of the first time totally visible on a really slow beat. Much laughter at my expense but I took it in good heart, Johnny made it very plain he meant it with love. Phew!

To begin with the show was the talk of the town and we performed on *The Wogan Show* – again at the BBC Theatre, Shepherd's Bush – but there was no cast album recording because we were a carbon copy of Broadway. Going into the Palladium for nearly a year on a daily basis more than made up for it, and David also gradually reduced his number of conducts per week until for the last couple of months I was waving for more than half the shows. I even got to conduct on the evening of my thirtieth birthday in January 1987. That felt pretty cool.

Just after the show opened there was another of those especially fortunate moments when Anthony Van Laast, choreographer extraordinaire, needed someone to play for rehearsals for a

Granada Television programme he was working on called *Return of the Antelope*, so off I went to LWT Rehearsal Rooms at the Oval for a few days while playing *La Cage* in the evenings. There were quite a few of these bonus jobs that turned up while *La Cage* was running. Stephen J. Colley, who played Hercule had a drag queen alter ego called 'La Morna Cove' and he devised a few shows with her which I helped with musically. My favourite was called *Boppin' in the Tropics* and we played it at the iconic gay pub, The Royal Vauxhall Tavern a few times. He took it to the Edinburgh fringe the following year, as well. La Morna was a bit like Lily Savage but with a killer voice, and she could sashay, boy she could sashay, Stephen was a fabulous dancer too!

The AIDS situation in London was getting worse and worse. It particularly affected ticket sales for *La Cage*, the coach parties from all around the country didn't seem to want to come to see a show about a gay club owned and run by a gay couple. Gradually it became apparent that our run was going to end and we played our final show on 31st January just after that thirtieth birthday.

La Cage was one of the biggest and most opulent shows I have ever worked on. I practically learnt my conducting technique (such as it is) while I was working on it and, of course, it was my first run at the Palladium – the Cathedral of Theatre.

EIGHT

WEST END PLUS...

Two mentors Dixon was once again looking for gainful employment after *La Cage* closed in early 1987 and fate must have decided that it was time for me to 'pay some more dues' because the next few ventures were short-lived episodes. Learning experiences, yes, but painfully brief.

Spin of the Wheel by Geoff Morrow and Timothy Prager seemed like a good idea. A game show musical. Hmm. David Firman had asked me to come on board as Musical Director – he was orchestrating – and after a quick try out in the Palace Theatre, Watford the show transferred to what was then the Comedy Theatre. Now known as The Harold Pinter. Sadly even with Maria Friedman and Teddy Kempner playing the leads and with Neil McCaul and Matt Zimmerman (the voice of Alan Tracy in *Thunderbirds*) amongst the rest of the cast, I am afraid it was destined to be another short six week run.

Then off to the Royal Exchange Manchester for the aforementioned *Bluebird of Unhappiness*, the Woody Allen revue. Again, close but no cigar, and the show had no further life after its short run there. There was one interesting connection on that show, though. Woody Allen's original was adapted for the stage by John Lahr. Another one of those anglophile types and the son of Bert Lahr who played the Cowardly Lion in *Wizard of Oz*. I had first met John during my *Look to the Rainbow* stint. Jack Gilford did a mean Bert Lahr impression and we had included *If I Only Had a Heart* in the show. Bert was a dear friend of both Jack and Dan Crawford, everything, you see, is somehow connected!

The autumn of 1987 brought with it another Mike Reed inspired job. Tommy Steele was taking his one man show, with ten dancers and a sixteen piece band, out on a tour around the UK and he needed a new Musical Director. Mike had been working with Tommy on and off for years following *Hans Andersen* in 1974 and had conducted the tour himself a couple of times so he suggested me.

Tommy can be quite a prickly character but we became bosom pals very early on in after a little cueing problem with stage management.

The band was on a raised platform at the back of the stage. I was on the deck conducting with Tommy, mostly, downstage centre. At the end of the first act there was a movie sequence where a screen comes down between Tommy and the band so that all the audience can see is Tommy, as if in a silent movie. We were playing with a 'click track' which enables everything to sync up with the movie as it played. Halfway through the sequence the lights are supposed to go out on stage allowing Tommy to make a quick change and complete the Chaplinesque moment which culminates in a huge explosion on the screen for which there is a stage effect known as a 'maroon'.

Unfortunately, on the very first performance, the sequence went wrong and instead of lights out on stage, the lights went out for myself and the band. A major hiatus for everybody, but the click track and movie didn't stop, so, in the dark, all I could do was shout a count in very loudly for the moment that the lights were supposed to come back up on the fore stage and by a miracle we all resumed exactly together for the end of the sequence and the pyrotechnic 'BOOM' worked. Of course Tommy had to fashion his quick change in a full lighting state in front of the audience! Ouch! Well, I am sorry to say that the stage manager had a very big and forceful 'bollocking' from Tommy – almost as loud as the maroon – but I completely 'got away with it' and was taken out for dinner after the show! We finished the tour in Norwich early November and for once I already had my next gig lined up.

It was off to Japan for me to 'sort of' play *Starlight Express*. I say 'sort of' because six of us were booked to sit under the stage and *cover* the show, which was all on tape except for the music under the races which we had to play live. We also had to be prepared to play at anytime if the tape failed.

We were in two venues over a period of three months. The first was the Yoyogi National Gymnasium in Tokyo, which back in 1964 had been built to house the swimming and diving events for the Tokyo Olympics, and the second was in Osaka just after Michael Jackson had performed his *Bad* tour, Osaka-jō Hall.

Japan, though seemingly westernised then, was in reality still a very 'foreign' place culturally. A lot of the cast stuck to their own nationalities for recreation but there were a few of us who befriended the Japanese crew and they loved joining in the fun and frolic with us and, of course, we got to see much more of 'real' Japan than those who remained insular. We had shows on Christmas Day and at midnight on New Year's Eve. It was very strange!

Back home from Japan in January 1988 and the next West End venture was all neatly linked in with the few days of work on *Return of the Antelope* for ITV the previous year. The Musical Director for *Antelope* was a go-getting hugely ambitious guy called Tony Britten and he contacted me to let me know that he had reworked Mozart's *The Marriage of Figaro* into a small scale Musical Theatre piece for small ensemble accompanied by string quartet and piano and would I like to join him and share the musical direction. It was a short season at the Ambassador's Theatre with Janet Dibley, Michael Sadler, Terence Hillyer, Lesley Duff, Prue Clarke & Stephen Tate, the piece was renamed *Figaro* and I loved playing it. Just the five of us playing the glorious Mozart and our actors with their focus much more on getting to the truth of the words than making the sweetest of sounds. It was liberating.

We did, however, misbehave a little on some shows. The dare was how fast can you play the overture? Well, the simple answer is 'too fast' and I apologise to any audience members who were in when we musos were in mid challenge.

Mozart was the direct opposite of the next theatrical venture. It was a new piece to play at The Half Moon Theatre based on events in the aftermath of The Great Train Robbery called *El Sid*. Chris Bond wrote the book and directed with Dave Watts writing the music. Gary Whelan, Carl Chase, Bernard Gallagher, Nicky Croydon and Vicky Licorish amongst the cast. A very good idea and exciting to be involved with what was really one of the first 'thriller' musicals. Sadly it didn't work, and I'm afraid it was followed by another one that seemed like a great idea at the time.

Nite Club Confidential was a musical from Los Angeles. Now that should have set the alarm bells going; there isn't really a theatrical tradition in LA. It was written, directed, choreographed and orchestrated by one man, Dennis Deal. He truly was a major talent, but wearing that many hats on one show should have made the alarm bells go completely doolally!

It was all about the Night Club culture of the 1950s and we were one of the shows that reopened the Playhouse Theatre after some thirty years when it had been used for BBC Radio recordings (*The Goon Show, Hancock's Half Hour, Steptoe and Son*) and pop videos (Queen's *A Kind of Magic*). The theatre certainly had a history.

Our illustrious cast, Ruth Madoc, Stuart Milligan, Kathryn Evans, Peter Bishop and Philip Gould took the bebop style of singing completely by the horns and we rehearsed in the old Decca Recording Studios in West Hampstead. *Goody Goody, That Old Black Magic, Something's Got To Give*, they sounded fantastic. Close, crunchy harmonies, and the sound absolutely authentic. The Film Noir aspect of the story was actually pretty accurate too, and we were hoping for a good run, at least six months or so. No, both Dame Audience and the critics made their opinions all too clear and we folded after – you guessed – six weeks! Devastated again, but there was something good to come out of the show.

I had booked a young trumpet player for the band, someone who knew the style back to front and someone who was already making a name for himself in the jazz world. Guy Barker. A stunning player and now an even more amazing composer and orchestrator. Our paths have crossed many more times over the years and I am pleased to be able to call him my friend.

Once the rancour of early closure had slightly subsided and I was used to being at home, what follows is a nice little reminder to any aspiring musician to always say YES if asked if you are available. It was a Wednesday evening at 5pm and the phone rang. "Mike, are you available to come into Marylebone Rehearsal Studios for a rehearsal at 7pm tonight with some actors who are learning to sing *The Threepenny Opera*? Someone has dropped out." Now my instinct was to say no, I was all set to have a lovely evening with Susie but I did indeed say yes and here's what happened.

*

The call came from vocal coach, Janet Edwards, and I went to Marylebone Studios that evening. There was an impish conductor called Dov Seltzer and a whole bunch of actors learning *The Wedding Song* and *The Army Song*. This was weird.

I met an imposing director called Menahem Golan and as we finished the rehearsal I was asked if I could also come in the following day. By the end of the week I was asked to be Assistant Music Director on the movie and by the end of the following week I was asked to go to Hungary for the twelve weeks of shooting to look after, amongst other things, the lip syncing of the actors on set, including a couple of hundred Hungarian extras who were going to be needed for the big crowd scenes! The stars of the movie were Raul Julia, Julia Migenes, Bill Nighy, Julie Walters, Roger Daltrey, Rachel Robertson, John Woodnutt and Anthony Hopkins as Peachum.

On the third week we were in CTS studios in Wembley recording the orchestra and the following week the vocal sessions. The orchestrations were in the most part by Nick Ingman and were very much based on the Kurt Weil version, angular and perfunctory but they worked extremely well. Dov did most of the conducting but I did get to conduct a little bit and then looked after all the vocal sessions.

Anthony Hopkins and Menahem Golan did not see eye to eye, there were various mutterings, sputterings and harrumphs and eventually Anthony left in high dudgeon at the end of the first vocal recording session. Richard Harris was asked to take over the role and there were frantic music rehearsals to get him up to speed quickly. As is normal in the film world all the songs had to be recorded first and then mimed on set. Julia Migenes – a mammoth operatic star – was playing Jenny and she wanted me to be in the room with her gently conducting and encouraging her as she recorded. Richard Harris didn't want to be conducted, he simply wanted me to point at him whenever he was supposed to sing – he wanted the same thing when we came to film his scenes – that was a challenge when the whole point of conducting is giving that sense of tempo within the upbeat. "I don't need all that flowery stuff!" he barked, so that's what I did, I just pointed at him when he needed to 'sing', eventually. This was all such amazing experience for me and I couldn't quite believe how quickly it all happened.

The twelve weeks in Hungary flew by. We stayed in Budapest and there were many late nights with Mr Harris taking centre stage. He was teetotal at this point in time but somehow managed to tell his stories as if he was on his fifth bottle of wine. Raul Julia loved taking us to restaurants with gypsy musicians and he would get up and join in with them at the drop of a hat. Bill Nighy as Tiger Brown was particularly fun to be around and simply enjoyed himself everywhere and all the time.

One of my duties was to teach the extras the big choral moments so that they would look like they were actually singing and to help me in that quest I had eighteen who spoke English well enough to be team leaders. As well as teaching them we had to find some children for the movie. The second camera operator, Gabor Szabo helped the search. I had made friends with Gabor early on in the shoot, basically I had to stand next to him an awful lot while checking the lip sync, and we became buddies. I was befriended by his family and Juli, his wife, suggested a school where there were enough English speaking children. I had one morning to audition them and in the afternoon I was teaching them the song before shooting the following day.

Funnily enough I loved my time with all the girls in the bordello – wonder why(?) – and along with Julia and some of my special extras including Éva Regenhart, there were some 'marvy old pros' like Louise Plowright, Liz Seal, Chrissie Kendall, Miranda Garrison and Julie T. Wallace to try to keep in some order while they larked around thoroughly enjoying playing 'ladies of the night'! David Toguri was choreographer, Jan Dorman was wig supervisor, and they made an unlikely pair as they created ad hoc dance classes and exercises while we were waiting for the next set up to be ready, but lots of people joined in, including me.

My favourite moment in the film, though, was the big battle scene in Soho Square. We were in Mafilm Studios about ten miles out of Budapest for most of the shoot and on one big soundstage a recreation of Soho Square from the 1800s had been built. In this one scene I had to stand beside the director of photography or DP, Elemér Ragályi, right beside his crane, to conduct the end of a big vocal sequence. As soon as I cut off Julia, Raul, Roger Daltrey and the two hundred extras on the last note, I had to leg it as fast as I could out of the way as twelve soldiers came galloping in on horseback firing their muskets full tilt while Elemér flew up on his crane. Who says conducting is a safe job! The scene continued into the Budapest Opera House in a sequence that was filmed about four weeks later, with yet more extras pretending to be in the audience.

Should you ever mistakenly see the film there is a sequence where Mackie (Raul Julia) is in prison, Polly Peachum (Rachel Robertson) and Erin Donovan (Lucy Brown) visit and have a screaming fight over him singing *The Jealousy Duet*, now in the background there are a few 'other' prisoners in shot. If you blink you will miss me, but I was there. It was such a tight set that the best way I could help get the lip sync right was to be one of the extras myself. Not my finest hour but at least an experience.

The film was launched the following year as *Mack the Knife* and had pretty poor reviews, was released on video very quickly and gently disappeared. The amount that I learnt and the experiences I had whilst working on it, though, were quite out of the ordinary and of course I am glad that I said 'yes' to that one rehearsal.

*

In the new year of 1989 there was a lot of talk about a new Andrew Lloyd Webber musical following on from the success of *Phantom of the Opera*, but this was to be a chamber piece based on a novella called *Aspects of Love,* published in 1955 by David Garnett from the Bloomsbury Group. So after I had recuperated from my time in Hungary I called mentor Mike and we had a chat about it. Mike had worked with Andrew on *Phantom* as the original conductor and he was also setting up a number of *The Music of Andrew Lloyd Webber* concerts, so I thought if anyone would know what was going on it would be him.

He told me that he was Musical Supervisor and was in the audition process of the show already, would I be interested in assisting him? Would I? Well, you can imagine I jumped at the chance and a week later I was playing audition piano in a room with Trevor Nunn, Andrew, Gillian Lynne, Mike and, rather bizarrely, Prince Edward. Edward was employed at the time by Andrew's Really Useful Group as a general assistant and he was around for a lot of the 'putting together' of the show – even handing out scripts on the first day of rehearsal – so he was there, with his bodyguard, sitting in the background taking it all in. Anyway, suddenly here I was in yet another scenario that I could only have dreamed about a few years before.

A few days later I was asked to meet Mike and rehearsal pianist Gareth Valentine with Andrew's long time orchestrator,

David Cullen and ALW at his apartment in Eaton Square to play and sing through the score for Trevor Nunn. That was totally surreal and, though I did join in, I kept on thinking about the unique bizarreness of it all. A few days before this meeting Michael Ball had recorded *Love Changes Everything* and we heard it for the first time there. Simple, memorable and immediately recognisable as an ALW tune but with Michael at full strength it was glorious.

We went into rehearsals with Michael as Alex, Roger Moore as George, Ann Crumb as Rose, Kathleen Rowe McAllen as Giulietta, Diana Morrison as Jenny and with an ensemble that was the best of the best. We rehearsed in Alford House, Kennington and I was assigned to work with Roger a lot of the time. Those particular rehearsals in the little downstairs room were memorable because in every hour there would be twenty minutes of solid work and concentration and the rest of the time I was regaled with hilarious and mostly unprintable stories involving all the amazing people he has worked with over the years!

Just before we moved into the theatre for technical and orchestral rehearsals I was also tasked with getting the understudy, Kevin Colson, up to speed. Although Roger could do it, there was a lot of anxiousness about whether he could sustain it and he was the first to admit that. There is a bootleg audio copy of the last run through in the rehearsal room and you can hear that hesitancy in dear Roger. My personal belief is that he would have absolutely got there and been wonderful but that final rehearsal in Awful House, as we called it, was his last time as George. Thereafter Kevin Colson, who was a very experienced musical theatre performer, took over the role and was, of course, superb.

I would like to break a little urban myth about dear Gillie Lynne here. Gillie was a great choreographer and before that had been a wonderful and highly respected ballerina with the Royal Ballet and a featured dancer in blockbuster movies – notably with Errol Flynn in *The Master Of Ballantrae*. I spent a lot of time in the rehearsal room with her and witnessed her invention at its best. In one song, *Hand Me the Wine and the Dice*, the time signature was basically 7/8, occasionally 7/4, but let's not split hairs. Anyway, naturally Gillie understood the way that the music should be counted and she was always so committed to making her choreography innovative that she would sometimes count across the beat to make some of her moves work. Cutting a long story short, she did indeed count in occasionally with, "One, two, three, four, five, six, se-ven," but we all 'knew' that she 'knew' and, more importantly, what she meant! (To explain: the number of syllables counted is actually eight when you split 'seven' into two, therefore making it a normal dance count of eight beats – hope that helps!)

Aspects of Love had a big computerised set and the tech rehearsal was long and arduous. Michael Ball could always be relied on to lift spirits and crack a joke though and we got through it. One of the centre pieces of the original set was a 'travelator' which was used throughout to give a sense of journey with some of the cast walking in the opposite direction on the deck of the stage. There was one very quiet moment in the score and I got a message from Andrew that was a little surprising. He wanted to know what key the 'travelator' was in. Sadly I had to report that the little electric motor that was audible to the audience emitted a tone that was right in the cracks between C and D♭. Hmm… The solution came a little later from David Cullen and the percussion part had a little finger snare drum roll written in at the point where the 'travelator' was so conspicuous. At the end of 2018 I was in Sydney watching a new production of the show and that little finger drum roll is still there. The 'travelator', of course, is not!

It was utterly brilliant being this close to the show's creation and to begin with I played keyboards in the orchestra. Mike conducted the first few performances and handed the show over to the Musical Director. Now begins a tricky tale.

I was happy to be Assistant Musical Director and I was hugely grateful to Mike for having enough faith in me to put me there; however, almost right after Mike handed over the baton there were mumblings and grumblings from the orchestra about the Musical Director. To be fair, Mike is a difficult act to follow, with such passion in his musicality and leadership, and anyone who takes over from him has a tough time finding their way. The MD had been around for most of the rehearsals, he knew the show but he simply did not engage with anyone. The murmuring gained weight when the cast joined in as well and I found myself in the middle of a maelstrom. No-one would say anything to Mike or anyone else from production. The consensus was that he was doing a great job of conducting the little bit of Maria Bjornson's set right in front of him but neither the cast nor the orchestra were receiving any of that musical fluence; in other words there was a total disconnect.

So two weeks after Mike left the show I took the bull by the horns and decided that I needed to say something. My Dad had always instilled in me that if there is a problem then the only way forward is to talk; communication is key. Here I was in a situation where there was literally no communication so I plucked up the courage to relay to Mike the full extent of what was happening in his absence. It was not a hatchet job, rather it was a rescue job for the show, and also my relationship with Mike was such that he understood that my impassioned plea to him was for the good of the show, so once I had broached the subject and said my piece I put my head back down from the parapet and hoped that things would work out for the best. The result was quick and by the end of that day I was asked to hold the fort and take over as Musical Director, initially for a probationary two weeks.

Aspects of Love is still the most difficult show to conduct. Because it is 'through-sung' the weight of the pace of the show is firmly on the shoulders of the conductor. It is also a show without rhythm section. The string quartet essentially becomes that driving force and therefore, as conductor, you have to be emotionally involved with the dramatic journey of all the characters and push the show accordingly. All of that makes it hugely rewarding to conduct and as dull as dishwater if you are not engaged. After those two weeks were up I was asked to become Musical Director permanently and I stayed with the show for two years.

Aspects is also where the whole question of 'where is one' or 'where is the first beat' comes from. An orchestra of classical players is a very different beast to an orchestra of 'pop' or dance band musicians and the lag between where you lay that first beat down and where it is perceived to be and played is one of the perennial questions. On *Aspects* I learnt so much and one thing is absolute. Good musicianship in all its forms is one of the greatest of all gifts and transcends language and religion in how it speaks directly to the heart and it also never fails to fill my spirit with joy.

The players on *Aspects* were particularly special, from John Marson, ex BBC Symphony Orchestra harpist, to leader and first violin, Rolf Wilson, the go-to leader of most of the big movie soundtracks recorded at Abbey Road, Anthea Cox on flute, Les Craven on clarinet, Jo Lively on oboe, Dave Lee, French horn from Covent Garden Orchestra, John Franci (remember him from *La Cage!*) on soprano sax, clarinet and flute, Ian Chopping on percussion, Tom Wakeley, Assistant Musical Director and keyboards, David Randall, second violin, Don McVay, viola and Robert Bailey on cello, all of them absolutely top notch musicians. Pianist Geoff Eales always played the really tricky solo piano part for the first verse and chorus of *Love Changes Everything* utterly breathtakingly. I know how difficult that was because I had to sit in and play it for one show when he was taken ill. I just about got away with it but I wouldn't have wanted to do it again! Our double bass player, Mike Brittain also holds the record for making the biggest noise in the pit after his bottom string snapped in the midst of a very quiet moment on stage. It was as if someone had fired a rocket in the pit. He said afterwards that it was the only time in his career that the low E string had ever snapped.

Aspects Of Love is also where on one particularly exuberant evening I raised my right hand clasping the baton and brought it down to give that elusive beat one without it attached. The baton and my fingers had parted company and it had gone sailing off behind me into the auditorium. My fear was that I would hear a cry at any point and some poor punter would be like King Harold at the Battle of Hastings! Fortunately about five minutes later the person sitting behind me in the front row gently tapped me on the shoulder and handed it back! I found out afterwards that it had landed benignly beside someone in the tenth row and it was carefully passed back to the front over those five minutes.

Which brings me neatly to another aspect of *Aspects*. There was no pit rail curtain on the show just the rail. The sound designer, Martin Levan, had decided that to make the chamber element of the show really work then the fourteen piece orchestra should be heard as naturally as possible. That's all well and good but the more red blooded gentlemen in the band (me included until I gave up my keyboard chair to be conductor) very quickly realised that there was an added bonus to no curtain. To put it as delicately as possible, any lady sitting in the front row needed to be careful that she wasn't showing us rather more than she intended. My wife, Natalie told me that she and her cousins had gone to see the show when she was in her early twenties and were seated in said front row and noticed that they could see the orchestra much more clearly than normal but had not put two and two together at all. No harm done except maybe a few heart rates in the pit higher than normal.

As the run continued my assistant, Tom, and I regularly frequented a little wine bar just down the road from the stage door of our theatre, The Prince of Wales. We used to go there in between shows on matinee days and often got chatting to this rather bright and funny chap called Tim Hancock. We talked about everything except the business and it wasn't until a couple of months into our weekly Wednesday yarns that I asked Tim what he did.

It turned out that he was an agent, working for his father Roger Hancock with offices just around the corner. Roger was the brother of the late, great and somewhat melancholy Tony Hancock and the agency had been set up in 1961 to look after him. Very quickly Roger added a few select comedy performers and writers and by the time I met Tim in 1989 it was one of the most respected agencies with people like *Only Fools and Horses* writer John Sullivan and *Dalek* creator Terry Nation on its books. At this point a couple of agents, Stephen Hill from The Stephen Hill Singers and David White from London Musicians, had been looking after my contracts and suchlike but I thought to myself, why not ask Tim? He knows everyone. When I did finally ask him he retorted with his usual huge smile and a wink, "Well, I wondered how long it would take you, of course I will you daft bugger!" Tim was my agent from 1989 right up until 2002 and we had many fun times together and he also helped me to get my feet in the door of the elusive TV market. Sadly he also had demons very similar to his famous uncle and he battled with them on and off and with varying degrees of success until his death in 2020.

Working on *Aspects* for this long time brought with it many new possibilities and, of course, another Cast Album. Mike conducted and I played keyboards and, because Equity took a few days to get their act together with contracts, we had a couple of days waiting around at Olympic Studios where we were paid for doing nothing. The fee I received was enough for me to buy a brand new Yamaha piano which is still my piano today. An afternoon at Reid's Pianos in Tottenham to pick my piano was a bit like being a child in a toyshop and a chocolate factory both at the same time.

A little word here for unsung heroes. Those of you that remember Elton John playing live at Princess Diana's funeral back in 1997 will have never imagined that perched behind the grand piano, out of view of the cameras and most of the people in Westminster Abbey, was a small sprite like Scottish man called Alex Brown wielding a piano tuning hammer primed and ready at any moment to jump figuratively into the belly of the piano in case something went wrong with the tuning. He had been there since four o'clock in the morning and did his final tune literally minutes before the funeral started. I met Alex for the first time when I was on *Mr Cinders* at The Fortune Theatre in 1983 when I was playing the six foot Yamaha C3 grand piano in the pit and since 1989, when I bought that piano from Reid's, he has been my piano tuner of choice and looked after it. He is a sparkling, spiritual man who will engage you for hours with his gentle observations of life. For years he tuned all the BBC pianos, studio pianos, theatre pianos, all the royal pianos in Buckingham Palace, Clarence House, you name it, he's been there and he has a story about it.

In the summer of 1989 I managed to get down to Cornwall for a short break leaving the show in the more than capable hands of my assistant, Tom Wakeley. There were no mobile phones at this time and Treyarnon had one public phone. I had given Tom the farmer's phone number in case there was an emergency and around 5.30pm on the Saturday I got a message to phone Tom urgently. I managed to get through from the caravan field and he told me that our wonderful leading lady, Ann Crumb, was involved in a catastrophic accident during the matinee. During a scene change blackout a first time understudy had accidentally steered her into the 'travelator' and the resulting damage was truly awful. She lost part of her foot, the show had to be stopped, of course, and her understudy played the next few weeks while she recuperated. The damage really was severe and she never got full mobility back. It was a shocking thing to happen and various safety measures were then incorporated into the running of the show to make sure that it could not be repeated.

Andrew took me aside one afternoon and told me that there was going to be a tribute segment to him on the forthcoming *Royal Variety Performance* being filmed in November at the Palladium and would I look after it for him. Paul Nicholas, David Essex, Rosemarie Ford, Michael Ball and Lisa Waddingham would sing some of the best known songs plus *First Man You Remember* and *Love Changes Everything* from *Aspects*. David Cullen did the arrangement and I was tasked with supervising it. Rehearsing it with them all was a breeze, and dear Gillie staged it with her natural class. Then into the theatre for the band rehearsal and camera rehearsal. This was my first sojourn on the Royal and it was still very much Musical Director Alyn Ainsworth's domain. All the parts worked, the band played it perfectly and he was a past master at dealing with major artists so all went smoothly. That year the Producer/Director was Ian Hamilton, another past master, and we have worked together many times since.

Over the course of my two years on *Aspects* there were many cast changes and for a while Sara Brightman played Rose with

Michael Praed as Alex but on my final conducting matinee the leading lady was the elegant Susannah Fellowes and at the beginning of Act Two as Rose she finishes playing *The Master Builder* and walks out of the stage door to sign a few autographs for the 'stage door Johnnies' who are jostling together to get her attention. Normally there were three in long coats and fedoras but on this matinee there was an extra one in a very long coat. The look of surprise on her face whilst singing, when she realised that the interloper was me was utterly priceless. I quickly got myself back to the pit, thanked my assistant, Tom, for conducting the beginning of the Act and got on with the matinee.

I had made a good connection with orchestrator David Cullen while working on *Aspects* and there is a recording of Julian Lloyd Webber playing *Tell Me on a Sunday* with the Royal Philharmonic Orchestra conducted by Barry Wordsworth with featured piano and there is a little story to tell.

David Cullen had orchestrated the album and was co-producing it and he asked me if I would like to play on the session. He told me it was 10am at CTS – or so I thought. I bowled up at CTS Studio 1, right by Wembley Stadium to find it completely empty. I was there early, of course, and this is why it pays to be early! The studio was empty because the session was at 10am at CBS Studio which was in Whitfield Street, just off Tottenham Court Road. Help! No taxis anywhere to be seen at Wembley, so quickly onto the tube and then a cab at Baker Street. I ran into CBS one minute after the session had started, in humungous panic, to see the piano on the other side of the studio. The walk of shame. An acknowledgment from conductor Barry to my obvious distress and my huge apology. A greeting with Julian on cello and we were off. So, should you hear that solo piano at the beginning of the track ever again just bear in mind that my heart was racing at some exorbitant rate and I thought that my career was over.

Julian loved my playing and in the break Richard Addison, principal clarinet, made a point of coming over to me and congratulating me on my 'musical' piano playing. That's about as good as it can get – in fact, I'd quite like it if my epitaph read 'he was musical', it is about the best compliment another musician can give you!

Harry Secombe was in full swing with his 'God Slot' programme, *Highway*, ITV's answer to the BBC's *Songs of Praise* and David Firman was the regular keyboard player. There was a pleasant day each week at Abbey Road 3 to record the musical accompaniment for the show and on a couple of occasions I 'depped' for him. On one of them I was able to have a chat with Harry about Roger Moore and the *Aspects* debacle. They were quite good friends. He was very wise and I was so chuffed to speak with my childhood Goon idol, Neddy Seagoon! A truly lovely man with charm and such a twinkle.

Other interesting moments along the way while *Aspects* was playing include a BBC *Hearts of Gold* with Esther Rantzen, a big excerpt from *Aspects* on *Pebble Mill at One* with our full band and an LWT *South Bank Show* end of the year special with Michael Ball singing *Seeing is Believing* from the show with me on solo piano. I even played piano for Andrew's wedding to Madeleine Gurdon in early 1991, where the Stephen Hill Singers, with Annie Skates and conducted by Mike Reed, performed a specially written choral work by Andrew. *The Benedicite*. We were in a freezing cold church in Suffolk and I remember having to wear mittens to play!

I think two years conducting a show is the optimum amount. There are plateaus that you reach as the show grinds on and to try to make it as fresh as possible you have to have time away from the theatre to keep your sanity. I am going to talk in detail about my private life later in the book but it was at this time that Susie and I parted and things got a little complicated so actually having the security of the show really helped me get through the emotional maelstrom, and I had a relationship with Andrew's PA, Jane Fann which helped to add extra fire to the mad turmoil that seemed to be consuming me.

Mike very kindly offered to let me have a room in his house in Chiswick and I stayed there for a few months until I bought a little one bed flat in Sutton Court, one of those Edwardian mansion buildings around the corner. Mike's house was very much a party house and friends like Kathryn Enticott and Lucy Bateman from Really Useful Group would frequent the almost religious Sunday lunch along with a number of Mike's friends. It always started with a visit to the City Barge pub on the river and sometime around four we would sit down to eat. Mike's dad, Peter, would also be there and I loved hearing his stories of derring-do – he had been shot down in the Second World War, held as a prisoner of war and after his return to London became a 'high-up' at Paramount Pictures – so his anecdotes were legendary!

When *Aspects of Love* went to Broadway Mike supervised it over there and at various times some of his musician friends from the States would pop up in Chiswick as well. The oboe player, Blair Tindall, whose book *Mozart in the Jungle*, about her experiences on Broadway and in the classical world became the inspiration for the Amazon Prime TV series of the same name, came for a holiday and we became very fast friends for a while. I had a fantastic holiday in New York with her and experienced that 'you have to see as many shows as possible' mentality that seems to pervade every theatre loving Brit on their first visit.

So life was busy as I continued to keep conducting *Aspects* and I had occasional meetings with Andrew when he came to see the show. I found him shy and self effacing but with an absolute will that holds firm and makes contradiction difficult. There was, however, a bond and I did feel that I was in that 'inner circle'. So much so that later in 1993 when a reworked version of *Aspects of Love* went on tour and had a short season in the West End – again at The Prince of Wales – I was Musical Supervisor with the quite astonishing Gale Edwards directing. This was a swirling drapes and beautiful emotionally driven theatrics version and actually, I think I preferred it to the original. Hilary Jane Parker, from the London Symphony Orchestra was leader and first violin on this production and Fiz Shapur conducted.

Back to the original *Aspects* and when it was announced that Andrew was going to put a revamped version of *Joseph and the Amazing Technicolor Dreamcoat* on at the Palladium I rather hoped that I might be asked to be involved in some way. Then I found out that Mike Reed was going to be Musical Supervisor and he asked me to be Musical Director and to take over conducting duties the day after Opening Night. Brilliant!

So, I was going to be back at the Cathedral of the Palladium and this time as Musical Director. The wonderful Steven Pimlott was directing with Anthony Van Laast choreographing. The race was on to find the perfect cast and at one meeting down at Andrew's place at Sydmonton he talked of Bonnie Langford as the Narrator, which would have been perfect. A little later, though, it was decided that Linzi Hateley should have the role. Linzi was also a brilliant choice and had great control and honesty when she sang and all the range that was required.

The role of Joseph was proving to be an interesting prospect, though, and one day I was asked to meet with Jason Donovan at Andrew's house in Eaton Square – he had moved from the flat where I had met him before those *Aspects* rehearsals. Jason was hot property at this point in time having had all the TV success with *Neighbours* and then the pop success, particularly, of course, with Kylie.

I met Jason in the piano room and we spent half an hour just gently playing through *Any Dream Will Do* and *Close Every Door*. He could obviously sing it all but this was just a little preparation before Andrew, Steven, Anthony and Mike came into the room to meet him and complete the audition. Jason had a cup of tea in his hand and I could see that it was shaking a little bit so I gently took it from him, put it down and he then sang to the rather daunting row of faces in front of him. It was all meant to be very relaxed but, really how could it be? Everybody warmed to him, he nailed it and so we had our very special *Joseph*!

The casting continued in the more normal confines of rehearsal rooms around London and eventually all was set and rehearsals began in Wandsworth. The search also began for our choir of schoolchildren. We needed fifty children per show and there were and are very strict rules as to how many performances children are allowed to participate in on stage and for how long. The call went out and loads of schools sent choirs to audition but there was one choir with one specific head teacher who particularly made an impression.

Red Hill School with Harvey Norton. Harvey bustled his kids onto the stage and there was a great sense of anticipation. They all looked at him with such affection and his yearning need for them to do well was self evident. He was even holding firmly onto a fluffy dog mascot for them and at the end of their audition Harvey most definitely set a lot of tear ducts into overdrive with his wonderful reaction to how well they had done. All the schools that we eventually used on Joseph were special and all the school kids very talented but there was something extra special about Red Hill.

John Cameron did the orchestrations for this super extended version of the show. However in rehearsals it became apparent that we needed to make changes to the pre-existing routines of the songs to go with this new vision of the show. Generally Andrew would talk through ideas with director Steven, choreographer Anthony and then Mike or I would jot down the idea but there were a couple of places in the score that needed longer and more involved invention. So at the end of *One More Angel* there is now an amazing Hoedown which Mike created out of Andrew's themes, Mike had also extended *Close Every Door* for *The Music of Andrew Lloyd Webber* concerts so that became our version for this show – the one with the huge key change and *a capella* ensemble moment – I extended *Go, Go, Go Joseph* during rehearsals with Anthony and one day we came to rehearse *Those Canaan Days*.

Well, Anthony had this crazy idea about creating a Parisian *Apache* for two of our amazing dancers, Michael Small and Amanda Courtney-Davies. I had already worked on the vocal arrangement of the song with Philip Cox who was playing Simeon, and all the other men with cod French accents and over stressed harmonies, so Anthony asked me if I could create something for the dance. On this particular day Mike was away with the *Music of ALW* concerts, Andrew was away too, so I thought, why not, and popped upstairs to the little piano room to see what I could come up with. Half an hour later I went back down and played Anthony my musical idea and he loved it. I expressed my concern about Andrew's approval and he simply said that I shouldn't worry and to play it to him later in the afternoon when he was due to arrive.

With a certain amount of trepidation, that afternoon, with Andrew sitting beside me, I played it with the suggestion of the violin intro setting the French feel and then in the middle of the song this ridiculous and very deliberate French pastiche. After the *Apache* I lifted the key up a semitone to complete the song. I think I was waiting for a "What on earth do you think you are doing to my music!" response, but instead I had, "Yes, yes, yes, but how about moving the key change to the start of the dance rather than at the end to help the change of mood?" That's what I then did and it was a stroke of genius from Andrew.

Along with various other interesting changes, including making *Poor Poor Joseph* into a 'kinda' rap with classical harmony interludes for the ensemble and choir, all of this went to John Cameron for him to put his inimitable orchestration stamp on the score. John is another of those ubertalented musicians and he found all sorts of fabulously inventive colours for the band to play in the resulting charts. John was the brains behind how *Les Miserables* sounds having been the original orchestrator both in Paris and London for Cameron Mackintosh, so the quality wasn't just good it was amazing.

Band rehearsals and technical rehearsals breezed through, however there was one moment of panic when we all had to evacuate the theatre very quickly because the Pharaoh Head dropped on its tethering and there was a worry that it might fall over completely. As it was something like fifteen metres high it would have caused a fair amount of damage! Mark Thompson's set design was elegant, witty and brilliant, though and he won an Olivier for it, most deservedly. When Princess Diana and her two young sons, William and Harry came to see the show early on in the run, they came backstage afterwards to meet us all and all the boys wanted to do was go on the revolve with the sheep AND the camel, the design was so mesmeric.

When I met Paul Maguire at the BBC in 1980 I could not have imagined that just a few years later I would be in a position to ask him to be Assistant Musical Director for me and yet that's what happened. We had met a few times over the intervening years and I just wondered whether he would be interested. He was the most perfect Assistant Musical Director, calm and perfectly assured, a great keyboard player and just a thoroughly nice guy. He stayed on the show until it closed in 1994.

I met my second wife, Jo Juson, while I was on *Joseph* as well. She worked backstage on the crew and we met frequently in between shows and hither and thither. She was a single mum with this little whirling dervish of a daughter almost magically called Lillie who loved eating 'Basghetti' in Anella's and who was all of four years old. Jo and I soon became an item and she and Lillie moved in with me in Chiswick in the autumn of 1991. More of that story in Chapter 10!

One of my main duties was working with resident director, Nichola Treherne, getting all the kids up to scratch and as the turnover of children was so high we were pretty constantly either rehearsing them or auditioning more schools to decide who would be next for their three month stint. I used to play games just before each show during my warm up with them on the Donkey Run. (The area just beside stage left and so-called because it was where the animals used to be held before making their entrance during the lavish pantomimes of yesteryear) I had a bit of a routine with them and would not only vocally warm them up but would also get them to dance around a bit – turning widdershins was a favourite! (anti clockwise for the uninitiated...)

The whole cast was so immersed in the show, it truly was an amazing time. From Aubrey Woods playing Jacob and Potifar to Patrick Clancy and Paul Tomkinson playing the Baker and the Butler to great comic effect, Steven Pimlott's vision of the show was tantalisingly fresh and different from what had come before. We even ended up with the first theatrical *Megamix* at the end of the show!

1991 Jason as Joseph, the waistcoat and Mum

Record Producer and trombonist for jazz funk band *Shakatak*, Nigel Wright, had just worked with Andrew on Timmy Mallett's version of *Itsy Bitsy Teenie Weenie Yellow Polkadot Bikini* and he had also just produced Jason singing *Any Dream Will Do* and Andrew asked him to see if he could come up with a great poppy clap-along ending for the bows. We met up to discuss and after a few chats and meetings the bones of the *Megamix* following the story of the show were laid out. John Cameron put an orchestration over the top so that in the pit we could play along for every show. Et voilá – the *Megamix* was born.

The making of the CD was a little more controversial because Mike had suggested to Andrew that it should be a LIVE CD recorded in the theatre. Andrew, following the success of *Any Dream Will Do* most definitely wanted it to be a pop studio album and he wanted Nigel to produce it. There was an impasse.

The result, after much wrangling, was that it was indeed a studio album, with Nigel producing, and I was asked to conduct it. The normal procedure would have been, as with *Aspects*, that Mike as Musical Supervisor conducted but as there was such a stalemate the baton was handed over to me, literally. The very first person I phoned after I had the call was naturally, Mike. He very generously told me to not worry and do the job, it would be good for me. So it is thanks to Mike that I have a Platinum Album of *Joseph* up on my wall!

The actual recording of the album took a couple of weeks and the orchestra was gently increased in size just to give more weight. I was always sad that, as it was a pop type album, the decision was made not to record the big dance moments and Mike's *Hoedown* and my *Apache* never made the cut. There is plenty to be grateful for, though, and the cast, kids and musicians made it sound really contemporary for the time. I worked well with Nigel and we had a ball in Westside Studios. One little admission, though. After we had sent everyone home on the last day we listened through to everything just checking all was spick and span. We got to *Pharaoh's Dreams Explained* and suddenly realised that we had forgotten to record the ensemble AND the choir of school kids. Help!

There was no way to get them back into the studio so the solution was that a brilliant session singer called Tracy Akerman, who Nigel had already used on many albums, was called in that evening and she and I sang nearly all that was missing. We did eighteen takes on each part to make it sound like enough people. If you listen very carefully you can hear that it is not the same sound as on the rest of the album – oops!! There was also one deliberate change from the show which involved Tracy, me AND Nigel. *Song of the King*, the Elvis pastiche number, sung by David Easter in our show, had backing vocal type harmonies, the *Bap-Shu-Wa-Du-Wa-Bap-Bap-Shu-Wa-Du-Wa* bits. We had recorded our cast but the three of us had a go at making the vocals sound a bit more authentically rock and roll and in the final mix the cast version was binned and it is our luscious tones that you can hear. Don't tell anyone...

The show was a mammoth hit and the rafters of the Palladium were completely raised every single night. For all of us involved it was breathtaking. I made my own waistcoat of many colours and gradually filled it with badges donated by the school kids and from some of the audience members! I even danced through the *Megamix* each evening, well I called it dancing.

There was a police cordon outside the stage door to keep the fans back, Jason was so idolised at this point in time. Some evenings he had to be snuck out the 'secret' exit in Argyle Street otherwise he would have been completely mobbed. The worry was that at some point Jason was going to have to have time off and, in fact, there was one show after a few months when he simply was not well enough to go on and the understudy, Peter Bishop, did the show instead. It was a brilliant show and Peter was fantastic but the audience had paid to see Jason and they were not best pleased that someone else was on instead. Poor Peter had to cope with a rough ride to begin with. I think this set red lights flashing for Andrew as contractually Jason was booked to have six weeks off seven months into the run, from January 14th to February 22nd 1992. Something drastic would need to be done and he is a genius at making Musical Theatre history by thinking completely outside the box, but en route to the decision I think there must have been some interesting discussions at RUG headquarters!

The first I heard was a very simple phone call asking me to be at RUG in Tower Street to meet Phillip Schofield (who at that time was presenting the biggest children's TV show – *Going Live* on Saturday mornings on the BBC) and just take him through *Any Dream Will Do* and *Close Every Door* to see if there was any chance that he could sing. His manager at that time was the radio DJ Peter Powell and he was there too – I think he was more nervous than Phillip, actually!

Phillip and I went into a little music studio in the basement at Tower Street and I asked him about his singing – had he ever done any? "No, apart from warbling in the shower," came the reply. So I gave him a very simple vocal warm up and then got him to sing a little bit of *Any Dream Will Do*. Well, he sang both with feeling AND perfectly in tune. He had such a natural charisma and warmth; it was genuinely touching. He'd obviously looked at the songs beforehand but there was incredible potential here. After we sang *Close Every Door* – even attempting the key change and the high F♯ at the end – it was apparent to me that:

Phillip would be sensational in the role and

This was a stroke of genius casting from Andrew.

We said our goodbyes and I immediately called Andrew and unequivocally told him that I thought Phillip could be brilliant – obviously with some work – but that the innate talent was there. Mary Hammond was the obvious choice for him to have lessons with – like Ian Adam, Mary was the absolute *numero uno* of vocal teaching and the go-to coach – so a series of visits were booked. After Phillip had done that, a secret meeting was held at the Lyric Theatre Hammersmith where Phillip auditioned for Andrew. I was there playing for him and after a shaky start he completely nailed it.

Andrew was thrilled. So Phillip replaced Jason for the six weeks and because of his high profile kids' TV presence the publicity was astronomical. Nichola Treherne and I even featured in the *Going Live* special that was transmitted just before Phillip's first show where there was much banter between Jason and Phillip, particularly about how to dance *Go, Go, Go Joseph* in the loincloth! I know that Phil was gut-wrenchingly nervous before his first show but he coped brilliantly and the audience loved

TURN AROUND AND TAKE A BOW

him. So much so that when Jason left in May 1992, Phillip took over the role for a year to hand over the *Dreamcoat* in May 1993 to Darren Day who came in just as I was leaving the Palladium to get on with *Grease* at the Dominion Theatre.

This whole period was incredible. To have conducted *La Cage* and then *Joseph* in this hallowed Palace of dreams, enchantment and entertainment, this Cathedral of Theatre even now makes me tingle with excitement, and it was all because David Firman and Mike Reed believed in me and gave me these two career defining opportunities and I am so very grateful to them both.

NINE

TELEVISION AS WELL

*T*he *Royal Variety Performance, The Eurovision Song Contest* and *Miss World* were three of the biggest annual TV shows as I was growing up. They were all massive events with huge ratings and, as my career has unfolded, I have been fortunate enough to have been Musical Director for all of them.

At the end of 1991 John Cameron was Musical Director for the *Royal Variety Performance* which was filmed at the Victoria Palace that year. I already had some experience from my involvement in 1989 so I was thrilled when John asked me to be his Associate on the show. John Kaye Cooper from London Weekend Television was producing it and Diana Ross was the headliner. Eric Idle sang *Always Look on the Bright Side of Life* and my overarching memory for the whole show was the day we put that routine together in the LWT rehearsal rooms at the Oval.

One of my responsibilities for John was to look after all things musical at rehearsals so I had already rehearsed with the original cast of *Les Miserables*, including the great Colm Wilkinson, Patti

LuPone and Frances Ruffelle, *Cats*, *Phantom* and *Evita* but the rehearsal with Eric took things to another planet entirely.

It started with an excerpt from *Madam Butterfly* with opera singer Ann Howard singing *One Fine Day*. She is interrupted by Eric dressed initially as Suzuki, her maid, with the familiar first strains of his song, '*Some things in life are bad, they can really make you mad*'. He loses his female Japanese garb to reveal the England football strip and continues singing. For no apparent reason the stage is gradually filled with a group of Sumo wrestlers, all the Royal Variety Dancers dressed as showgirls, the Sixties Tiller Girls, a dwarf carrying a placard with LIFE written on it and finally The Dagenham Girl Pipers. Really! Literally over a hundred people. During the mayhem Eric walks towards the front of the stage and eventually down the front steps into and out of the auditorium, followed by everyone on stage except Ann Howard, who is left downstage centre to give a cod operatic finish to the song. It was completely bonkers and even more bonkers in the rehearsal room where choreographer, Alan Harding, was trying desperately to get everyone into some order!

The orchestra and singers were all tucked under the stage for this show, not in the pit, so communication was of paramount importance and I spent the entire time with headset on listening to the director, Alasdair Macmillan, calling the show from the mobile production control room or 'scanner' and relaying any extra info to John as he needed it whilst he conducted. This was invaluable experience as two years later that was going to be me, but before that a couple of trips to Abbey Road and the start of *Grease*.

At the beginning of 1992, whilst continuing my regular job as Musical Director of *Joseph*, I was asked to conduct some sessions for Expo 92 which was happening in Spain that year.

It was my first time in the cavernous Studio 1 at Abbey Road, which of course had been the place where Elgar conducted *Land of Hope and Glory* for the grand opening in 1931, and this was a day with me conducting the Royal Philharmonic Orchestra. The piece written by Javier Navarette was called *Tierra!* and has the distinction of being the only time that I have ever worked with orchestra and a hurdy-gurdy player!!

I continued my Spanish connection for a couple of days with the Wren Orchestra in Studio 2 for a recording of Albert Guinovart's *Flor de Nit* for the Dagoll Dagom Company of Barcelona. Both of these recordings were engineered by a wonderful man called John Kurlander who had been an assistant engineer on most of the Beatles' Abbey Road recordings. It was John who pointed out to me that the stairs down from the control room onto the studio floor are the very stairs that the Goons used in the *Ying Tong Song* when they are running to and from the microphone before the '*Take me back to Vienna*' explosion. (If you don't know the *Ying Tong Song* that last statement will be complete gobbledygook, I fear!) David is a real gent and so quick at getting a sound in the control room that corresponds to the sound the orchestra actually makes in the live room. That kind of craft and expertise is rare and I have only come across a handful of people who can do that so quickly and efficiently.

In early 1993 I was asked to be involved in a new production of *Grease*, so I made my way to Wimbledon to meet up with director David Gilmore to talk about it. This was to be the very first time that the additional songs from the movie, *Sandy, You're the One That I Want, Hopelessly Devoted to You* and *Grease is the Word*, were going to be allowed to be used on stage. Our producers were David Ian, Paul Nicholas and the impresario of all impresarios, Robert Stigwood, and it was because he owned the rights to the movie that we were allowed to use those songs. David Gilmore talked to me about not wanting to make it a carbon copy of the film but instead he wanted to create a brand new and original version. Arlene Phillips was booked to choreograph and her reputation for innovation was legendary, so when David started talking through his vision of the show and asked me to be in charge of it musically I was beside myself, this was the big step up. I was to be Musical Supervisor, Musical Director and write the new vocal and dance arrangements! It felt a little bit like being let loose from Mike Reed and David Firman's apron strings that had held me secure for the previous few years and I suppose I felt that this was the right time for that to happen.

We were to open at the Dominion Theatre – a huge barn of a place – and a few weeks later I met with our sound designer, Bobby Aitken in that auditorium with its wide stage and even wider aisles of seating. Bobby, with his huge amount of experience and dour Scottish wit, completely nailed it when he said, "This'll be tough!"

Rehearsals were on the South Bank of the Thames just east of Tower Bridge and with Craig McLachlan and Debbie Gibson as *Danny* and *Sandy*, Sally Ann Triplett and Shane Richie as *Rizzo* and *Kenickie*, Richard Calkin and Charlotte Avery as *Sonny* and *Marty*, Tamzin Outhwaite and John Combe as *Patty* and *Doody*, Liz Ewing and Drew Jaymson as *Jan* and *Roger* plus Gary Martin and Myra Sands as *Vince Fontaine* and *Miss Lynch* and a class ensemble, this was a prodigious cast. Arlene's choreography had just the right amount of a nod to the movie and along with her brilliant assistant, Karen Bruce, they moulded the cast into a highly polished troupe with hints of fifties authenticity all the way through. The surviving member of the pair that wrote the original piece, Jim Jacobs, was around for most of our rehearsals and was really engaged with us in making this hybrid version work. The really interesting thing about *Grease*, when you analyse it, is that it is a show written in 1971 about the genesis of the rock and roll culture of the 1950s but, through our viewfinder from 1993, that can give a somewhat skewed view. David Gilmore very much wanted this production to have truth but we ended up with what was sometimes viewed as a show of caricatures though ultimately it moved the audience sufficiently well for all that. Subsequently I would always get whoever was playing Sandy to really think about making *Hopelessly Devoted* work as a piece of prose. All the repetitions of the lyric 'hopelessly devoted to you' have to be thought through as if you were saying a Shakespeare soliloquy – each one needs a different thought process and yet you have to deliver it as a pop song as well. When done well you should be able to achieve both, of course, and I think our Debbie Gibson, Sonia and Samantha Womack (Janus) really did achieve that.

I had asked Paul Maguire and Roy Moore to work with me in rehearsals and Broadway orchestrator, Larry Wilcox was writing the orchestrations. My young assistant, Oliver Ashmore, completed the music department. During the main bulk of the rehearsal period I would meet Larry each lunchtime to talk through all the changes made to the score. Larry sat with his wife Barbara, smoking profusely, taking it all in his stride and listening to me playing through the changes. We were fundamentally changing routines right up to dress rehearsal really – it was imperative to get it right. I am particularly proud of a few moments in the score, notably, the *Overture*, *Sandy Opening* going into *Grease is the Word*, *Greased Lightning* and *Born to Hand Jive* dance breaks. They most definitely seemed to make our version different from what had gone before.

About halfway through rehearsals David Gilmore asked me if there was any music to bring Vince Fontaine, the DJ from Radio Waxx in the show, onto the stage. In the original score there wasn't anything there that he wanted to use so I suggested that I could write a little jingle for the moment. I did my, 'let me pop into the rehearsal room for half an hour,' routine and came back with '*The sunny sound of radio in your own neighbourhood. Vince Fontaine, the main brain on Double-U-A-X-X Now!*' in full four part harmony and David loved it. I recorded it to be played into the show and those are my sultry tones singing it all, should you ever hear it – *The Radio WAXX Jingle!*

Our cast, though, made a glorious noise in the rehearsal room and it was one of the best full throated sounds I have ever had the privilege to put together. For the final run through I was really chuffed and exhilarated, this was going to sound magnificent on stage! Unfortunately none of us had bargained for the sudden curve ball that Stigwood threw at us once we got on stage.

Bobby Aitken had designed a sound system for a piece of musical theatre as had been talked about in pre-production. Robert, quite rightly in the end, pointed out in no uncertain terms that we needed to be thinking major rock and roll sound here. Chests pounding and all the chandeliers rattling. There was a very difficult meeting after the first run through on stage where he put that to Bobby as only Stigwood could. Bobby told him that there was no way he could open thirty-two radio mics on stage plus the band and make anywhere near a rock concert type sound because everything would feedback and howl, it would be a disaster.

The only way that he could get the band loud enough, and the cast on top even louder, would be to use hand held mics for principals and I suggested a backstage booth of professional singers to sing all the harmonies. The cast on stage would sing those harmonies too, but they would be lower in the mix to mitigate the danger of all that feedback flying around. So that evening some frantic calls were made to Annie Skates, backing vocalist supreme. My Music Associate, Roy Moore, was extricating the vocal parts out of the score and the following morning I was working with two teams of eight singers while a booth was being made on the first floor beside the pass door and Bobby and his team were rebuilding the sound system to make it take the roof off the building. That following night Annie's folk were actually singing during the show and we were on our way to making the Dominion Theatre really rock. With the booth up and running, some hand held mics used judicially and Bobby cranking up his system, Stigwood was happy and we had our BIG sound.

A couple of months later the room beside the pass door was requisitioned for VIP events so the vocal booth was moved down into the basement of the building. It was always one of my favourite places to go when I was on a show watch, such a luxury having terrific vocal talent on tap like this. (When the show started its touring life a few years later the booth had to be replaced by pre-recording the cast singing the harmonies which would be played into the show – known as 'click tracks' because the band plays along to a metronomic click which ties everything together and the music stays in sync.)

While I am mentioning Robert Stigwood there is one other little story to tell. The band was up on a moving bridge at the back of the stage which trundled downstage to the front for a couple of moments in the show, most notably the *Overture*. The bridge was raised as it went back upstage, thick sound proofing curtains came in and finally we were cut off from the cast and almost in a studio environment, where we played 80% of the show. After the first two weeks of previews I took the band and the booth singers out to the Chinese restaurant that used to be accessible just outside the stage door of the theatre to say thank you. We went on the Saturday, in between the matinee and evening show. It is fair to say that, as the drinks were my treat, a few gentle libations were imbibed and as I started conducting the evening show just afterwards I started playing around a little with the band and at certain key moments in the *Overture* I got some of them to stand up. The audience clapped along as they did on every show but on this Saturday I actively encouraged it from my conducting position with the spotlight on me and they went wild. The band truck trundled backstage and we got on with the rest of the show. In the interval the Company Manager, Peter Roper, called me in my dressing room to say that Mr Stigwood was in and would I please go and see him at the end of the show. Gulp…

You can imagine that the second half of the show my mind was somewhat distracted again with images of P45s floating around and pictures of sacks dancing before my eyes. Anyway, we finished the *Band Playout* and I made my way up to the back of the Circle where Robert had his private office. When I say office, I should say it was like walking into the Kasbah. Inside the room was a pink Bedouin tent with a large Jukebox one end, a live feed from the stage the other and in the middle an elaborate bar. I knocked on the door, with a certain amount of trepidation, I may say, and Robert's voice boomed a "Come in!" I opened the door to be greeted by Robert handing me a bottle of Stella Artois and saying, "Whatever you did with the band tonight, you have got to do it every night, it was fantastic!" Well I mumbled some suitable words of thanks, drank my bottle of Stella, said that I absolutely would, bade farewell and went back to my dressing room to change out of my costume with a pretty good bounce in my step and a huge sense of relief in my heart! A tradition on *Grease* was born that evening – the *Overture* always went with a bang. However, we did take a little while to go back to the Chinese again!

This was one of the last shows that Orchestral Advisory Management or Chick Norton and Allen Franks 'fixed'. They were the pinnacle of the West End orchestral contractors – now superseded by Sylvia Addison and her company, Music Solutions Ltd. In 1993 Chick and Allen ruled the roost and you knew that if you had them on your show you could book the best players and they would be looked after. After our early discussions about my preferences they suggested this line up of players:

Assistant MD/Keyboards: Ollie Ashmore
Piano: Bill Worrall
Keyboards: David Mellor
Guitars: Keith Airey and Keith Jenkins
Bass: Jo Meacham
Drums: Tony Bourke
Saxes: Barrie Shaw, Alan Wakeman and Maggie Gray,
Trumpet: Stuart Brooks
Trombone: Colin Hill.

Tony on drums had become one of my favourite players and there were some nice tie ups. Colin Hill had played trombone on the tour with Tommy Steele, Keith Jenkins had played guitar on the *Joseph* I did in Belfast and Bill Worrall and Maggie Gray were both ex Trinity. Stuart Brooks was one of the most sought after trumpet players in the business and we were very lucky to have him with us. We gelled pretty well up on the bandstand. They loved the moments of glory where we were moved on the bridge down stage and into the limelight. We even had to wear specially made jackets so that we could be the Radio WAXX Showband! One very strange thing happened during band calls, which were held in the first floor bar of the theatre. Maggie Gray had left her baritone sax in situ overnight after we had been assured that the theatre was safe, and the following morning all the other instruments were there – guitars, drums, keyboards and all the music and music stands – but there was one thing missing. Someone had taken that sax, it had been stolen. To this day no-one knows who or why – it was certainly a very 'niche' and 'large' item to steal! Poor Maggie.

After the Gala Opening Night, which had been so successful, the second show started as normal and the band truck moved us all downstage centre. We were getting close to the end of the *Overture*, when the truck should start to trundle back, instead there was a little jolt and it suddenly stopped. Beside me on the podium was a set of lights and a telephone – a direct link to stage management in the prompt corner – I looked down and the red light was blinking furiously. I knew that I had to stop but I waited until I got to the end of the *Overture* and gently picked up the phone, knowing that I was still in full view. I was informed that basically the truck we were on, which weighed four tons, had failed, the manual winch had not yet been fitted and on top of all that it had stopped over the little flap where the computers that controlled it were located. There was quite a lot of noise from the auditorium, shuffling and whispering – people could see something was wrong. I managed to clamber off the back of the truck (out of sight of the audience) and got down to prompt corner. As it was literally the show after opening night all the production team were there. I was not alone in suggesting that we continue the show as a concert, with the cast in front of the band, but unfortunately the producer, David Ian, had to make the decision to cancel because if we had performed it like that we would have been in breach of our insurance contract and completely illegal. Craig and Debbie went out onto the stage to deliver the sad news that we would have to cancel, Craig took his guitar and for a few minutes they entertained the crowd. Naturally, most of the audience accepted the news with disappointment but good grace. Sadly there was a small faction that caused problems with our front of house staff and the police had to be called to disperse them. It got a bit ugly. We were all sent home early and the following morning two things happened. Firstly all the red top newspapers had the fact that we had cancelled the show on their front pages – great publicity for the show, of course – and secondly, the stage crew plus a few more able bodied people from the production company making thirty or so chaps managed to manhandle the truck back upstage. The manual winch was fitted and the computer brain was relocated so that the same problem couldn't happen again!

Any young Musical Directors reading please ignore this paragraph and move onto the next… I have explained a little bit in this book about long runs and reaching plateaus before and on *Grease*, because we were in a studio environment for such a large amount of the show, we had to find ways of filling the time between numbers. I had a TV monitor and two little stereo speakers right in front of me so that I could see and hear the stage but on this particular show, around three months in, I was playing Scrabble with some of the band. Yes, I know I shouldn't have been, but there you are, I was and I had a particularly good set of letters so I was just about to put a killer seven letter word down when I suddenly noticed two things at exactly the same time. Jo Meacham on bass guitar was stage whispering my name very pointedly and Charlotte Avery, playing Marty on stage, was seemingly speaking the words to the next song *Freddy My Love*. The realisation of what was happening dawned slowly and, yes, I had completely missed her cue line into the song. After a small hiatus she realised I wasn't paying any attention (my image was on a TV screen hung from the rail at the front of the Circle) and so she started speaking the lyrics. As I realised I called out to the band, threw my arms in the air and we ploughed into it and after a few seconds, which felt like about three hours, we continued the song, successfully with Charlotte, to the end. In the interval I girded my loins and ran up the back stairs to her dressing room in full knowledge that there was nothing I could say to redeem myself or to make this right. So I knocked on the door, opened it and immediately fell prostrate in front of her intoning 'Mea Culpa' a few times. To be fair to Charlotte she took it with good grace. Of course she was angry but we made our peace. What was funny about the episode is twofold. Firstly, I never knew what that Scrabble word was in the aftermath and secondly, the song itself was cut a couple of months later! Maybe my cock-up was an omen.

All the way through rehearsals Arlene, David and I were really positive about our version of the show, but we thought we may be lucky to get around six months out of it. The fact that it ran in London until 1999 and toured the UK until 2017 just shows you how little we know!

We recorded the album of Grease, again with Nigel Wright producing, in Whitfield Street Studios. The very same place – then known as CBS – where I had recorded Tell Me On a Sunday with Julian Lloyd Webber. Unlike Joseph, on this recording I was able to insist that we record the full routines of the big numbers. So there is the full version of Greased Lightnin', with Craig playing the guitar solo himself – he used to mime it in the show while Keith Airey actually played – Born to Hand Jive and so on. My only regret is that we never recorded the Overture for this recording, but I did get an opportunity later!

Around the time we opened I was contacted by Rachel Williams, who ran the music department at London Weekend Television, again they were producing the Royal Variety Show, they wanted to do an excerpt from Grease and they wanted me to be Musical Director for the whole show. This news really hit home – one of the three biggies and I was to be in the 'Alyn Ainsworth' or 'Ronnie Hazlehurst' position. I asked Roy Moore, who had worked with Mike Reed on a couple of BBC Royals, if he would be my associate so I knew that I had a safe pair of hands assisting me. This was also the first of the Royals that I wrote the theme for.

The show was hosted by Cilla Black and a couple of weeks before rehearsals we had a meeting at the Mermaid Theatre with the guys from Right Said Fred plus Frank Oz and Brian Henson (Jim's son) from The Muppets to routine a little section where Cilla is talking with Miss Piggy and Kermit. The conceit was that Cilla introduces them and they were going to sing a song, there and then, but they needed someone to play for them and they call for the band and on comes Right Said Fred. Everything goes wrong and eventually Right Said Fred perform a short medley of their hits with all sorts of big and small Muppet creatures joining in.

So, in rehearsal this had to be 'routined', as we call it, in other words put together musically and physically staged. I sat at the piano with Frank Oz to my right and Brian Henson to my left, we talked for a few moments about what was required and then I played a little arpeggio and, in that little theatre, and almost right in front of my eyes something miraculous happened. Frank Oz ceased to be Frank Oz and instead, with no puppet or prop, he *became* Miss Piggy. The same with Brian on the other side, he *became* Kermit. It remains one of my treasured memories. As Frank delivered the cue line, "Oh, Kermie, I can feel myself Falling in Love Again," he really and truly morphed into his alter ego. However the story doesn't stop there. A few days later we were in Metropolis Studios creating the track of the medley with Richard and Fred, from the band and a few of The Muppet people. We needed to replace some of Right Said Fred's lines in the songs and also add various grunts, oohs and ahhs in Muppet style. I was asked to join in with the Muppet guys so some of the noises on the track are me. I was an honorary Muppet for that one time. I was even given a Kermit the Frog watch by Martin Baker from Jim Henson's Creature Shop to prove it!

When LWT moved into the theatre to record the show *Grease* was cancelled for a week so that the TV set could be built and all the camera equipment could be set up. *The Royal Variety Orchestra* was too big to fit onto the band truck that we used for *Grease* so we needed to split it into sections. I was on the truck conducting with rhythm section, brass and woodwind (sixteen players including Guy Barker on trumpet), in front of me, then the string section, harp and percussion (eighteen players) were in the room that Stigwood had used as his 'office' for the first couple of months of the run and finally I had Annie Skates and her eight singers down in the vocal booth below stage. Three separate positions for forty two people and I had video and comms to all of them and an audio link to the producer John Kaye Cooper, director Nigel Lythgoe and sound supervisor Mark McLoughlin. Lots of buttons to press if I needed to talk to all of them and, thank goodness, two years before, on the 1991 Royal, I had made sure that I experienced wearing headphones and listening to the director, so I had some idea of what it would feel like.

Timing is everything on a *Royal*, from the Queen's entrance and the playing of *The National Anthem* right through to the closing of the show with everyone on stage. In the interval I had to record some of my theme music so that on the edit it could be placed under a piece about Brinsworth House and the Entertainment Artistes' Benevolent Fund. I had just finished and communicated on my comms link to the orchestra that they could take their quick 'comfort' break when suddenly on the director's link I heard that the Queen was coming back into the auditorium. Most of the players were already gone but a few were still there as I shouted on the comms that we were about to play the Entr'acte because the Queen was early. Fortunately it was only to be used for the theatre audience and was not going to be included in the TV edit, which was just as well as it probably sounded like the orchestra was suddenly reduced to piano, bass, drums and kazoo!! After the show was finished I found out from

Nigel Lythgoe that we weren't the only ones caught out. Half the camera operators weren't at their stations either and the first item, which was an excerpt from a show called *Forever Plaid*, wasn't completely filmed. In the edit they had to use sections from the Dress Rehearsal. Another salutary lesson!

The headline act on this show was Michael Barrymore and his routine with 'A Company' The First Battalion, The King's Regiment of *Will You Still Love Me Tomorrow* brought the house down. The rehearsal, back in the old LWT rehearsal rooms at the Oval, was hysterical. Alan Harding was choreographer again and between him and me, we had to get the army chaps to look like they were actually singing. Particularly the Sergeant Major who had solo lines direct into camera, 'Meets the morning sun', and had to be drilled into doing it right. Alan's choreography based on their own marching routine, is classic and Barrymore, who was at the height of his fame at this point, was brilliant. The real vocals were sung by the boys in Annie Skates' vocal booth, way down under the stage, by the way, though you would never know.

Some of the other highlights for me on this show were working with the Bee Gees – the orchestra joined in with their band for *Massachusetts* – and Harry Secombe and Roy Castle on the excerpt from Cyril Ornadel and Leslie Bricusse's *Pickwick*, choreographed by Gillian Lynne, in which I got to conduct dear Harry singing his iconic song *If I Ruled the World*. There was also a spot on the show for emerging new comedy talent and the three chosen were Bradley Walsh, Joe Pasquale and Darren Day. The opera singer Lesley Garrett sang *And This is my Beloved* from Kismet and Brian Conley did a Blues Brothers routine in his own unique way. It's not called a Variety show for nothing, but the quality of musicianship that was needed, think about it, one minute the orchestra is playing a song from *Grease* and the next it's playing an operatic aria – and it has to be perfect every time, stylistically as well as just playing the notes – the musicians who do this are the best of the best, and in my career I am so fortunate to have worked consistently with such talent.

1993 Royal Variety – The Queen with John Kaye Cooper,
Arlene Phillips, Gillie Lynne and Brian Henson

As soon as the show finishes there is the line-up to meet the Queen. All the Heads of Department from the TV show plus all the main performers get to shake hands and she rather brilliantly manages to make everyone feel completely special for that moment. As I was Musical Director this time and not Associate MD I was on that line-up. Beside me were Arlene and Gillie and the other side of me were Brian Henson and Frank Oz. I was one of the lucky ones and the Queen actually made conversation with me. We had a little chat about where the orchestra was and she said that she had seen me on the TV monitors which were hung from the circle. Rest assured there was no playing Scrabble on this gig! Now, if you shake hands with the Queen then the

Handshakes of Separation go off the scale of course, and, to top the whole evening off, at the Gala Dinner later I was on one of the top tables and found myself sitting next to George Martin, with Cilla Black and her husband, Bobby Willis opposite. All in all it was the culmination of an extraordinary few days!

A couple of weeks after the *Royal* I was in London Studios with *The British Comedy Awards* for LWT, produced by the enigmatic and notorious *Top of the Pops* director, Michael Hurll. A smaller band hidden away but nevertheless live. This was the year that there was a fair amount of controversy when Julian Clary announced to Jonathan Ross that he had been backstage 'fisting Norman Lamont'. I had a direct feed in my ears of the control room, as usual, and when he uttered those words the comms feed went completely silent for five seconds and then it erupted! Alasdair Macmillan, directing, was calling shots left, right and centre to try to get as many of the reactions as possible. My wife at that time, Jo, was working on the show as a runner and at the very moment that Julian said his infamous phrase she was sitting right next to Mrs Norman Lamont who turned to her and said, 'What does fisting mean?' Fortunately I think her answer was drowned out by the loud reaction of the audience all around them!

In early 1994 the people who ran Theater an der Wien in Austria suggested that they wanted to produce another version of *Grease* in Vienna. They didn't want to replicate the London show instead they wanted to use my version musically and re-work the show for an Austrian audience. When I say my version, of course I mean my vocal and dance arrangements and Larry Wilcox's orchestrations. Everything was agreed and I went to Vienna for auditions. I was greeted by the casting director Doris Fuhrmann, an imposing woman with pince-nez and with a shock of red hair, director Michael Schottenberg, who was the spitting image of Steven Spielberg and American choreographer Denis Callaghan, who had just recently choreographed the huge Christmas show at Radio City, New York. There was a great synergy amongst us and I loved the weird juxtaposition of auditioning and then rehearsing a full-on rock and roll show in the same place that Mozart had premiered *The Magic Flute* and where a few years later Beethoven had actually lived!

Although we rehearsed at Theater an der Wien, we played the show at the nearby Raimund Theater. The cast was a mixture of nationalities and it starred Susanne Eisenkolb, Pia Douwes and Andreas Bieber. Very different from the London version and conducted by the rather enigmatic and forever smiling Christian Kolonovits who was famous in Vienna with his crossover work with the Vienna Symphony Orchestra. We even made a promotional event for the show at the Vienna Opera House – again what a juxtaposition of styles!

Our director, 'Schotti' as we called him, had an equally interesting assistant called Sigrid Markl who had this fascinating dominatrix-like quality about her. She was really good company and kept Schotti and his quite harebrained ideas in place. The show was such a success that it was decided to create a German version as well. This eventually played in Dusseldorf at the Capitol Theater after touring around Germany. Denis Callaghan directed with his brilliant and funny assistant, Sue Delano, and Michael Brenner and his company BB Promotion produced it. Delano and I became great friends and we had some mad evenings usually culminating in a musical theatre sing-song. She had been on tour with Liza Minnelli as one of her two dancers and she had the piano vocal score from that show – well I just HAD to play through it and she just HAD to sing it, glorious fun!

Just as in Vienna we hired a lot of American actors but unlike Vienna, where the orchestra was a full time entity and

I had to pick who I needed, in Germany they imported a lot of American musicians and I had to audition them. Fortunately there were some terrific players, like guitarist Greg Dinunzi and the Musical Director who had the longest tenure, John Opfar, looked after the show impeccably and became a great friend.

While the show was at the Capitol Theater, Michael Brenner and his partner Thomas Krauth managed to get Olivia Newton-John to visit the theatre to help promote it. We had a quite crazy afternoon when she appeared in the rehearsal room at the very top of the theatre while I was taking a little refresher music call for the ensemble. Naturally when she walked in, after everyone had cheered wildly, I got her to join in with us all singing *You're the One That I Want*. It was a magical half an hour and she was just the most gracious and lovely presence in the room. A proper *Star*, in the best sense of the word.

We made CDs of both the Viennese and the German version and I made sure, as this time I was producing, that the *Overture* did indeed get recorded!

My association with Michael Brenner continued until his untimely death in 2011. He was one of the 'good guys' and a really tuned in producer, with a cherubic smile, a quirky sense of humour and an inner rod of steel, I really liked him. He always called me 'Mikey' and for some reason I liked that. On my regular visits to *Grease* in Dusseldorf we would meet up and review the show and he asked me to take a look at a piece he had just started producing based on the *Beauty and the Beast* story and nothing to do with the Disney version. It was written by a German composer called Martin Doepke and starred Friederike Krum as Bella. She was stunning and with her translucent mezzo-soprano voice brought a delicacy as well as the obvious sultriness to the role. Michael wanted me to simply give the show an appraisal but in the end I spent time whenever I visited *Grease* working with the cast of *Die Schöne und das Biest* which was running in nearby Cologne at the Sartory Theater over a two year period from 1995-1997.

Though I stayed conducting *Grease*, London until the middle of 1994, I had a lot of time off to pursue this burgeoning TV career as well. Over the next two years I found myself working for both LWT/ITV and the BBC. I did a series of *The Brian Conley Show* in 1994 as Musical Director and composer, with Ian Hamilton directing, Colin Edmonds script editor and executive producer and Nigel Lythgoe producing, and then in 1995 a series with Jimmy Tarbuck called *Tarbuck Late*, where my house band and I played for 10cc, Mica Paris, Paulette Ivory, Darren Day and Elkie Brooks amongst others and a little later in the year, *An Audience with Jimmy Tarbuck* where I was asked to look after the song *Johnny B Goode* for Jimmy to sing. The band that LWT put together for me to play *Johnny B Goode* was probably the starriest band that, even to this day, I have ever worked with. Rick Wakeman on keyboards, Hank Marvin and Justin Haywood on guitars, Jon Lodge on bass guitar and Kenney Jones on drums. All I had to do was suggest the key and they were off!

A one off show with Ronnie Corbett called *The Entertainers* provided a little extra entertainment for some during rehearsals. Ronnie wanted to do the routine from *Swan Lake* that he had made famous in *The Two Ronnies*. I had pointed out to both him and the producer, Mark Wells, that this would be a big ask for a seven piece band but they wanted to do it. I had programmed some keyboards and actually in the control room it sounded not too bad, considering. On the studio floor, however, it sounded rather thin and Ronnie came over to me during rehearsals and tore me off a strip in front of everyone with me trying to defend myself by telling him politely that the music was working in the control room and that the TV audience would hear it properly.

The band was on a slightly raised platform so to everyone else it must have looked a little bizarre. A short and very famous comedian dressed in a pink tutu haranguing a tall and very long haired Musical Director trying to defend himself and his musicians!

This was my second time at the famous TC1 studio in BBC Television Centre, because earlier, in April 1995, I was Musical Director for a show recorded to commemorate the fiftieth anniversary of VE Day on 8th May 1995. It was a 1945-style concert featuring music & comedy from contemporary entertainers giving an affectionate portrayal of the stars and household names of WWII. With Marti Caine playing *Gracie Fields*, Ronnie Corbett as *Arthur Askey*, John Inman as *Frank Randle*, Max Bygraves as *Bud Flanagan*, Su Pollard as *Cecily Courtnage*, Mike Yarwood as *Max Miller*, Samantha Womack who was playing Sandy in *Grease* at the time, singing *I'm Going to Get Lit Up,* as *Zoe Gail* the wife of the writer Hubert Gregg, Maureen Lipman as *Joyce Grenfell* and Richard Stilgoe and Peter Skellern as the *Western Brothers* along with Gary Wilmot and the cast of *Me and My Girl* – it was quite a starry affair. I wrote the title music *Call Up the Stars* with lyrics by director David G. Croft. It was very much written as a pastiche of a wartime song. The orchestra was at the back of the stage and I had both Paul Maguire and Roy Moore with me again, oh, and it is the only time that I have had to wear a hairpiece when performing. My hair was too long and, rather than cut it, the producers, Bill Cotton and John Fisher, allowed me to wear a short haired wig!

A week after this show I was in Dublin for that year's *Eurovision Song Contest* – yes, I got to tick off No. 2 on that list of the three biggest annual shows. Kevin Bishop was producing the British entry for the BBC and he asked me to be involved. Some say it was a weird choice for that year – almost a rap – but it had a really good hooky chorus, *In the morning, when the sun shines…* It was written by Stephen 'Beanz' Rudden and performed by Jay Williams, Yinka Charles (a.k.a. 'Reason') and Paul Hardy, with 'Beanz' on keys on stage with them, the song and the band were called *Love City Groove*. This was back in the heady days when the orchestra HAD to be used. Only some items, percussion and a small amount of backing vocals were allowed to be on track so I orchestrated the rest of it to be played by the RTE Orchestra. We were in a huge building near those docks in Dublin where my Grandfather had his close shave with the IRA back in the early 1920s. It was called The Point but it is now known as 3Arena.

The event itself was a week long festival and the really brilliant thing is that every night there were national parties put on for all the people involved and every country was trying to outdo everyone else to make their party THE BEST. The rehearsal schedule was very drawn out so there was a lot of spare time. We had good vibes about how everything was going, in fact our song was favourite to win, so we made sure that we partied well, and I had to experience proper Guinness for the first time too. On the Thursday afternoon we had finished our first main rehearsal with the stage, lighting, cameras and orchestra and the next thing on the agenda was a trip outside Dublin for a photoshoot. Everywhere we went we had Special Branch with us, the 'troubles' were still happening across Ireland and there was always a level of threat, so protection was vital.

While we were on the shoot Kevin Bishop from the BBC had a call from the TV people back at The Point asking us back in to check over the recording of the rehearsal, they just needed Beanz, Paul Hardy and myself, there were some sound issues that they wanted to get right. The window of opportunity was quite small so we mentioned to our police escort that we had a predicament and could we get back to The Point in ten minutes – it took us thirty minutes to drive where we were, by the way. Our police officers looked at each other, smiled and agreed to take Beanz, myself and Paul in their car, leaving the others and their entourage there with the coach and two police outriders. The three of us got into the back of the police car, our two Special Branch officers in the front said, "How about some music, lads?" promptly turned the siren on and we zoomed back to The Point in four and a half minutes, flat! The precision and speed of their driving would have put them on a par with a certain Lewis Hamilton, it was breathtakingly quick. I sat in the middle and I'm sure I must have looked just like the cat who got the cream for those five minutes. Our meeting was wrapped up really quickly and all was well so we met up with everyone else and resumed both the photoshoot and the continuing partying!

On the Saturday it was all loins girded for the show. The dress rehearsal had gone well so we were ready. There was a young Irish chap who I bumped into a couple of times backstage called David Hayes. He was working with RTE Television as a Musical Associate and he was very courteous and we chatted – he later became Musical Director for the *Riverdance* International tour and our paths have since crossed on *Angela's Ashes*. A huge musical talent!

Come the show and I was escorted round to the orchestral platform just before our allotted time. Then it was the look around to camera for the 'Conductor's Moment', with a hand signal especially for Lillie, and we were off. *Love City Groove* gave it their all and the RTE Orchestra did their best to make it work musically. It was so exhilarating, this was me conducting the *Eurovision Song Contest* and I still get a frisson of excitement thinking about how it all felt. The fact that we only came tenth overall really doesn't matter, in today's terms that is a very respectable result, isn't it?

*

Granada Television in Manchester and Shane Richie – who had progressed from Kenickie in London to playing Danny on tour in *Grease* – had an interesting concept for a TV show. Three couples compete on a live show and the winning couple get married there and then. Compared to all the reality TV there is nowadays that actually sounds quite tame but in 1995 it was pretty radical. We recorded and transmitted a pilot episode in 1995 and then a series in 1996. My band included Keith Airey, again, on guitar and Steve Pearce on bass guitar plus three vocalists, Hazel Fernandez, Louise Marshall and Tommy Blaize. Highlights were working with The Osmonds, Lulu, Status Quo and Tammy Wynette.

As 1996 dawned it became apparent that on top of the continuation of the *Shane Richie Experience* there was going to be a lot more ALW in my working life. Having left *Joseph* back in 1993 suddenly I found myself in a meeting talking about a new version of *Jesus Christ Superstar*. Gale Edwards, from the second version of *Aspects,* was directing and I loved working with her. She is a rare breed, a director who understands the music in a Musical. She had been Trevor Nunn's associate on *Les Miserables* when it originally went over to Sydney and he then asked her to direct the Viennese production a couple of years later. Her pedigree is impeccable. I love her direct approach and how she interacts with actors, like all the best directors she finds a way to achieve her aims by empowering the performer after first sifting and sorting the thoughts and narrative that is required. So Gale directed, with the legendary John Napier designing and Aletta Collins choreographing.

Casting Steve Balsamo as Jesus was central to the production – he was stunning – but our Judas, Zubin Varla, Mary, Joanna

Ampil and Pilate, David Burt, were equally impressive. Before we started rehearsing with the cast though, the decision was made to make the cast album. Normally the cast album is made when a show is up and running but the idea here was to remake the concept album as Andrew did in the very first place with the original *Superstar*. This was hugely exciting and with Nigel Wright producing we set about making it.

We recorded the rhythm section first over a few days in CBS – now Whitfield Street – Studios. A stunning rhythm section with Ralph Salmins on drums, Steve Pearce on bass guitar, Fridrik Karlssohn and Paul Keogh on guitar, Pete Adams on piano, Andy Lynwood on keys and Keith Fairbairn on percussion. Andrew gave some great advice and wanted this version to feel like it was brand new, the first time it had been played. He said that he had always felt that the original concept album was out of his control and he wanted to redress the balance. So that was what we did. Every moment in the score was approached as if for the first time. It was thrilling putting it together and I think the results really speak for themselves, there is some astonishingly brilliant playing.

I spent a few days with the main cast members, basically coaching and teaching but also helping with interpretation and the narrative. Then they came into the studio to record. This was mostly done at Metropolis Studios and Air Lyndhurst. On one sunny June day dear Tim Rice had asked to come in and slightly 'tidge' a couple of lyrics that had been bugging him over the years. We held Steve and Zubin in the studio and gently waited for him to appear. To while away the time in the control room we casually turned the TV on to see Tim, as bold as brass, sitting in the VIP box on Centre Court, Wimbledon. That neatly coincided with a call from his PA apologising profusely, but Tim had been inadvertently delayed and wouldn't make it to the studio. When he did come in the following day I wanted to whisper in his ear that *'we knew where you were yesterday'* but I didn't have the *cahones*. It wasn't until many years later when I was conducting *My Life in Song* a BBC concert entirely about Tim's lyrics that I finally told him in rehearsals that we had found him out on that day back in 1996! Anyway, in *Heaven on their Minds* the lyric *'I am frightened by the crowd, for we are getting much too loud'* became *'and our conquerors object to another noisy sect'*. The change is really rather good and conveys the sense of oppression that this version of Judas, who is essentially a resistance fighter in an occupied country, must have felt.

Finally we added the choir and orchestra. Sylvia Addison assembled a simply stunning group of eighty or so players and Annie Skates booked sixty singers to make the choir, with Simon Lee as chorus master. The time had come to conduct the *Overture* and all the major orchestral moments to complete the album. Funnily enough this was in CTS Studio 1 right by Wembley Stadium where I had mistakenly gone a few years earlier for the Julian Lloyd Webber session!

If I had to single out one moment in my career that I could keep, and have to ditch everything else, this would be that moment. My personal history of *Superstar*, from sitting in Karon's back room listening to the original album on that B&O system, right through to 1978 and sitting in with Bill Worrell at the Palace Theatre, but deciding that it was too soon for me, to this time in 1996 and actually conducting this moment for posterity, I cannot fully express how astonishing this was and is to me. I am so proud of this album and truly grateful to have worked with such a stunning group of people in its creation.

Before we went into rehearsal I had a couple more visits to Abbey Road, Studio 2. This time it was two consecutive Saturdays conducting the orchestra for the movie of *Evita*. Nigel Wright was again producing with Andrew and, although by the time

I was in the studio, all the vocals and all the rhythm section had already been recorded. John Mauceri had conducted *Don't Cry For Me Argentina* and a significant further amount of the score. What was left, which was around a third of the movie, I conducted. Madonna recorded her vocals in Whitfield Street with David Caddick and then with her dulcet tones in my ear we added the orchestra on top. There was one near disaster because on my second day we came to record *Eva's Final Broadcast* when Evita's decline is most evident and there was no click to enable us to tie everything together, just a guide piano and Madonna's voice. The orchestra were not allowed to hear how Madonna sounded – it was all a bit 'hush hush' – so, because I had arrived at Abbey Road in plenty of time, I was able to create a safety click just before the orchestra turned up. I had actually flown up from Newquay airport on the early flight because I was on holiday at Treyarnon with Jo and Lillie. Thank goodness I got there early!

After the *Evita* sojourn it was into *Jesus Christ Superstar* rehearsals. On the CD Alice Cooper had sung *Herod's Song* but for the show proper Nick Holder played him with a wicked sense of impropriety. Steve Balsamo and Zubin Varla on stage were even more engaging and magnetic in their performances than on the album. One of the morning rehearsals I asked my friend from school, Tim Thornton, who was now Principal of North Thames Ministerial Training Course, to come in and we had a full and frank talk about the Christian viewpoint of the story and a very interesting Q and A session following. Gale Edwards, very cleverly, linked his historical perspective to her vision of the show and it was really illuminating for all of us.

The show was set to reopen the Lyceum Theatre after a complete refurbishment. At the end of the rehearsal period I had three days of band rehearsals. The orchestra for the show was much smaller than the recording, of course. Eighteen players in all, which was quite a reasonable size, all things considered.

The first time that the band and cast sing through the show together is traditionally referred to as *The Sitzprobe*. The name comes from the operatic tradition where the cast all sit on the stage and sing the score, literally translated as 'seated rehearsal'. Generally in Musical Theatre the *Sitz* occurs wherever the orchestra have been rehearsing. For this show we rehearsed the band at the old BBC rehearsal studios in Park Royal and so that's where everyone congregated. Andrew with quite a large entourage and all the various departments turned up, so it was quite some audience. I conducted the rehearsal and we essentially performed the whole show in concert form. It was exhilarating and even more so when Andrew, in a hugely ebullient way, congratulated us all, he was so enthused by it.

Next was The Tech – always very slow and tedious but so necessary! Cast only with rehearsal piano, John G. Smith and Paul Maguire playing, with Simon Lee, who was to be Musical Director, now conducting. It became apparent very quickly that my original intention, which was to conduct the previews and opening night, as Mike Reed had done on *Joseph*, was really not going to be an option. I needed to be out in the auditorium with Gale and Andrew using some of the diplomacy skills that I had inherited from Dad to keep order between them. There were a few tricky moments within the show and I suppose I was best placed to translate Gale's intention into musical terms for Andrew and if I had stayed at the back of the stage in the band position, conducting, I would not have been able to gently pour oil over the troubled waters!

I had a little meeting with Andrew in that favourite haunt of mine, Joe Allen, during one of the tea breaks. The entrance to Joe's was literally opposite the stage door so we didn't have far to go. At the meeting I explained my thinking, that it would be much better for the show if I stayed out front and properly supervised while Simon conducted. Andrew graciously listened and accepted my proposal, however I had to make peace with myself about it all. Because of the aforementioned 'Dixon' history with the show I was *so* looking forward to conducting the Opening Night, it was a huge wrench to pull myself away. I knew it was best for the show but, oh boy, it hurt. At least I had the knowledge that I had conducted the CD and that was how I came to accept the situation. It was tough, though.

During previews it became apparent that this newly refurbished theatre had some major sound issues. Once the orchestra was in place and Simon was conducting, our sound designer Richard Ryan tried to balance the vocals with the band but the high ceiling just made everything swirl round and round. There was no detail or crispness to the sound it was just a 'mush'. Richard's idea to rectify the situation was to suggest that we needed to place some sound deadening material high in the ceiling. Much like the mushrooms in The Royal Albert Hall. It was agreed that this was the best plan and, of course, it would take a few days for the pieces to be built and then installed. In the meantime we just had to cope.

The previews continued and the next evening I was sitting next to Andrew in the auditorium, with audience all round us, when he started getting agitated. The sound issues, of course were not yet resolved and the inevitable frustration spilled out of him like a mini volcano. I could see that audience members were noticing – and after all Andrew is difficult to miss – so I said very forcibly to him that he should come out of the auditorium and to the relative calm of the stalls bar. We were only a couple of rows from the exit so I practically dragged him out with me. Once we got there he started venting his frustration and I very loudly and in the nicest way possible told him to *'shut up!'* and I explained that of course the sound was not yet right, the sound deadening pieces had yet to be fitted as we had discussed. As I was saying this to him the Managing Director of the Really Useful Group at the time, James Thane, came running into the bar. He had been sitting upstairs but had seen me take Andrew out and knew there was something up. He was completely aware of the situation and took over gently cajoling Andrew. I made myself scarce – this was really above my pay grade – and went back into the auditorium for the rest of the show.

During previews the tradition on *Superstar* was that all the heads of department would meet in a little restaurant around the corner to discuss the issues that needed resolving, so I made my way there as normal, fully expecting to receive my P45 as I sat at the table. To Andrew's credit the first thing that he did when he came into the restaurant was to come over to me, apologise and thank me for taking him out of the auditorium, thereby saving him from embarrassment. I was mighty relieved and I also really did appreciate his good grace that evening.

Superstar ran at the Lyceum for a couple of years after receiving good notices and over the next year Steve Balsamo was lauded for his performance as Jesus. He performed *Gethsemane* a number of times on TV and I played piano for him on a few of them. Just after the show opened I was again in studio, this time to record all the titles music and stings for a BBC show hosted by Gaby Roslin called *Whatever You Want*. A gentle day at Air Studios and by the end I think all of us had really had enough of Status Quo – in the nicest way!

To round off 1996 Andrew asked me to help with a performance on *Children in Need* and there were a few weeks working on a very novel version of *Starlight Express*. First, *Children in Need*.

ALW was going to use a song from his forthcoming show *Whistle Down the Wind* as a charity single for the BBC's flagship philanthropic money maker. Harvey Norton and his Red Hill

Kids were the choir to sing it and I had helped a little with the recording which was produced by Nigel Wright. When it came to performing on the TV show I asked Harvey if Lillie could join the Red Hill Kids for one night only and sing with them. A plan was gently hatched and Lillie, who had just had her tenth birthday, learnt the song. It is also fair to say that she had practically learnt it by the time I had finished telling her that she was going to be in the choir! For the live TV transmission there she was singing her heart out and, thanks to Harvey, dressed in the requisite tee shirt as well. I was hidden behind the cameras conducting the choir and very proud to have her in front of me. She was beaming!

Then came *Starlight Express*. This version was on ice, choreographed and directed by Winter Olympic Gold Medallist, Robin Cousins, for a tour in the States. The skaters mimed everything so the full score and vocals had to be recorded. Again Nigel Wright produced and I conducted and again we used Sony/Whitfield Street Studios. All the orchestral sessions were completed and then Nigel, his engineer Robin Sellars and I decamped to Los Angeles for two weeks to record all the vocals in Westlake Recording Studios, West Hollywood. We spent those two weeks soaking up all the positive vibes in that amazing studio. The place where *Thriller* was recorded and where Quincy Jones practically resided. A warm and hugely talented man called Stan Beard was our vocal fixer, coach and chorus master. He brought in some brilliant vocal talent and I think at one point we had half of the backing vocalists used on *Thriller*! A lovely young girl called Aspen Miller sang Pearl, and Stan's son, Landon sang Rusty. I never saw the show but it toured the States for most of 1997. Whilst in L.A. with Nigel, I finally got to have dinner with Alan Parker. Our paths had never crossed on the *Evita* recording sessions so it was good to sit with him. Nigel had already mentioned to him how I had finished the recording sessions with the orchestra and he was extraordinarily kind and appreciative.

After returning from L.A. on December 19th a heavily pregnant Jo and I went to the opening of the *Evita* movie and just after we got home from the huge party, joy of joys, little Meg decided it was the perfect time to be born! The final mix of the movie was very loud so that is what must have piqued her interest in the big wide world!

Andrew loved how Aspen sang *Starlight* on the recording used for the ice show and in 1997 when he was putting his annual Sydmonton Festival together he brought Aspen over from L.A. to sing in the concert. I was Musical Director and it was a very varied affair. We had a group of instrumentalists from the Brit School who performed with the electric violinist Linda Brava, Steve Balsamo sang and to finish the concert Dame Kiri te Kanawa sang *The Heart is Slow to Learn*, with lyrics by Don Black, which was intended to be part of *Phantom II*. The song has had quite a life because after Andrew used it here he then used the tune in *The Beautiful Game* as *Our Kind of Love* with lyrics by Ben Elton and then much later in 2010 it appeared again, but this time in a similar guise to the version that we did in 1997, as the tune formed part of the song *Love Never Dies* used in the eponymous musical, which was effectively *Phantom II*! When Dame Kiri was asked to sing the song back in 1997, we met up in Abbey Road Studio 1 with a large symphony orchestra booked for the afternoon and recorded it. Don Black was there too and as we hadn't seen each other since *Aspects* it was good to catch up. He truly is, in all the best senses of the word, a 'nice' man. David Cullen had written a beautiful orchestration and the song sounded glorious. At the Festival performance Dame Kiri sang to the backing track though the full recording was used on Andrew's *Divas* album which was released, I believe, in 2006.

Early in 1998 I had another Julian Clary moment, this time it was simply to write the theme and incidentals for his ITV show, *In the Presence of Julian Clary*. It was a hugely camp affair and as I recall the little piece I wrote was mostly harp glissandos!

Spring 1998 was full of joy and laughter. I was working for the second time with director Steven Pimlott and choreographer Aletta Collins and we were starting to put pre-production ideas together for a new stage version of Leslie Bricusse's movie musical *Doctor Dolittle*. In a little music studio round the back of Marylebone High Street, my old college haunt, I was playing and singing through the score with them both and trying out dance music to *My Friend the Doctor* with Steven and Aletta joyfully dancing Irish jigs and whooping along. Paul Gregg and Adrian Leggett from Apollo Leisure had decided to produce the show and, fresh from his success playing Joseph, Phillip Schofield was going to be *The Doctor*. Again I was writing new vocal and dance arrangements as well as being Musical Supervisor and I also agreed to stay and conduct the first three months of the show.

My first meeting with dear Leslie Bricusse was in Hammersmith, in the bar of the Lyric Theatre, just after a day full of auditions. I was intrigued to meet Leslie who was one of that extraordinary group of talented people who had such amazing success but also managed to stay safely in the shadows and not deal with all the unpleasant side effects that fame can bring. He and his elegant wife Evie were married in 1958 and were just about always together and always smiling. From the late 1950s his list of songs, musicals and movies is awe inspiring. To have written *My Old Man's a Dustman* (using the pseudonym Beverley Thorn), *Feeling Good* with Anthony Newley and to have won two Oscars is amazing enough without adding to that the lyrics for two Bond songs, *Goldfinger* and *You Only Live Twice*. He has collaborated with all the greats and was a real gentleman, urbane, clever and kind. This is the man who on his first movie musical, *Doctor Dolittle*, had Alexander Courage, who wrote the *Star Trek* theme, as his Musical Director and on his next musical, *Goodbye Mr Chips*, had a young film composer and arranger recommended to him by André Previn called John Williams! The *Trekky* universe and the *Star Wars* universe have their own Hadron Collider in Leslie!

I needn't have worried on that day in 1998, I was immediately put at my ease when we met and I am happy to say that we remained friends until he died in October 2021. My *Handshakes of Separation* were again in overdrive when he told me about a very early visit to New York, after he was taken under the wing of Beatrice Lillie. She introduced this young whizz kid to everyone who was everyone on Broadway, but one day the introduction was a little enigmatic. "Go to the concierge of the Harkness Pavilion Hospital at 5pm and just tell him you're Leslie Bricusse. I will meet you there."

Leslie duly appeared at five with Evie and they were ushered into a private elevator which took them to the seventh floor. The white carpet in the elevator was as sumptuous as the carpet in the long corridor that met them as the door opened. At the end of the wide, windowed passageway, which was akin to being on an ocean liner, was a chaise longue facing into a bay window. A wisp of smoke was coming from a long cigarette holder that was held aloft by a senior gentleman in a silk dressing gown and as they got closer to him he turned, smiled and Bea introduced him. "Leslie, this is Cole Porter."

"Please call me Cole," he said and apparently, after Leslie had finished hyperventilating, they had a wonderful two hour conversation over a huge tub of Beluga caviar and two bottles of Roederer Cristal Champagne, and Leslie was presented with the recently published *Cole Porter Songbook*, signed, naturally, which laid the foundation stone of his lifelong passion for collecting rare and inscribed books.

Leslie had recently been working with Frank Wildhorn on *Jekyll and Hyde* for Broadway and suggested that we use his orchestrator, a large and ebullient man called Kim Scharnberg. I was very happy to agree to that and very soon afterwards Kim came over from New York with his family to work on the production. We had decided on an eighteen piece band for the show. Any smaller in this venue would not have done the music justice. Michael England, a young, up and coming conductor was hired as Musical Director to take over when I left and our Assistant Musical Director was Corin Buckeridge, a wide eyed deeply enthusiastic man with bags of energy. It was a terrific music team to make Leslie's music soar.

Doctor Dolittle was even bigger in scale to *La Cage aux Folles*. The theatre was the Hammersmith Apollo, which is, in London, second only to the Royal Albert Hall in terms of size of auditorium and seating and Mark Thompson's set made use of just about every inch, with a specially built walkway from the stage all the way round the edge of the Dress Circle and back again, so that the circus performers and Pushmi-Pullyu could parade during *I've Never Seen Anything Like It!* There was The Great Pink Sea Snail on stage and The Giant Lunar Moth that flew from the very top of the Upper Circle down to the stage and back again, it was huge.

Leslie suggested that he use his formidable connections to garner the services of Julie Andrews to play the role of the parrot, Polynesia. Yes, that's right, Dame Julie Andrews. She is and has been a great pal of Leslie and Evie, along with her late husband, Blake Edwards. She agreed to do it and the idea was that she would turn up for a couple of days and record her dialogue. There were also a few lines to 'sing' in a couple of the songs, so on one fine sunny day I found myself sitting at a piano in those old LWT rehearsal rooms at the Oval to rehearse with Dame Julie. At this point in her career she was very much still in the throes of getting over the botched surgery that had completely broken her vocal cords. Although the sound she was making was croaky and, of course, she was trying to sound like a very wise supercentenarian parrot, it was still Julie Andrews sitting next to me.

I did stop at one point and physically pinched myself, then I looked at her and said, "Just checking that I'm not dreaming and that it really is you here with me!" She laughed and gave me the warmest and most radiant smile, squeezed my knee and we carried on working. The next day we were in Angel Studios to record *Talk to the Animals* with Phillip and once that was done all the rest of the dialogue that she had in the show. She and Phillip worked together as if they had known each other for years and years. It was brilliant. He had been really good when he was playing *Joseph* but here as *Dolittle* his sense of performance and both his acting and singing became more and more assured. Julie instantly recognised his talents and they hit it off, there and then. It was an immense pleasure and privilege to have spent that time with her, and I still pinch myself!

1998 Doctor Dolittle Cast and Crew plus Julie Andrews in cap, centre

The parrot puppet was part of the Jim Henson's Creature Shop responsibility on the show, along with a myriad of other animals including Gub-Gub the pig, Chee-Chee the chimpanzee, Sophie the seal, Jip the dog, Dab-Dab the duck and of course that Pushmi-Pullyu. They were created with a system they called animatronics, which was *electrickery* of the highest order, brilliant model making and simply the best puppeteers on the planet. This was, of course, my second time working with the Creature Shop after my brief episode as a Muppet back in 1993, but this time I got to visit the workshop itself and see the creation of these amazing puppets. Even the Pushmi-Pullyu slightly paled into insignificance when in Act 2 the Great Pink Sea Snail appeared. I think twelve people were needed to physically make it seem to be alive – it was beautiful.

For the brief period of three months I conducted the show before I handed it over to Michael England to take over but there were two wonderful audience moments that I have to recount here. Audience members really do forget that if they are sitting in the front row that person waving their arms around in front of them and conducting the show is actually flesh and blood and can see and hear them…

Firstly, on one Saturday matinee, right behind my conducting rostrum, in the front row a young lady sat with her new born baby on her lap. She must have booked before she knew that she would have that brand spanking new infant, maybe it had arrived slightly early. Anyway, it was not going to stop her seeing the show and in Act 1 it was plugged into her left breast, as quiet as you like, and then when I returned to conduct Act 2 she had plugged it into the other one. Brilliant. The baby was completely content and it wasn't until near the end that there was any noise, and even then it was just happy giggles and a few yawns.

Secondly, one evening there were a couple of senior people right behind me who were very gently talking most of the way through the show. In Act 2 when the action reached Popsipetal Island and the cast are all dressed in white on a set that is also predominantly white the lady of the pair turned to her husband and quite loudly said, "Oh Arthur, isn't it colourful?" I did chuckle to myself.

When the time came to record the show for the Cast Album we devised a very canny way to make it happen. Right next to the stage door of the Apollo was a small recording studio called the Pierce Rooms. It had a fully functional control room with all the state of the art equipment needed and with some very careful wiring to the theatre we were able to record the orchestra in situ in the pit, the cast on stage and with Michael conducting, I produced it from within that control room. When we needed to overdub solo vocals we were able to use the live room there and it worked a treat.

The show was a massive success critically and Phillip was a masterful Dolittle with Sarah Jane Hassell as Emma Fairfax and Bryan Smyth as Matthew Muggins, along with Dame Julie's recorded performance and a supporting cast full of hugely talented performers, it looked like it would be there for a long time. Sadly the theatre, though ideal for the spectacle, was not known for its West End credentials. It was too far from all the action of the West End and there was practically no 'footfall' whatsoever. There was a lot of speculation as to why the show ended up there but whatever the reason I think a lot of us were of the opinion that if it had opened at The Dominion Theatre, for example, it would have run for years. As it was it almost made the one year and ran from 14th July 1998 to 26th June 1999. Quite respectable but it could have been so much more. A National Tour followed so that was a little recompense.

The rehearsal period for *Dolittle* flew by and I think some of the musical arrangements of Leslie's music that I wrote are some of the best that I have ever done for a theatre show. I really worked hard at creating underscore using related motifs from other parts of the show and Kim's orchestrations brought out all that musical thought with his unswerving loyalty to both Leslie's original and my adaptation. Alexander Courage would have been pleased that we also honoured some of his original textures and musical brilliance in the score, as well.

Once *Dolittle* was up and running I was able to help Leslie with another of his projects. He had written a musical treatment of *Noah's Ark* a few years before, but the demos that he had were a little jaded and old fashioned. I made new tracks for twelve or so of the songs from the show and we then had a week of recording in the Pierce Rooms beside the Apollo. This time, as we were only recording vocals, we were able to use their small live room only. I was able to cherry pick some of the amazingly talented people I had worked with before and we ended up with a pretty impressive cast for the recording. David Burt and Zubin Varla from *Superstar*, Linzi Hateley from *Joseph,* Gary Martin from *Grease* and Annie Skates brought her team of singers, some of whom had been singing in the booth! A song called *Peace on Earth* was the stand out tune in the piece and though, as yet, the musical has not been professionally produced, at least, when we came to create a special *Friday Night is Music Night* for Leslie in 2011, we were able to perform it with a beautiful new orchestration by Roy Moore and sung in full throaty glory by John Owen Jones.

Just after I had finished producing the demo of *Noah* I spent a few days just outside Nice at Leslie's French home in Saint-Paul de Vence on the Côte d'Azur along with his then PA, Bronia Buchanan and film director John Stephenson from Henson's Creature Shop to talk through some ideas. John had practically story-boarded the whole thing and the animals, Ark and all the set pieces looked simply amazing. As with so many projects the ideas were all there, all that was needed was the finance and sadly, as with many similar scenarios, that finance never came, so Leslie's *Noah's Ark* is still a work in progress.

Of course 1999 loomed large and for most of the year I was busy auditioning and then conducting all the music sessions for a new talent show for the BBC called *Star for a Night*. Jane McDonald hosted with the irrepressible Barbara Windsor along with record producer Nigel Martin Smith as the two regular panelists. Over two years we had two series of twelve shows each plus a kid's special where two rather notable young performers did rather well. Alexandra Burke came second and Joss Stone won. I remember both of them appearing for their audition and being enthralled by the natural talent that they both had. Joss, with her almost uncanny natural soul voice and Alex so bright and vivacious. Truthfully they both should have won!

In between auditions and recording the first series Dan Crawford from The King's Head called. "Mike, before Vivian Ellis died (in 1996) he asked me to have a go at his other hugely famous opus, *Bless the Bride*, so will you join me?" Well, it was dear Dan asking and he had managed to get Martin Charnin, conceiver, lyricist and original director of the musical *Annie* and one of the first *Jets* in *West Side Story* on Broadway, to direct. How could I refuse! It was a gentle relief from the frenetic time I was having and it led me to work with one of the most gracious creatures in the history of British entertainment. Judy Campbell. She played an older Lucy Willow and at the end of the show with her younger self played by Tiffany Edwards they sang *This is my Lovely Day* together. Judy was the first person to sing *A Nightingale Sang in Berkeley Square* when she performed in the revue, *New Faces* in 1940 and she had been Noel Coward's muse for a number of years. Her daughter, Jane Birkin, came to visit one evening, which also caused a flurry of excitement, though she was as gracious, warm and lovely as her mother. We had a cast of 'marvy old pros' and Martin had reworked the book so I had to rework the score and also write new arrangements. Just piano and woodwind, very gentle for the tiny auditorium made out of that old boxing hall at the back of the pub. It was a really enjoyable time though and a welcome respite.

Star for a Night was pretty relentless. Tom Gutteridge from Mentorn Television was producing for the BBC and we had been on an audition tour all over the country. When we auditioned in Birmingham there was a rather good and very young piano player who had been booked to play. Chris Egan was his name and though I didn't work with him again for a few years I kept a note of his details. His amazing facility and musicality was to come in very handy for a considerable part of my career, later.

We recorded all the tracks for the show at Whitfield Street Studios, but this time I booked Steve Sidwell to orchestrate and Mike Ross was the recording engineer. Steve Sidwell and I had known each other since those early *Royal Variety* shows. He was a regular number one call on trumpet and a couple of years later, when he was in my band for the Brian Conley series, I needed an arrangement of *September* by Earth Wind and Fire and I remembered Steve had mentioned to me that he had started writing orchestrations so I asked him to do this for the show. It was really good, it played straight off the page and when I needed someone to look after all the arrangements for *Star for a Night* he was the perfect choice.

The way we worked was that I would spend a couple of days with the contestants and Tom, the producer, deciding which song would suit each person best. I would quickly sit with them routining how much of the song we needed, usually around two minutes, but, of course it also had to make sense musically. Once the routine was done then off it went to Steve to orchestrate and then the following week we would have a further two days at Whitfield Street recording the band/orchestra but we would also record the artist singing a guide vocal so that the TV director had something to go on to make the camera script. For the show proper the contestants had to sing live, naturally, and one of my jobs was to help them feel as much at their ease as they could be and to give the best performance possible.

Star for a Night was a bit of a trailblazer for all the talent shows to come, *Pop Idol*, *X Factor*, etc. In fact, one of the columns on our audition sheets was headed 'The X Factor'. It was frequently used to help us make the final differentiation between some of the better singers. The show spawned a couple of spin offs. One of them, *Stars Sing the Beatles* from 2000, couldn't be called one of the finest television programmes ever produced. Jane McDonald hosted a number of celebrities singing their favourite Beatles song. I won't dwell on this too long, it hurts! Anyway, Englebert Humperdinck sang *Penny Lane* – the song that he kept off the number one spot with *Please, Release Me* – the newsreader Anna Ford sang *Here, There and Everywhere*, Sid Owen (Ricky in Eastenders) sang *Let It Be* – to be fair he sang it rather well – but you get the picture. The positives were recording all the tracks in Abbey Road Studio 2 – and working with all the great musicians who were booked to play.

By the end of 1999 I had also started work on another TV series, this time for ITV again, a chat show with Jerry Springer hosting. After the talk show series with Jimmy Tarbuck I always rather liked running the house band, creating music to bring guests on and accompanying performances. To be a Harry Stoneham or Laurie Holloway, who were the Musical Directors for Michael Parkinson's show, was a musical goal, I suppose, and on this *Jerry Springer on Sunday* show I got some way to achieving it. Mike Woolmans, who was 'Mikey' from Steve Wright's 'posse' on BBC Radio 1, wrote the theme and my band was a mixture of all my favourite players at that time. Steve Pearce on bass, Tony Bourke on drums, Keith Airey on guitar, Pete Adams on keyboards, Phil Todd and Snake Davis on saxes, Stuart Brooks on trumpet and Colin Hill on trombone.

The first show was recorded in autumn 1999 at Teddington Studios and the standard of the guests was set pretty high with Tom Jones, Glenda Jackson, Robbie Coltrane and Martine McCutcheon. Other guests in later series included Tony Curtis, Jane Russell, Hugh Laurie and Wyclef Jean. Even more cool. I think the show reached its sell by date a couple of years later, though, when *Puppetry of the Penis* were featured, however, the face made by trumpeter Stuart Brooks, in a brilliantly timed close up by director Geraldine Dowd at one point, tells such a story that it was almost worth it!

My TV career was moving pretty quickly and I was still involved in a lot of musical theatre so there was an awful amount of juggling and spinning plates involved. It was hugely exciting and, at this point leading up to the Millennium, I had no idea that it would get even more busy and more frenetic with the addition of some truly extraordinary events in the early part of the 2000s.

However, before I get onto those I'm going to take a pause, reflect and gently explore life, losses and loves.

TEN

LOVE AND MARRIAGE

Natalie is the third and final Mrs Dixon but it was quite a journey to actually find her, woo her and marry her.

Back in 1980 on that eventful tour of *Hair* when Susie and I got together, I was twenty-three and she was just eighteen. We were very much in love and it felt so completely right for us both to live together and then marry. Susie's Mum and Dad, Maureen and Joe, both had an entertainment background. Joe as crooner Ken Swane, and Maureen one of the best little tap dancers in the business. They formed a double act and Susie actually went on stage with them when she was a toddler, with a Beatles guitar, so it was inevitable that she would literally follow in their footsteps. They lived in Wigston, Leicester and that was where we were married in 1985. Mike Reed offered to play the organ for the wedding and he played Walton's *Crown Imperial* for us, brilliantly.

Maureen was working for Everard's brewery and was able to get Leicester County Cricket Ground as the venue for our wedding reception. Even though it was the eighties I still followed correct protocol and actually asked Joe (and Maureen) if I could live with and then marry their daughter. Fortunately they agreed!

When we moved into our little house in South Tottenham we were completely together and even though our careers were taking off and we were away a lot, we managed to keep meeting up and giving each other loving support. Our friends in the vicinity, Steve and Helen, from that first panto and Trinity, Janthea, from *Mr Cinders*, her husband Steve, and all our direct neighbours were quite a little band of support for us and we had good times. We even had a proper little boozer around the corner from our house and if I timed it right I could usually get back from whatever show I was working on just in time for last orders, and occasionally a 'lock in'. Those close neighbours and proper Tottenham chaps, Roy, Keith and Bert would have a pint or two ready for me.

Susie made a strong presence for herself first at The Oldham Colosseum and then at Nottingham Playhouse. Kenneth Alan Taylor was the common denominator here, he was Artistic Director at Oldham and then moved to Nottingham and he was very much a standard bearer for Susie's talent, both as a straight actor and as Principal Boy in Pantomime. He was a great exponent of the art of Panto and a lot of Susie's success later at Hackney Empire comes from what she learnt at the hands of dear Kenneth. There was also a lovely link here because Kenneth's wife, Judith Barker was in Andy Capp both in Manchester and London, so I had been working with her. It was a happy time and then suddenly I had to deliver to Susie the worst news imaginable.

She was in Oldham working with Kenneth and also staying at their house, I had been out for the evening with our neighbours Bert and his wife, Maggie. It was one of those slightly boozy evenings, Bert was in the Freemasons and this was his Ladies' Night. So I got home to our little house in Gorleston Road to find a number of messages on the answerphone from Susie's mum for me to call her urgently. I immediately phoned – of course no mobile phones in the mid eighties – and Maureen told me that Susie's dad, Joe, had suddenly died. He had been a hugely active man and as well as doing a lot of amateur dramatics he also had his 'day job' working for Tetley, where he used all his entertainment industry experience in his unique selling technique. He had retired from Tetley six months earlier and was looking forward to being able to follow his beloved daughter's career even more keenly. He was so, so proud of Susie. When Maureen gave me the news I knew that there was only one option. I had to drive to Oldham and tell Susie face to face.

So off I went on the four hour journey with my heart pounding and full of such profound sorrow. It was the worst journey, the miles dragged on, but gradually I got closer and when I was around an hour away I stopped at some services and called Kenneth and Judith. It was the early hours of the morning and they completely understood when I explained the reason for my unannounced visit. They were my amazing support team when I finally got there and delivered the achingly sad news. It truly was the most difficult time and Susie, naturally, was devastated but, as with all these life changing moments, some sense of acceptance of the awful truth prevailed and even though she was full of grief she appreciated immensely that I had got the news to her personally and as quickly as I could have done. There was a certain irony in the episode, though, because Joe was one of that rare group of people who knew and was regularly asked to sing the Ladies' Song for Lodges around the Midlands. Nothing would necessarily have changed but if he had been singing at Bert's Ladies' Night…

We continued to work and both of us progressed carving our own particular niches in the entertainment business. We always respected each other and I think we both tried our best to make it work but sadly we gradually found ourselves growing apart. I certainly fell into the trap of using our increasingly long times apart as an excuse for finding solace elsewhere and by the time I started *Aspects* I had decided that, though Susie and I would always be bound by our years together, it was time to move on and that we had to bring a close to the relationship.

It was in all ways a difficult time but we had grown out of each other. I was only just starting to deal with my own particular demons. Demons that had been created for me as a child, yes, but that were still lurking below the surface and not really fully acknowledged as yet.

Though I would not change a moment of our time together I am sorry that I caused hurt, but I am also pleased that we both have found our complete happiness elsewhere and I am proud of what Susie has achieved beyond measure. Her continuing career as a director, writer and as an actor, plus, of course, her life as wife to Sharon D. Clarke and their trailblazing time together. She has achieved so much and is a proper person in the very best sense of the word. Proper.

*

Once the decision was made we got on with things, I had my short relationship with Jane Fann and after a few months of living as Mike Reed's lodger I finally bought my own one bedroom mansion flat in Sutton Court, Chiswick. When I started conducting *Joseph* a couple of years later I was somewhat struck by a member of the stage crew called Jo. She was very feisty – and needed to be working in such a male oriented environment – and she also would frequently bring to the theatre, in between shows, this utterly captivating little girl called Lillie. Lillie was four and knew absolutely everything there was to know about everything, and, as I wrote before, she loved her Basghetti!

It wasn't long before I asked Jo out. I had been told by one of her pals in the crew that she was frequently seen watching me conduct the show in the monitors at the side of the stage and it wasn't to learn about conducting technique, apparently. So we embarked on a relationship which, of course, involved little Lillie as well.

Things progressed pretty quickly. Jo and I hit it off extremely well and Lillie seemed to magically make good things happen. While Jo was at the theatre Lillie was looked after, mostly, by a fantastically eccentric lady called Zoe. Zoella, as I call her, has remained close and kept her wonderful counsel with us. A lady of great fortitude and one of the best bakers I know!

It was in a matter of minutes, it seemed, and Jo and Lillie had moved in with me at Sutton Court. This was very grown up – Lillie was getting close to school age and it felt right and proper to make a home happen very fast.

Jo and I got married in September 1992, around a year after we had started our relationship. Our wedding at St Paul's Church, Grove Park, Chiswick was very much a *Joseph* affair, but this time I asked Mike Reed to be my Best Man rather than play the organ. On my stag night, which he organised along with assistant Best Man Derek Wade, an evening in a rather sprauncy restaurant in Notting Hill, I was furnished with a ball and chain at one point and while I was laughing about it I suddenly realised that the key to the ankle clamp had been thrown out of the window – we were on the first floor – and there was no spare key. Not best pleased, I had to wait until we got back to Chiswick before I could get a hacksaw to get myself out of the predicament. Notwithstanding that, the whole wedding event was full of laughter and I felt happy.

The first of three life changing events happened around three months into my relationship with Jo. Lillie was sitting on the end of the sofa with me, we were playing a game and up to this point she had always simply called me Mike. She stopped what she was doing, looked at me with the serious gaze of a four year old going on twenty-seven and said, "Mike, can I call you Daddy?" She had obviously been thinking about this moment for some time. Well, you could have picked me up off the floor, I was totally banjaxed, hugely flattered and full of love for this little soul with the shock of dark hair and the smile that could melt a glacier. Knowing that Lillie's birth father had never been around and that she had never called anyone by that name I said to her that I would be honoured to be her Dad and that she could call me by that name at home to begin with and gradually, if everything progressed as well as it was going with her mummy, in just a few months she could call me Daddy all the time. I think I held out for about three weeks. I was her Dad.

A couple of years into the marriage and we had gone through a court process enabling Lillie to take my name and for me to assume parental responsibility. It was as close to adoption as was possible and Lillie was the one who instigated it. I love that.

It would not be disingenuous of me to say that Jo and I ended up having quite a difficult marriage. We tried to make things work. There were many wonderful times but there were also some really gut-wrenchingly horrible times, for both of us. We moved into a lovely ground floor flat around the corner in Thames Village and we made our peace together. We both tried hard and, for a period in 1996, we seemed to have found an equilibrium in our relationship that was much more positive and full of joy. Jo announced that she was pregnant and at the end of 1996 we moved into our house in Wolseley Gardens.

Then the *Evita* movie opening and the second of those life changing moments happened. Our daughter, Meg, was born. As I said before it was obviously the loudness of the *Evita* score had got her interested in the big wide world, but I now had my two wonderful daughters. They continue to be there and they continue to fill my heart with joy. They are both very different but they have such an open musical ear. Whether it be nature or nurture – in fact it has to be a mixture of both, doesn't it? They have as eclectic musical tastes as I do and they are both such musical souls as well. They sing, and, most importantly, they can only sing if they are telling story. They both have honesty, a great sense of pitch as well as unique tone. They don't sound like anyone else is essentially what I mean.

1997 With Lillie & Baby Meg

For a short while all was OK between Jo and me, and our relationship held firm for the first year or so, while Meg was a little baby. It was not to last, sadly, and early in 1998, as *Dolittle* was starting, I am afraid we came to another impasse, and this time it was the start of the end. I did try later in the year to confront those demons of mine and I embarked on a six month stint of counselling which did enable me to look at the whys and wherefores of my inability to remain faithful but it was not going to save our marriage. In the early part of 1999 I decided that if we continued like we were it would be no good for any of us. So in early July it was the end of the road. I was desperate that Lillie and Meg were protected as much as possible, but naturally they had witnessed some of the unpleasantness between Jo and me and I knew that the only way to make sense of it all was to agree to part ways and finish our relationship as quickly as possible.

*

After that I stayed in the house for a couple of months and found an interim flat to rent which I moved into in September. Of course, in the midst of those two months I had met Natalie at Trethias and it wasn't long after I moved into my little apartment in Beaver Close (don't snigger), that I called her and we very gently embarked on our journey of discovery together.

That very weekend, when I moved out of Wolseley Gardens, I also finally gave up smoking for good. It was as if there was so much change, angst, worry and heartache going on in my life that adding a simple little thing like stopping smoking made the process of giving up easier. My main worry was for my girls and leaving them, somehow giving up smoking paled into insignificance and it was actually easy.

One of the pacts that I had made with myself was that I would give up when Meg was born. Just as my Dad had given up when I was born, I suppose. I failed that one and had to wait nearly two years before I actually made it, so that weekend was momentous and the one really good thing is that Meg cannot remember me smoking.

In 2006 as I was getting close to my fiftieth birthday I had a Wellman check up – a full MOT, if you like – and in my results I was referred to as a NON smoker. I was expecting to still be an EX smoker, but, no, I was officially a non-smoker. That really was a milestone after being so tethered to the unpleasant habit for so long. Before I moved out of the house Jo and I had discussed how things would work and we agreed that I would have the girls every other weekend and, naturally, I wanted to be as open about this new relationship as I could be but not try to suddenly play happy families.

For one thing, Natalie had a huge lot of ground to cover in accepting that she and I were a couple – I had tried my very best to talk openly about my demons and she has always been so very understanding – plus here was I with my two children, this completely bonkers lifestyle with every second that I had full of auditions, studio, theatre, television. It was a huge and momentous lifestyle change for her. Totally different from how things had been in her career working at Mars Confectionery, and totally different from any relationship that she had been in before. Her natural calm and analytical way prevailed. Dad had always instilled into me to talk through any problem, don't let it fester. It really is the only way and, because that was the same with Natalie, it was easy to achieve, we quickly resolved any problems and, finally, I found myself in a happy place.

By the time we got to the end of 1999 I was totally in love with her and although the divorce going through was not the easiest of things to deal with, somehow we made it on into the 2000s. Meg and Lillie also managed to embrace her into their lives and, I suppose, they could sense that here was a love and stability that hadn't been so obvious before and they could see how happy I was now. Quite different from some of the bad times earlier.

After a few months I moved into her little flat in West Harrow and early in 2001 we started searching for a house together. Grange Cottage appeared on the market and we both loved it. However the serendipitous fusion of Treyarnon and lasting friendships played a part in that, as well.

The difficulty was arranging a time when we could see it both together because I had more daytime free and Natalie was ensconced in chocolate in Slough. A phone call came from the estate agent asking if we were available that afternoon. I was, but Natalie just couldn't get away so she made a call to our own particular cupid – Lucy Davies née Pelham – to see whether she could accompany me. It wasn't that Natalie didn't trust my judgment just that she didn't *yet* trust my judgment, if you see what I mean. Lucy would be able to give her the unemotional analysis required. So, thanks to Lucy we did indeed buy Grange Cottage and on May 4th 2001 we moved in.

The first time I ever lived in a detached house – it was bliss! No danger of neighbours banging on the walls if they didn't like me playing some Poulenc or Beethoven, with enough space for Meg and Lillie to stay with us and for them to feel at home too. Grange Cottage has proved to be a great place to live, close enough to London to make travelling in on the tube easy and rural enough with a fabulous meadow and gardens right opposite. The house itself dates from the fifteenth century but only became a dwelling in the late 1800s. We even have gas lamps in each of the main rooms that still work and I adore them because they are so reminiscent of early times in Cornwall with the caravan.

Later in 2001 I decided that it was time to ask Natalie if she would marry me. She had come with me on a BBC jaunt for a *Friday Night is Music Night*. After the gig I was so hyped up that I simply couldn't wait and ended up asking her, there and then, after we got back to our hotel. All well and good you may think except that we were in that most romantic of towns, Grimsby, for the gig. It's a city known rather more for its fishing fleet and port than its romantic heritage but not for us, for us it's as romantic as, well, Grimsby. Fortunately, the 'where we were' didn't matter and Natalie said yes. We waited for eighteen months or so and in June 2003 we were married.

2003 Third & Final Wedding to Natalie in Cornwall –
With Meg and Lillie

By this time my friend, Tim Thornton, had become a bishop and I asked him if he would be able to officiate. Because I had been married twice before he couldn't perform the 'marriage' but he was, instead, able to bless our nuptials after we had been to the Register Office. Our Register Office was Truro and the church where our marriage was blessed was St Merryn Parish Church which is the closest church to Treyarnon. Tim is probably the only Bishop who has managed to work the 'strap-line' *A Mars a Day Helps You Work Rest and Play* into a wedding sermon. Natalie was very impressed! Local family and friends joined us for the fun and frolic. Pasties and sparkling rosé were on the menu and the following day we had a little marquee behind our caravan and the festivities continued. Lillie was a star singing Natalie's favourite song, *The Girl From Ipanema*, and Meg (aged six) loved being a bridesmaid.

We had some time together for a 'sort of' honeymoon and then the following Sunday Natalie's Mum and Dad, Patricia and Colin, had arranged a separate party at their favourite haunt, the Old Merchant Taylors' Sports Ground, Durrants. To this event a lot of other friends and relations were invited and, of course, as this was very much *We Will Rock You* time for me, a few of the cast, including Sharon D. Clarke and Tony Vincent, came too. Sharon had a dual role as she was there also as Susie's other half. Brian May and his wife, Anita Dobson, were guests as well and there was the inevitable entertainment spot where, when Tony Vincent sang and I accompanied him, Brian joined us in a brilliantly ad hoc way. Borrowing our friend Mike Prendergast's guitar – which he hasn't cleaned since – Brian came up to the stage area and we were suddenly a trio. I think it was one of those fabulously serendipitous moments, the stars aligned and our own very special and unforgettable Wedding moment happened. Lillie again sang *Ipanema,* my niece, Sara, sang a song that she had written for us and I wrote a song for Natalie as well. Brother in law, Paul, was best man and he also played drums with us in the entertainment. It was a fabulous day.

Durrants was the scene for my fiftieth birthday party in

January 2007 and I am particularly pleased that along with family, friends, Treyarnon folk and musicians there was a separate and very select group of people at that party. Natalie was joined by both Susie and Jo, so all three of my very special ladies were there at the same time.

Three wives is most certainly enough, but as I reflect on the times gone by and what the future may hold, I am certainly most honoured that love, hope, loss, joy and life has been shared with them all, but, as I say, Natalie is my third and FINAL wife. I love her beyond measure and cannot begin to express how happy and content I have been since 1999.

The lyrics below are from the song I wrote for Natalie at our Wedding and they hold true just as much now as they did then:

When I saw you it was just like in a dream
When I held you were we both just seventeen?
Seventeen?
Was it a dream or are you really here?
When I held you were we both just seventeen?
My Queen
Not a dream
It's real my love for you is so clear

When I saw you it was just like in a dream
In a dream
You mean everything to me
I want you
Give me your hand
With you I feel strong
We belong together now you and I
You and I

Now I see you and it's not just in a dream
Now I hold you and we're not just seventeen
My Queen
Not a dream
It's real my love for you is so clear
When I saw you we were not just seventeen
No no
Now I love you and we're not just in a dream...

©MD June 2003

ELEVEN

EXTRAORDINARY
EVENTS

The year 2000 started with a bang and my first job was the closest I ever got to working with Morecambe and Wise.

The BBC was celebrating the fortieth anniversary of BBC Television Centre and produced a special show called *Night of a Thousand Shows* hosted by Michael Parkinson. I was credited as Musical Director but actually I was only involved in one section.

There was a very famous sketch in which Tom Jones sang the song *Exactly Like You*, with Morecambe and Wise miming along to the backing vocals, *Yeah, Yeah, Yeah*, and inevitably larking around beside him. For this show they wanted to recreate the sketch with Tom, of course, and Reeves and Mortimer as Morecambe and Wise. We recorded the track at Angel Studios and I was able to get hold of the original orchestration, which was in the BBC Music Library, written by the legendary TV Musical Director and arranger, Peter Knight, who had worked with Morecambe and Wise from 1969-1977 – pretty much through their golden years on TV. A hand crafted score turned up at the studio and it was almost like having the Dead Sea Scrolls in front of me. He had a reputation for writing arrangements that played straight off the page and this was no exception. It was a perfect orchestration.

Tom, naturally, sang it on screen perfectly and my only regret was that Reeves and Mortimer didn't really embrace the comedy with the same rigorous work ethic that Eric and Ernie are known to have had. They rather fudged at the routine, trying to be funny, instead of just being themselves. Anyway, I was still chuffed to bits that I had helped to recreate Peter Knight's arrangement and it sounded great!

The year continued with more *Star for a Night* and *Jerry Springer on Sunday* shows plus the ongoing supervision of *Grease* and I had also been approached about a new BBC project to find the *BBC Voice of Musical Theatre*. An elegant, forthright and quite brilliant lady called Kate Jones was producing and singing teacher Mary Hammond and I were the initial adjudicators. The process involved sifting through around five hundred videotapes to get down to around fifty or so who would audition in person. The tapes were from all corners of the globe and it was interesting sorting out the better people. Basically it was seeing who told story with the best voice. The process continued with the final fifty coming to Cardiff and auditioning for us at the New Theatre just with piano played impeccably by Paul Maguire, but now in front of an audience. Once we had decided the top twelve (actually it was so tight we ended up with thirteen in that first show) we then had a Semi Final and Final with orchestra and a panel which over the years included Julia McKenzie, Peter Polycarpou, Mary Hammond, Simon Callow, Elaine Paige, Michael Ball, Edward Seckerson and, from the BBC, Lewis Carnie. The shows were hosted by that legend of the airwaves, Ken Bruce. I ceased my role as adjudicator at that point and became principal conductor for the section with orchestra. David Firman and I shared the conducting during the Semi and I went on to conduct the Final.

This was my first time waving for the BBC Concert Orchestra and though it was really a rather frantic event as there was so much music to organise, it was an amazing competition to have held the musical reins for. Laura Michelle Kelly, who went on to play *Mary Poppins* at Drury Lane, was our first winner and in the subsequent competitions of 2002, 2005 and 2006 the winners were Loren Geeting, Tom Solomon and Aimie Atkinson. All were worthy winners and it was a great shame that the competition was axed after the 2006 event. It should have become a regular biannual competition but it was expensive to run and, I suppose, it just wasn't cutting edge enough.

After the first competition in 2000 finished I was approached by Alan Boyd, who had been one of the producers on *Friday Night is Music Night* for seemingly centuries, to see whether I would be interested in conducting a special in Grimsby. (Remember Grimsby!) So in February 2001 I made my *FNIMN* debut with singers Claire Moore and Graham Bickley, the BBC Concert Orchestra and the Black Dyke Band. A few months later a second *FNIMN* and it was my first visit to BBC Maida Vale – where the pioneer electronic musician Delia Derbyshire, assisted by Dick Mills, had worked on Ron Grainer's theme to create that most iconic bit of TV musical history, the *Doctor Who Theme* – this time the concert was presented by newscaster, Richard Baker. Of course, I knew him from the 'telly news' of my youth, and it was so lovely sharing a stage with him and chatting in between rehearsal and performance. The awful disaster of 9/11 had just happened in New York and he had been there on holiday with his wife. He told me that they were due to go up the twin towers that very morning but half way through their journey on the subway he realised that he had brought the wrong glasses with him and they turned around to go back and get the correct specs. As they got back to their hotel the first aeroplane hit the tower and the disaster unfolded. It wasn't until later in the day that the enormity of their close shave really sank in. This gig was literally only a month afterwards, his acceptance of how close they had been to calamity was very sanguine. A true gentleman. Since then I have conducted well over forty concerts for BBC Radio 2 and there are a fair few of them that most definitely count in the Extraordinary Event category and I will get to them anon.

A couple of weeks before the gig in Maida Vale my friend, Tim, had been ordained Bishop of Sherborne at a truly ancient and extraordinary ceremony in Southwark Cathedral. When he told me a few months before that he was to be made a Bishop I told him straight out that there was no way that I would be kissing his ring but I did agree to write some music for him to be played at the service. He suggested the Recessional Voluntary so I wrote a piece for organ called *Tempus Fugit* which did indeed get played for the final moments of the service as the Archbishops, Bishops and all the other clergy processed out of the cathedral. I was very proud seeing my old chum from Devonport High, form 1w, there in amongst this motley crew of all the senior clergy in the Anglican church. He later became Bishop of Truro for eight years and ended his career as Bishop at Lambeth, Bishop to the Forces and Bishop for the Falkland Islands. Natalie and I went to Truro and then to Lambeth for those Installations as well.

I did seem to be involved in a lot of TV Talent shows but all of them paled into insignificance compared to the next project. *Pop Idol.* Simon Fuller's creation with Ken Warwick and Nigel Lythgoe producing. It was hot off the heels of the success of *Popstars* with their winning manufactured band, *Hear'Say*. I was Musical Director and pianist for the second stage of this competition where the top fifty were whittled down to ten. I worked alongside vocal coaches David and Carrie Grant in a sort of boot camp where we coached ten artists a week to create a show to be transmitted each Saturday where they sang one song with just piano. Very exposing for them all.

The panel of Simon Cowell, Nicky Chapman, Pete Waterman and Neil Fox critiqued each performance and the winners of each heat would be decided by a live phone vote. We filmed everything at Thames Television Studios in Teddington and, apart from very quickly having to get used to about eight camera and sound operators following our every move, it was really fantastic being so much part of the creation of new format television. Ant and Dec (Anthony McPartlin & Declan Donnelly) were the main hosts with Kate Thornton fronting the 'behind the scenes' aspects and the *Pop Idol Extra* show on ITV2. All hugely professional and so good at this kind of pressurised work.

David, Carrie and I would work for a couple of days deciding what song each person should sing and then give them some coaching on that song. It involved me very quickly routining the song, working out the best key for them and creating a piano version. Always tricky with pop music but worth the challenge! Carrie and David were fabulous to work with and we became a good team for those five weeks.

After the two days of sorting and coaching it was time for the 'as live' show. The panel were the only audience and I sat at the little Yamaha grand piano on the other side of the studio with my pile of hastily written charts. This was the point at which the eventual winner, Will Young, famously talked back at Simon and really caught the attention of the public. On the Saturday the show was broadcast, followed by a live results show where the two winners of the heat, who would go into the final section, were announced.

Out of the fifty people that David, Carrie and I worked with there were some really stand out singers. Will, of course, along with Gareth Gates, Darius Danesh, Zoe Birkett, Hayley Evetts, Jessica Garlick and Andrew Derbyshire and all of them have gone on to work professionally in either the music business per se or in Musical Theatre. Maybe the sometimes vitriolic comments helped to prepare them for the future or maybe it was the whole immediacy of it all, whatever it was I know that David, Carrie and I certainly wanted as many as possible to succeed. The show led to a whole raft of similar competitions, and, ultimately, Simon Cowell's empire which was built on the back of Simon Fuller's original idea. But even before I began on *Pop Idol*, a train of events had started that would take me away from talent shows almost for good.

In the summer of 2001 I had a call to go and meet a certain rock guitarist, his manager and a theatre director. It was to talk about my possible involvement in a new show based on the music of Queen and written by comedy genius, Ben Elton. I had my meeting in Paddington with Brian May, Jim Beach and Chris Renshaw and I felt that the meeting had gone pretty well. As is normal in our business this was followed by silence. Silence for over two weeks and then suddenly a phone call asking if I would like to be Musical Supervisor and Musical Director on the show. I remember hearing once that the best part of ANY job is the moment when you are told that you have got it. Well, strictly speaking, that is true but in this case being told that I was to work on *We Will Rock You* was the start of an adventure that kept giving for a considerable amount of time.

My agent, Tim, had called me with the news. I put the telephone down, told Natalie and we played *Bohemian Rhapsody* as loudly as we could in our musical dining room and head banged our way through it with the most inane grins on our faces!

The audition process started a couple of months later at The Venue in Leicester Square. Boy George's musical, *Taboo!* which had been directed by Chris Renshaw, was playing there at the time. Chris had asked me to have a musical look at the show and I spent a couple of days as musical consultant on it, so I was familiar with the place. On the morning of 9/11 we had been auditioning people for our ensemble, along with choreographer Arlene Philips, and after coming back from lunch we had just started again when the stage manager came into the auditorium looking ashen. There was a TV monitor just where they were and the news of the first plane hitting had just come up as a news flash. Of course, the auditions were halted and everyone was sent home.

I walked from Leicester Square to Charlotte Street to meet with Tom Gutteridge to talk about preparations for the next series of *Star For a Night* and it was quite unsettling walking through the centre of London because it felt like we were in some sort of apocalyptic reality. It was as if everything had stopped. My meeting was overshadowed by events and I made my way home.

Arlene, Chris and I resumed auditions the next day, somewhat in a state of shock. Things proceeded well as far as finding our original cast but Galileo and Scaramouche were proving to be elusive. We found Scaramouche first, and she had been staring us in the face because she was in the cast of *Taboo!* Hannah Jane Fox had practically been born for the part. Brian May and Roger Taylor loved how she sang and Ben Elton was totally knocked out with her comedy timing. That just left Galileo. For the next couple of months there would be occasional calls to go and see, pretty much, the cream of the West End. No-one had that something that would enable them to be Freddie, without being Freddie, if you see what I mean. Galileo was not Freddie reincarnated, rather he was subconsciously inspired by him and just as the lead singer in a rock band is the frontman so was Galileo for *Rock You*.

It wasn't until Christmas Eve 2001, after my involvement with *Pop Idol* had finished that this elegant, gaunt and supremely talented guy from the States appeared in front of us. Tony Vincent really had all the (rock)star quality that we needed and on that Christmas Eve I worked with both him and Hannah Jane to see how they could sing *Who Wants to Live Forever* together. We were all blown away, there was immediate simpatico between them and we finally had our first 'dream team' casting for the two principals.

Meanwhile I had started to write the Vocal Score based on Ben's libretto, with all the songs given their position in the script.

The original idea was that we would slightly 'musical theatre-ise' the songs but that was pretty hastily binned in an early meeting with our two resident Rock Gods, Brian and Roger. In hindsight, even though it meant that some of my invention was lost, it did mean that the show gave a much more authentic Queen experience. Bobby Aitken was again designing the sound but this time the parameters were set early on. By the end of the show you are in a full on Rock Concert and Bobby absolutely delivered that in spades.

Chris Renshaw is a really good theatre director and I liked him a lot but it was his vision of the show that Brian and Roger most objected to and, in the end, he was somewhat marginalised so Ben took over directing duties. I now have to make mention of one individual without whom the show would never have happened. Tony Edge. I had worked with him before as he was Resident Director in the West End for the whole run of *Grease* and he was in the same position here on *Rock You*. Tony would take all the information from the director and assemble it in his methodical mind to make cogent sense to deliver to the actors. He was able to pour oil on the many troubled waters and without him the show would have been an even more untamed beast than it was.

Lucie Pankhurst assisted Arlene in the choreography department and, as usual, Arlene's stamp was very firmly and joyfully put on the show. Roger was not best pleased when I managed to get references to *Radio Ga-Ga* in the middle section of *One Vision* but Arlene loved it. Although they were expunged from the show musically you can still hear them on the Original Cast Album.

Arlene also worked a great deal with Mark Fisher, who was a mammoth designer in the rock world with credits including concerts for The Rolling Stones, U2 and Pink Floyd, but who was not used to the rigours of musical theatre design and the demands that having thirty-two cast members cavorting around, on and off stage, puts onto the overall vision. Mark embraced it with his ever present optimism and, apart from one moment when some hasty changes had to be made as the subterranean set piece that was Tottenham Court Road Station lurched to a halt when it appeared with all the *Bohemians* gyrating and writhing around on it, created a design that stood the test of time and was adapted for all the successive versions of the show throughout the world.

To say that our producers were unused to Musical Theatre would be quite an understatement. Although they learnt very quickly, there is no finer example I can give than my discussion with them late in 2001 about the Music Department. Yes, I was booked as Musical Supervisor and original Musical Director and I was arranging the songs and creating the Vocal Score, but when I said that we would need an orchestrator they were somewhat flummoxed. "All the music exists on CD," they said, "surely you can just give that to the band?"

Now it is true that in the pop and rock world not much music is written down but I had to tread very carefully as I explained to them that in Musical Theatre and even in 'Rock' Musical Theatre to be able to recreate the show quickly and authentically everything indeed had to be written down. Keys were being changed to fit the voices, routines were being changed to enable the storytelling and choreography plus duets and ensemble pieces were being created to open up some of the set-piece moments. The original Queen line-up of four had already been extended with the addition of Spike Edney on keyboards when Freddie was alive, so adding more musicians to the *Rock You* band was accepted and we ended up with Piano/MD, Keys 2/Asst MD, Keys 3, Keys 4, Guitars 1 & 2, Bass Guitar, Drums and Percussion. Nine players in all. I asked Steve Sidwell to orchestrate and, following the success of our previous collaborations, this worked extremely well.

Early in 2002 we started cast rehearsals in dear old Alford House, yet another return visit. Day one was notable because the morning was taken up with a script read through and a look at the set model and costumes and the afternoon was, well, it was my time to prove to Rog and Bri that thirty two theatre luvvies could actually sing *Bo Rhap* (as it came to be known) and make it sound as good as Freddie, John, Brian and Roger did back in 1975 when they recorded it and overdubbed it, time and time again.

So after lunch I sat at the piano with the full company in front of me, my newly minted arrangement on the music stand, Brian sitting beside me and Roger the other side of the room. After about forty-five minutes of me teaching everyone their parts in the cod operatic section, Roger was out the door. Mind you he only left after sending me an enormous thumbs up and a huge smile. Brian stayed for most of the afternoon, also beaming, and his attention to detail and memory of being part of the creation of those harmonies in the first place was invaluable. A pattern started that afternoon that continued through all the rehearsals.

Brian was very much hands on and Roger let us get on with it. Roger, though, when asked if we could alter some lyrics in a few songs, most notably *Radio Ga-Ga*, was first to offer suggestions and to push that particular envelope, so, in truth, they were both absorbed by the process.

In the second week we were working on the backing vocals for *Somebody to Love*. The big gospel harmonies had to be curtailed because they were only being sung by eight girls playing the *Teen Queens*. The sense of them also had to change as, instead of being lyrics that supported the lead vocal as in the original, they were lyrics that had to be sung as if *opposing* the lead vocal. Over the course of three days I created twelve different versions that the girls had to learn before we settled on the one that we ended up using which worked best with Hannah Jane Fox's amazing lead vocal and Arlene's 'bitchy' girl choreography.

Just after we started rehearsals we also had to decide on our initial *Rock You* band. In normal circumstances I would have had a good discussion with our brilliant fixer, Sylvia Addison, and I would have left her to get on with it. These were extraordinary circumstances and with Roger and Brian around it was inevitable that finding our band would take a different route from the norm.

We assembled a mixture of rock and theatre players and auditioned them. I had recommended some, as had R'n'B and Sylvia. Then they were all assembled in Metropolis Studios, put into separate groups and the plan was to play *One Vision* and *Who Wants to Live Forever*. The former to show proper 'rock chops' and the latter to see whether they could follow a conductor, and after that it was a simple rock twelve bar in A, where I would nominate soloists to take a chorus each. I know 'conductor' and 'rock' are not normally mutually inclusive but our band was going to be on two separate sides of the stage, raised up on platforms, working on headphones, looking at a TV monitor of me waving and would have to be able to understand how to respond to a conductor or at least show willing!

At the end of each set up I would go back into the control room to meet with Brian and Roger and we'd go into separate corners and write down our notes. At the end of the session we correlated everything. Roger paying most attention to drums and percussion, me, keyboards and Brian, naturally, guitars. The three of us compared notes and we all had selected the same players as our first choice. I was amazed and delighted, it felt like validation for me. This was also the point when Brian and Roger coined my *Rock You* nickname – Reg. (At the end of *Seven Seas of Rhye* Queen used the *Oh I Do Like to Be Beside the Seaside* as the fade out – the song had been made famous by Blackpool Tower Ballroom Organist Reg Dixon!)

My drummer friend from *Grease*, Tony Bourke, was unbelievable that day. I so wanted him on the show as I knew how diligent and supportive he was. I also knew that he was a really good drummer, but I was not prepared for how gushing the praise from Roger and Brian would be. He was compared to Ginger Baker by Brian. Roger could 'hear himself' in the playing. I was so pleased, but obviously couldn't tell him right there and then. The other players decided that day were all offered the job and with one exception they took it. Jamie Moses, guitarist from Brian's band, had commitments he couldn't get out of, so we went with our second choice.

Here is the original line-up:

MD/Piano – Me
Asst MD/Keys – Andy Smith
Keys – Spike Edney (Queen's keyboard player and MD)
Keys – Jeff Leach (Session player and programmer)
Guitar A – Laurie Wisefield (Wishbone Ash, Tina Turner)

Guitar B – Alan Darby (Asia, Robert Palmer)
Bass Guitar – Neil Murray (Whitesnake, Black Sabbath)
Drums – Tony Bourke (Session player)
Percussion – Julian Poole (Session player)

This process became THE process for most of the subsequent productions and, although it was unusual to use an audition to find theatre musicians, what it did was to enable us to find players that wouldn't ordinarily have been in the mix. Players that the regular contractors wouldn't have found. It was particularly useful in Madrid, where at our first band audition we rejected everyone. There was a hushed silence when we returned a few weeks later and started the whole shenanigans again. This time I noticed a rather unusual Spanish keyboard player who seemed to be utterly committed to the music, with great presence but no finesse. Pablo Navarro – I asked him if he had experience in theatre music in any way, he replied that he didn't but he was so compelling that I asked him to take over MD duties from the guy who had been recommended to us and, lo and behold, he was brilliant.

The band that was assembled for Madrid would have rivalled any of the other production's bands, but if we had followed normal procedure we wouldn't have found Pablo and we wouldn't have had such an inspirational group of people playing their hearts out along with him.

We found incredible people in Moscow where we performed a promotion for the show in The Kremlin (!) and I must say that my first visit, along with Brian and Roger, was one of the few times that I have been VIP'd into a country and the only time I have been on an audition panel that was furnished with vodka shots both mid morning and mid afternoon! On my second visit a month later, the production manager greeted me with a cheery, "Thank goodness you're on your own!" When I pushed him for an explanation he told me that the restaurant where we had been taken by the Russian (mafia) producers on our last day of the first round of auditions, had a most extensive and expensive wine selection. Some wine was chosen by Jim Beach for us all to drink, Gavi de Gavi I think, and, according to Ruslan, the wine bill that evening came to $2000 for four bottles. I wish I'd known it was a $500 bottle of wine as I was drinking it! Well, he didn't have to worry this time, the band that we picked just took me to a couple of straight forward beer houses while I was there, so no more outrageous wine bills.

Over the next few years in Cologne, Sydney/Melbourne, Las Vegas and Johannesburg we also found amazing players who were all stunned to find that both Roger and Brian were not just approachable, they were completely committed to spending time with them, offering gems of wisdom from the heady days of playing those iconic gigs with Freddie and sharing some of the secrets of their amazing technique. In Vegas we had John Miceli and Paul Crook, the drummer and guitarist from Meat Loaf's band, plus Killer Queen was played by Patti Russo, his female lead vocalist. All in all it was a completely 'bonkers' time.

Back to rehearsals in London in 2002 and along with Tony Vincent and Hannah Jane Fox playing Galileo and Scaramouche we also had the most wonderful and assured Sharon D. Clarke playing our Killer Queen, Kerry Ellis as Meat, Alexander Hanson, (who had been the lead character, Alex, in the National Tour of *Aspects* way back in 1993) Khashoggi, Nigel Clauzel, Brit and Nigel Planer as Pop. Over the years many brilliant people have been part of the *Rock You* alumni and it has been a real treasure trove of talent.

In those early months of 2002 at Alford House, when no-one knew how it would or could work, that very first rehearsal period continued to throw up obstacles and challenges but along with those occasionally mind numbing obstructions we experienced a sometimes joyous development of what was to become a classic show. All the songs were worked and reworked in some way or another and Brian was at my side for an awful lot of rehearsals keeping his detailed almost encyclopaedic brain-box always on tap. We only fell out once and that was about the music for the bows. I wanted to mould a musical montage together and he wanted to use an adapted version of the rarely played fast version of *We Will Rock You*. In the end, naturally, Brian's idea was used and it really was the perfect soundtrack for that adulatory moment at the end of the show.

After the exposure of Day One and 'will *Bo Rhap* work', the final day in the rehearsal room was notable for a different reason entirely. Robert de Niro was an executive producer on the show and on that afternoon of the last day and the final run through in the rehearsal room with only me on piano accompanying them, our cast performed the show for him. There was a surreal moment just before we started when he came over to me and gently and graciously introduced himself. "Hi, I'm Bob," he said and I almost responded with, "Yes, I know!" But I managed to stop myself and we ended up having a very pleasant short conversation.

We then moved lock, stock and barrel-organ into the Dominion for the dreaded technical rehearsals. Many changes were made to the structure of Act 2, mostly libretto related, though some were musical, and naturally there was a large element of tension given that a lot was riding on the show so tempers were a little frayed.

One meeting that we had nearly caused a loss to the music world of megalithic proportions. The Creative Team, including Ben, Brian, Roger, Arlene, Chris and yours truly had been summoned to the next door hotel lobby. Firm words were being spoken by producers and after half an hour or so a resolution had been found and we gently made our way back into the stage door of the Dominion. When we got back down to the stage

Brian casually asked, "Mike, have you seen my guitar?" He was talking about his 'Red Special' – the only one in the world – the guitar that he and his father made together – I say again – the only one in the world...

Now I remembered that Brian had taken the guitar in its case to the meeting and that he had popped it behind the sofa in the lobby where we sat but that was all. I recounted that information back to him and as I did so there was almost a cartoon like '*Geh-Doinnnggg*' as Pete Malandrone (Brian's 'Keeper of the Guitar') rushed up to us, listened to what we were saying and, with his features ashen grey, suddenly legged it as fast as he could off stage, up the stairs and back to the aforementioned hotel lobby. Before we had time to even take a breath Pete and the 'Red Special' were back in the theatre, beside Brian and the crisis was averted. A blessed relief for us all!

For a considerable amount of the tech I had to be in two places at once. I needed to be involved with what was happening on stage but I also needed to take the band rehearsals. At the Dominion at this time there was another secret room and it was one that I had not come across in my time on *Grease* nine years earlier.

2002 We Will Rock You Band rehearsals and Lillie

Outside the front of the theatre at the top of the building just behind the outstretched arm of the Freddie Mercury statue are the windows of the room we used for our band calls and the *Sitzprobe*. It has since been made into a rather nicely appointed rehearsal room but back in 2002 it was a tacky, distressed and unloved room with plaster damage all around and wallpaper peeling off the walls. It was the perfect place. I could run out to see the stage whenever I needed to and also get down there pretty quickly. We could also make as much noise as we liked without causing any interference to the cast, crew and other creatives while the Tech slowly trundled on.

Along with Roger and Brian, Steve Sidwell and his brother, Richard who was our copyist, were with us, plus a guitar tech and a drum tech. It was a well filled room, especially later when the cast joined us for that *Sitz*! All the band worked really hard, some were more used to the process than others but there was one player in particular, on that first iteration, who was beyond excited and in an almost religious fervour. Our drummer, Tony Bourke. As was expected, his playing was brilliant, but I hadn't realised just how much of a Queen fan he was. He was in seventh heaven working so closely with Roger, who was only too happy to pass on little nuggets of technical skill and musicality whenever he popped by.

Tony also told me one morning, towards the end of the Tech, that at the end of the band rehearsal the night before, he had stayed on later than anyone else up in that room. He was with his girlfriend, now wife, Chris and while he was showing her this wonderfully distressed place, full of the mad musical gubbins of rehearsal, I was down on stage with the cast and the continuing technical rehearsal. To leave the theatre he and Chris had to walk from the rehearsal room via a corridor beside the Circle, through the pass door and down to stage door. On their walk down as they got to the entrance to the Circle they saw a black and white harlequin figure run from the auditorium, across the corridor and then out of sight. They got to where the figure disappeared in just a few steps and were completely banjaxed to see that there was no doorway visible for the phantom to have gone through. It was as if Freddie had popped in to make sure that all was okay with the show, was disturbed from his secret viewing and vanished into thin air after Tony and Chris had seen him. We took it as validation and chalked it up as our very own *Kinda Magic* moment. Once Tony told me we decided that we should keep schtum about his Freddie visitation and it wasn't until a couple of years later that I told Brian. He looked at me, smiled with just a little hint of sadness in his eyes, and nodded sagely. He didn't need to say anything, we both just knew it was okay.

It was now time for the *Sitz*. I always try to keep the cast away from band rehearsals so that when they finally hear the musicians at full tilt it is as exciting as it can be. As I said before, this was a well filled room and now it was even more busy. Microphones, cables, loudspeakers, mixing desks were added to all of our band paraphernalia, courtesy of Bobby Aitken and his team. Producers, director, choreographer, heads of departments, and, of course, Brian and Roger were all assembled. I only wish that the rehearsal had been filmed. The cast didn't just love singing with the band they were completely astounded to hear *Queen*'s swaggering rock music in all its raw glory played by our band. We felt that we were riding a wave and that continued when the next day we all moved back into the theatre for sound checks and over the next couple of days the final run throughs and Dress Rehearsals before Dame Audience was due to arrive for the first set of previews.

It didn't take long to get used to our new position on either side of the stage, the main difficulty we had as a band, was that we were completely cut in two. I was on stage left with all the keyboards and percussion and on the other side the guts of the band held sway, drums, guitars and bass guitar. We all had to use in-ear headphones at all times and I had a camera pointed at me so that both the band and the cast had an image of me on their TV monitors which for the band were right in front of them and for the cast were backstage in the vocal booth, right next to the quick change area, either side of the stage and, of course, on the rail at the front of the Circle overhang. Sound and stage management also had a feed of this video because, naturally, in a musical most cues are driven by the music.

On the very first preview everyone was on tenterhooks. Ben Elton, Roger, Brian, all of us really had no idea how the show would be received. Our cast, led by Tony and Hannah, were supremely gifted and the whole technical wizardry of the set, video and sound design along with our masterful band were brilliant. One of the other innovations that Roger and Brian insisted on was that at the end of the show, after the cast had taken their bow, the band came onto the stage to also receive their applause. This was especially good as it gave the band an enormous buzz, proved to the audience that the band were real and meant that for once, in a piece of Musical Theatre, we were not relegated to just a cursory wave from the cast. The response to the show was electric. They were standing for most of the end sequence of the show and when we started what essentially was the epilogue, *Bohemian Rhapsody*, they were singing along as well. On the second preview we had a proper rock'n'roll visitation up on the bandstand from Roger. He was carrying a little tray with a glass of Champagne for each of us, first on my side and then over to the really noisy side. Class act, that Roger. Of course there were things that we all had to improve upon during those previews but by the time we came to the grand Opening Night we were feeling pretty positive and ready for whatever the critics were going to say.

The Premiere was a start studded event and at the party afterwards, where Spike Edney's *SAS Band* and Roy Wood from *Wizard* entertained us, the overall feeling was so good and positive that when the reviews hit the following morning the sense of incredulity was heightened to the extreme. Were those critics watching the same show? With two exceptions they completely vilified it. Ben's script was particularly savaged but actually the notices pretty much rubbished everything and everyone. The only two critics who seemed to 'get it' were The Financial Times and The Sun. Two rather interesting extremes.

This all really served to feel like a mammoth kick in the teeth and naturally the box office seemed to take the brunt and suddenly we all realised that we were in jeopardy. You simply can never tell, when you are so close to the creation of a show, what its life will be. We were saved by two events. A *Parkinson Show* on BBC1 and The Queen's Golden Jubilee rock concert, *Party at the Palace*. Both of which happened quite soon after the Opening.

The *Parkinson* TV event also had Ben Elton as one of the guests which meant that he was able to use his formidable wit to answer some of the vitriol that had been spouted. The full cast and band performed and we raised the roof of Television Centre. Straight after it was transmitted the box office started to look healthier but after the Jubilee event it rocketed.

Back in rehearsals for the show, designer Mark Fisher had mentioned to me that he was designing the set for the Queen's Golden Jubilee Concert and he also told me that he thought that we would all be performing an excerpt but that it wasn't public knowledge as yet. Brian had also told me that he had to go to the Palace for a recce as he was going to perform *The National Anthem* from atop the Palace. All this knowledge meant that when we were officially informed a plan was able to be quickly put in place.

Although Brian's *National Anthem* was a completely separate part of the event it has become so iconic that it is forever linked with the *Rock You* appearance. His bravery, to perform live and with the orchestra so far away on the concert stand, is now a thing of legend. As far as our *We Will Rock You* excerpt we had to work with both the BBC and the event producers to make it something extra special and not just an advertisement for the show. The section was therefore built as a *Queen* concert that gradually morphed into a full on plug for our show. First of all we had to find someone other than *Rock You* cast to sing *We Are The Champions* and I was one of the people to suggest Will Young. Of course I had just worked with him on *Pop Idol* so I was able to use that experience to be able to give a hands on opinion of his ability. We also had the interesting conundrum of having a rather starry house band drummer available to us in Phil Collins.

We rehearsed first of all in our favourite little distressed rehearsal room at the Dominion and it was here that the full magnitude of what we were putting together hit me. This was to be the first time that Roger and Brian had 'performed' with us all. Up to this point their involvement in the show had been very hands on, yes, but this was something very different. It was as if we had been co-opted into *Queen* for the duration and the dynamics were very different. This was their gig not a Musical Theatre representation.

Just before the rehearsal started Roger came over to me, he asked me if I wouldn't mind taking him through the middle section of *Bo Rhap*, the cod operatic section. I was somewhat taken aback until he explained. Basically they had rehearsed it in mid 1975, it was recorded in autumn 1975 and from that date whenever they performed it with Freddie they always scarpered offstage to get changed at that point in the song. It was for ever the video that was used. Then they would come back on stage for the head banging hard rock section and perform to the end. This was a double whammy. Of course I was more than happy to 'take him through it' and it always makes me smile to think about it.

We then rehearsed the whole section and all got comfortable playing together. I was playing piano throughout and leading but every so often I had to pinch myself, this was Freddie's piano part, particularly the famous *Bo Rhap* crossing hands start. This was a big deal. To have Phil Collins and Roger playing the song *We Will Rock You* was particularly cool with the two drum kits sitting in mirror image (Phil Collins is a left hander and his kit was set out the opposite way round from Roger, a right handed player) and that came after Roger had sung *Radio Ga-Ga* with Phil playing drums so that Rog could be out front, singing.

Our second rehearsal was at Air Lyndhurst Studios with full cast as well and then it was a rehearsal out the back of Buckingham Palace where the set and 14,000 seat auditorium had been built. As it was filmed by the BBC there were a lot of my TV allies around and the next day literally just before I was about to go on stage for the actual gig Toby Baker, the floor manager, gently whispered in my ear, "Have a good one Mike, don't worry mate, only about 150 million people watching worldwide..." If you look closely during one particular closeup of my hands you can actually see them shaking!

So this was it, all of us in it together. Roger and Brian in their natural habitat with Will Young and soloists Tony Vincent, Hannah Jane Fox and Sharon D. Clarke along with our full cast in their Bohemian costumes looking and sounding great. The backstage 'village' of dressing rooms and hospitality suites was awash with star performers and their hangers on and there was a surreal quality to it all. I was lucky enough to be invited to the party actually inside the Palace after the gig where the surreal met the pomp and circumstance, if you like. As I have experienced when meeting the Queen at *Royal Variety Performances*, the 'Firm' trumps everyone and everything else, of course, and quite rightly.

Incidentally, twenty-five years earlier at the Queen's Silver Jubilee, I was with my friend from the Devon Youth Orchestra and the Royal Academy of Music, Phil White, and we were pretty much the closest people to the gates of Buckingham Palace. After helping a rather senior Canadian lady to get close when the police cordon was lifted as the Royal Party came out onto the balcony, Phil and I started the ad hoc *Land of Hope and Glory* that followed their appearance. That moment was used in many TV clips at the time and Phil and I vowed that we would do the same for the Golden Jubilee, should it happen. Well, events were taken out of my hands, dear Phil, though I would have repeated it if I could have!

The success of *Queen* and *We Will Rock You*'s appearance at the Golden Jubilee Concert was evident very quickly because suddenly the box office was ridiculously busy and even though we had been panned by those critics we became a huge hit with Dame Audience. Apparently it is a knack perfected by *Queen*. After all, when *Bohemian Rhapsody* was released it was also mauled by the music press and then went on to become one of the biggest songs on the planet, perhaps even THE biggest.

One of the major positives that came out of all of this is that Ben Elton never sat on his laurels, well, to begin with there were no laurels to sit on anyway, but instead he gradually honed and updated the script so that it became tighter, funnier and fresher. Small changes that really continued throughout the life of the show and, of course, as the show gradually went through its international existence any changes that weren't simply pert to the locale were also imported back into the London version. I really enjoyed witnessing Ben's wit at work, such a clever man and someone who really is genuinely smart.

Being up close and personal with Brian and Roger was also really illuminating. As the show was rolled out around the world I spent quite a lot of time with them both. Fascinating watching Brian's reaction in a Madrid department store as they played *Crazy Little Thing Called Love* on every single TV screen in the store and whilst we were in Madrid we were even treated to going backstage for Springsteen's gig at the Estadio La Peinata. Not sure that being with Brian for the *Air Guitar International Final* in Melbourne in 2003 will go down as one of the most extraordinary things but it was certainly weird, however being '*Fandangoed*' by Eva Maria Cortés who played Meat in Spain, at the end of the first round of auditions was most definitely an extraordinary if slightly disconcerting thing to happen. A really incredible visceral sound to witness so close at hand especially from Eva, who has one of the best voices I have heard, ever. Watching Roger go up to the band platform in Vegas and spending ten minutes retuning the drum kit that was being played so masterfully by John Miceli and suddenly making it sound like his own kit in that one fell swoop was also more than a bit special.

Brian also has the distinction of being babysitter to Lillie and Meg one evening when they were in watching the show at the Dominion. Lillie, who was in her teens by now, ended up sitting with me and playing tambourine in July 2002 when we performed in Hyde Park for *Party in the Park* – full cast and band this time and an unashamed plug for the show. That was one of the few occasions when John Deacon was backstage with us as well.

A month after the whole Buckingham Palace gig I was once again in Lyndhurst Hall at Air Studios but this time with a different member of *Genesis*, keyboard player Tony Banks. He had written a suite of orchestral music which came to be known as *Seven – A Suite for Orchestra* and the brilliant Simon Hale had orchestrated it all for the London Philharmonic Orchestra to play. The project, which was two days of conducting this amazing orchestra, was the total antithesis of the previous few months with this music very much in the pantheon of modern British classical. It was recorded by Naxos and for a brief period of time, after it was finally released in 2004, it was number one in the classical charts. Tony has a very individual musical voice that is obviously doused in the progressive rock heritage of *Genesis* but somehow it lends itself to an orchestral interpretation and Simon managed to meld wonderful colours, textures and timbres so that my job, which was essentially the arbiter of musicality with the orchestra, was straightforward and joyous.

For the remainder of 2002 I stayed conducting most of the *Rock You* shows but I did have a little time off to work with my *Pop Idol* buddies, Will Young and Gareth Gates, as music consultant for their tour in September and also round the same time a show for ITV with Cilla Black called *Sing With a Star*, *BBC Voice of Musical Theatre 2002* and a *Friday Night is Music Night*. I have always found that making my musical life as varied as possible and keeping busy helps to keep the 'long run blues' away.

We also made the *We Will Rock You* CD as a 'live' album. A really good idea to make it this way as it differentiates neatly and completely from the great original *Queen* CDs. We recorded three shows and then Brian and his recording engineer, Crispin, got to work tidying it up and making it sound the best it could sound. It's a pretty good representation of the show though it is a shame that *Crazy Little Thing Called Love* and *Fat Bottomed Girls* aren't on it. Two very separate reasons why. The way that we ended up routining *Crazy Little Thing* for the show never pleased Roger so the easiest thing was to leave it off the album and at the point that we recorded the live shows we had yet to use *Fat Bottomed Girls* except as one pre-recorded chorus so it actually didn't exist. I am proud of the overall result and also happy for the gold disc that I have to join the others on my wall.

2014 With Brian on last day of WWRY London

*

2003 was full of the start of international *Rock You* as well as that most important third and final marriage to Natalie, but later in the year I was able to tick the last box of those three annual TV shows from my youth: *Miss World.*

It was around October when I got a call from producer Peter Usher. He was looking after *Miss World* for Julia Morley that year and they had decided to make the Talent Show part of the contest a Fast Track section rather than just a 'show us your party piece' which it had previously been. Peter knew me from my *Star For a Night* days and I also knew a lot of the production team, Ken Warwick from *Pop Idol* was executive producer and Alasdair Macmillan from the *Royal Variety Show* in 1991 and the *British Comedy Awards* from 1993 was directing. The event ran over four weeks with the Live Final coming at the very end, naturally. What I didn't know then was that this was to become another of my major long term commitments.

I arrived in Sanya, a holiday resort at the southern most tip of the island of Hainan, China at the end of November just as the final section of the bikini round was being filmed – yes, they still had a bikini round then. One hundred and six of the most beautiful girls, all representing their country and all in outfits designed by Miss World 1975, Wilnelia, Lady Forsyth-Johnson, on a beach, on a tropical island with seemingly hundreds of camera operators and assistants milling around. It was certainly an extraordinary introduction to the whole *Miss World* experience. The next morning I was taken to a small theatre in the less salubrious part of town to meet with all the girls who were going to take part in the Talent Show. All went well and after a couple of days of honing and coaching we filmed it. There were a few girls who could dance really well, a couple of singers and a magician so the mix was quite fun. Bruce Forsyth was also there to support Wilnelia and he couldn't help himself, suddenly he wasn't just an adjudicator, he was also tap dancer in chief on stage as well! His inherent talent in front of a crowd always at the ready even a crowd that only spoke Chinese!

All was going well and I was getting ready for the twenty-four hour flight home on the next day when out of the blue Ken Warwick came to meet me in somewhat of a panic. "Mike, the music that was commissioned for the show really doesn't work and we need *Walk Down* music for all the girls for the beginning of the live final – but we need the music to rehearse with them tomorrow, is there any way that you can you help?" Well, quite by chance I had taken a small midi keyboard and my laptop with me, so I naturally said yes and that I would give it a go.

I asked for a framework to work with, tempo, bar counts, that sort of thing and overnight I wrote and made a little demo of a four minute piece and at 8.30am, an hour before I needed to leave to catch my plane, I played it to Kenny and his choreographer, the legendary dancer Donna Derby, in my hotel room from my computer. Fortunately they loved the concept and it was approved. It was the bare bones with enough rhythm and melodic information on the track for Donna to work with, so I hastily bounced it down to a CD, hightailed it for the airport with the promise that I would get the finished piece to them in the next few days after I had returned home. After no sleep I was very relieved that it was the right sort of thing and though I didn't finish it until I did get home, I still found enough time, while I was waiting for my plane connections, to add quite a lot of flesh to those bare bones in transit.

I finished the track and sent the file back to them in Sanya and it was indeed used for the opening of the show. The city council there had built a special auditorium to house the final – shaped like a crown, naturally – called the Crown of Beauty Theatre and the winner of the beach wear contest ended up winning the whole event to become Miss World 2003, Rosanna Davison. That first year I was very much part of the crew for my week there but after completing the track and saving a difficult situation, the following year I was asked to write the music for the whole show as well as look after the Talent Show.

I was now part of the core team and stayed with them all at the Sheraton Resort working closely with Donna, who had taken over as Stage Director and choreographer, and with both Julia and Steve Douglas Morley. I knew Donna from a few of the TV shows that I had MD'd back in the 90s and also because Bradley Walsh is her husband. She is brilliant, gorgeous, has a wicked sense of humour and this fabulous way of getting the best out of all the contestants, whether they think they can dance or not! I delivered the music, did the Talent Show and again couldn't stay for the main show – but this year no overnight writing sessions just before my flight home!

In 2005 I simply didn't have the time with all my other commitments to go, so I sent the tracks for Donna to work with and was on the end of a phone when needed to make any little changes. It was very strange being remote like this but then everything changed the following year.

Natalie and I were driving from Treyarnon to Bude during our summer holiday when out of the blue Julia Morley called, she told me that *Miss World* was going to be in September 2006 rather than November/December, not in Sanya but in Poland and would I be able to come out for the duration, look after the Talent Show and write the music again but this time stay for the final as a Judge! Well, we looked at each other slightly askance but, as ever, the musician's reply is always in the affirmative, so I gratefully accepted.

Amongst that judging panel were Louis Walsh, Dame Kelly Holmes, Krish Naidoo, Karan Johar, Wilnelia, Lady Forsyth-Johnson and Denise Van Outen and the show was hosted by Tim Vincent, Angela Chow and Grażyna Torbicka, with Westlife, Robin Gibb and Amici performing on the stage of the Palace of Culture and Science in Warsaw. Angela Chow has become one of the regular presenters, she has an elegance and surety about her and as she is multi-lingual and can flit from English to Chinese mid sentence, she is perfect for the global television audience.

I think I caused Tim Vincent to wonder whether my sanity was intact when he came over to the judges, microphone in hand and asked me a simple question, "Mike, what is it that you're looking for tonight?" My reply included the phrase, "*Miss World* is all about superlatives, the best girls, the best charity work, all these girls do such fantastic things from the plains of Patagonia to the wilds of Warsaw…" What on earth was I on?

Now is the time to 'fess up'. My mother-in-law, Patricia, posed me a challenge after Natalie and I told her that I was going to be a judge, and that challenge was if I was asked a question, live, on air, then my reply had to include the word Patagonia. Somehow. So, dear Tim, apologies, but that was why I flummoxed you with that reply! The irony is that because the show was only transmitted on satellite in the UK, Patricia didn't even see me *brilliantly* incorporate her word.

For a number of years Donna and her assistant Sandy Hamilton, were my major allies on the show and along with Head of TV Production, Dave Morgan we became quite the inseparable 'band of brothers'. It has to be said that, though Julia Morley is an absolute power house at the helm of the organisation, there is always a sense of spontaneity in the preparation leading up to the final show that a lot of people would find challenging. Julia's energy and drive are second to none and her focus on the charity side of *Miss World*, *Beauty With a Purpose*, is the main reason that I will always defend the show. Through Julia's tenacity and vision, more than one billion dollars has been raised over the last twenty-five years and each country's franchise holder is encouraged to develop and create new charity initiatives with the girls. Some of those actions over the years are truly astounding with girls setting up sustainable and renewable schemes, raising awareness about major world problems including all forms of global warming, lack of clean water, famine, serious insect transmitted disease, human trafficking, renewable products for menstrual hygiene, domestic abuse and child abuse.

The days of the swimsuited girls in high heels who want world peace and to be kind to animals have long since gone and the event really focuses on ability, empathy, talent and communication skills along with drive, ambition and positivity of spirit. Steve Douglas Morley, Julia's youngest son is now the Event Organiser and has great enthusiasm and ambition for the future of the show. It is watched worldwide by up to a billion people each year and remains the best known of all the 'Beauty Festivals'. It went out of favour with the major UK TV companies through the late 1990s and since 2001 has only been transmitted to the UK via satellite. With its current emphasis on female empowerment maybe it is time that one of the big stations had the foresight to take it on again.

I look forward to my *Miss World* fix each year and though I don't write much of the music anymore, as we tend to use existing tracks for the big routines, I still get to work with Donna in creating a *Dances of the World* segment where I creatively edit together some of the contestants' National music to make a spectacular and exciting part of the show which Donna choreographs with her consummate skill, especially given the numbers of bodies that she has to manage. Along with Donna's brilliance there is the ever present Andrew Minarik who looks after the hair, make-up and overall styling on the live final. He is with us the whole time, keeping us entertained with his brilliantly camp repartee and making sure that his army of make-up artists and hair stylists are drilled to perfection.

We have had some highlights over the years and have visited many parts of China, Washington, Poland, Indonesia, Inner Mongolia, South Africa, The Philippines and a lot of the UK. The girls are always challenging and interesting to work with and I still love my time on the Talent Show each year. In 2009 it was won by the representative from Sierra Leone, Mariatu Kargbo, who was a fire eater and quick change mask artiste. Her routine involved such precision and dexterity with split second facial mask changes on top of some elemental use of fire sticks. Mostly, though, it is dancers or singers who win and just occasionally the talent winner becomes Miss World. In 2019 we had a set of really good singers – so good that I took them to Abbey Road to record a new version of *The World in Union* which we used that year as an anthem for the contestants – and the representative from Jamaica, Toni-Ann Singh, won Talent with her rendition of the Whitney Houston classic *I Have Nothing* and then went on to become Miss World 2019. The fourth Miss World from Jamaica!

We have also had some extraordinary talent performing on the shows over the years. From Robin Gibb, Sister Sledge, Lionel Richie, Dave Koz, Ramin Karimloo and Rodrick Dixon to Sky Blu, The Vamps, Donel, Diversity and Celine Tam.

For Celine, who performed Lin Manuel Miranda's *How Far I'll Go* in 2017, we suggested that she perform the song completely live not with a backing track. That was quite something to achieve as we were in Sanya, China, again, but I agreed with Celine that we perform the song very simply with me on piano alongside a solo cellist. A piano was eventually found and brought over but finding a cellist was proving to be more difficult. Steve Morley Douglas's Chinese assistant, Michelle Gong, finally found someone who might be suitable. A wonderful lady called Sun Xin Yang who had played cello with the Beijing Symphony Orchestra but who had recently moved to Sanya with her husband and young child. Lo and behold, her husband was a musician too and we had a glorious afternoon rehearsing in their little studio. This is when the power of music is stronger than any other power in the universe. Here was a beautiful Chinese musician with no English and me with no Chinese and yet as soon as we sat together and started playing my little arrangement of the song that wonderful magic happened. Then when we played with Celine – an immensely talented young singer from Hong Kong who had recently won

America's Got Talent – the magic became almost divine. It was a wonderful moment in the show.

Also in 2017 Julia had decided to give a special award to an extraordinary man, Father Marciano "Rocky" G. Evangelista from the Tuloy Foundation in Manila. He had set up a remarkably unique orphanage in the Philippines for street children back in 1993 and the Foundation that he created has saved thousands of children from a life of violence, street crime and depravation on the streets of Manilla. Julia knew him very well having spent time with him on a few of her *Beauty With a Purpose* visits. His favourite song was *You Raise Me Up* as sung by Josh Groban and we also found out that the whole school knew the piece so it was inevitable that we make something musically special happen. I knew nothing of all this when I arrived in Guangzhou that year but as soon as I got to our hotel I was accosted by Steve who, in his exuberant and frenetically individual way, told me that at 6am the next day we would be flying to Manilla to meet Father Rocky and to record and film all five hundred of the children singing the song. Ouch! I'd only just arrived after a twenty hour flight…

It was another sleepless *Miss World* night for me as I had to create a track that could be used for the filming and which also could be used for the soloists live on the show, Celine and Jefferey Li. So, at 6am, Julia, Steve, our camera operator and insert director, Joe Warwick, and yours truly set off to fly to the Philippines to meet with Father Rocky and all the children at the school. I rehearsed with them all and a rather surreal six hours later we had recorded and filmed all five hundred of them in their hand built church at the campus and we returned post haste to China. I have to say that witnessing Father Rocky alongside Julia talking to these kids, seeing his strength of purpose and the results of his devotion in the way that every single one of the children responded to him was truly magnificent and awe inspiring. A few weeks later we were back in Sanya for the live final and Father Rocky received his award. Celine and Jefferey sang with consummate style and the children of Tuloy took prominence as the recording of them all singing was now embedded in the track and in full Technicolor glory on the huge video wall across the whole back of the stage. Profoundly moving.

The calibre of the Production Team and crew on the show is also remarkable. Ian Hamilton, my chum from the Brian Conley series, was a regular director along with the late Stuart McDonald, Simon Stafforth, Russell Norman and Derek Wheeler and we have a great support team of South African camera and sound operators who have been associated with the show for years and who understand how the four week bootcamp of rehearsals and Fast Track events work. Glen, Sven, Len, Ken, Ruan and Kevmate – somehow they always come back for more. Our editors, led by Simon Graham, have an uncanny knack of creating the best inserts in the show and their workload seems to increase each year as the show develops on this global stage. However there is one editor, Roger Stevens, with whom I have a slightly different relationship…he, like me, is a *Doctor Who* fan and at any opportunity we can, when the other is unaware or concentrating on something else, we sidle up behind and make a Weeping Angel pose. It can be an unnerving sight at breakfast but I think over the years I am just in the lead in the ongoing competition!

Obviously the event was cancelled in 2020 but Julia and Steve were determined to celebrate the 70th Anniversary in 2021 and a deal was made with two sets of sponsors in Puerto Rico for the final to be on December 16th 2021 at the José Miguel Agrelot Coliseum in San Juan. With an assurance that Covid protocols would be adhered to, we arrived at the Hyatt Regency

Grand Reserve Hotel, about an hour drive from San Juan, on November 26th. In the end ninety-seven or so contestants arrived, which was something of a miracle given the situation. Everyone had their PCR test on arrival, everyone had to show proof of vaccination to get into the country, so all seemed ok. Rehearsals for the main show, the Head to Head rounds and auditions for the Talent Fast Track started well. Amongst all of us, crew and contestants, there seemed to be a sense of 'wow' we are actually here and we are actually going to do this. The atmosphere of positivity was palpable and almost visible to the naked eye – and then Covid made a guest appearance….

The representative from Tanzania arrived late and, though her PCR test was negative on arrival, two days later she registered a positive result. As you can imagine things moved very quickly and it wasn't long before a small number of girls also tested positive. Only a couple of days later, that number also included our 2019 Miss World, Toni-Ann Singh, Miss World 2018 Vanessa Ponce, and some of the TV Crew. What was even more worrying was that our sponsors were insisting that we proceed with all the events as planned. We were also still rehearsing with everyone, without knowing whether they were negative or positive. It is true that as soon as anyone was positive they were put into isolation, but, with testing on every other day and the results only coming in late afternoon, the big problem was that events and rehearsals had to continue before the results were known. We were all inadvertently being exposed and we felt that we needed to address this with Julia and Steve.

After an early morning meeting, our core team of Donna, myself, Andrew and Donna's assistant, Simon Coulthard, made plain what we felt on behalf of everyone. Rehearsals and events were curtailed for a couple of days as the whole 'campus' of *Miss World* pretty much shut down. Though this was good practice and surely must have made things safer, I am sorry to say that it became apparent a few days later, that the horse had indeed bolted. That was after our sponsors insisted that two further events MUST happen.

One was the *Areytos Sunset Female Empowerment Music Event* with a huge drone show, and the other was a fund raising Gala for 600 people at the Fairmont Hotel, where the contestants were supposed to sit at tables with people who had paid substantial sums of money for the privilege. Our Talent Finalists also performed on stage. Miss Mongolia – a contortionist of some considerable ability, Miss Chile – a beautiful en pointe ballerina, and Miss Japan – a very talented contemporary dancer. We reluctantly agreed to attend, but did say very carefully and firmly that we felt this event could put the Final in jeopardy. There was no social distancing and most people were without face coverings. Some of the girls voiced their concerns and indeed made their feelings very plain by not sitting at the tables as was expected of them. This was eventually sanctioned by Julia Morley, who is usually very much their champion, and so a lot of the girls kept themselves as safe as possible by sitting together, away from everyone else.

By the time we got to final rehearsals in the stadium however, yet more girls were isolating, as well as three of the editing team of six, and one of our sound crew. Then, on the day before the Live Final, we were informed by Steve that Julia had tested positive! Even after this news the expectation was that the show would go ahead. We, however, were certain that this was the death knell for the live final. How could we go ahead without Julia as Chair of the Judges and announcing the winner, which she has done since Eric Morley died in 2000? It was unheard of. So, after a very difficult meeting with Steve, a plan was made to see how many of the set pieces in the show involving all the contestants we could record on that dress rehearsal.

Unbelievably, two more Molotov cocktails were thrown at us before we could even start. Firstly the director, Simon Staffurth, and his crew were locked out of the outside broadcast truck until the owners were paid by the sponsors. Without the truck in operation nothing could be filmed, no sound or videos could be played in, zilch. Hastily and quietly, as if by a miracle, after a forty-five minute stop we were informed that all was well. The delay was appreciated by ALL the contestants, who were running round trying to get ready for the filming on an evening that they thought was simply going to be a rehearsal, and by one of the sponsors, Crystal Pierce, who was also going to be a judge. If this was going to be filmed then it had better be filmed with her on the judging panel in the $20,000 dress bought specially. So during the hiatus there was a lot of activity going on, not quite headless chickens but you get the picture.

Then the second Molotov cocktail... the Puerto Rico Philharmonic Orchestra wouldn't play until their contract was amended, signed and sealed following the possibility that this would be 'broadcast' and not just 'rehearsal'.

I should explain a couple of things... this was the first time for many years that we had been given the chance of a full scale orchestra playing for the show. Since I started in 2003 and a good time before, it was always filmed with pre-recorded tracks. The *Miss World Orchestra* had played when the show was transmitted on terrestrial television and it was the late, great Phil Tate wielding the baton, but those were the glory days in the UK. Here we were in Puerto Rico, about to utilise all 65 members of the Puerto Rico Philharmonic – and along with conductor Angel Velez, who works mostly in Hollywood but hails from Puerto Rico, we found ourselves sharing conducting duties for this, the 70th *Miss World*. Angel was conducting all the 'Latin' segments in the show and I was conducting some of the music that I had written over the years and a new orchestration of W. Pritchard's *Coronation Anthem*. (Julia Morley's father, incidentally!) We had also planned for Toni-Ann to bow out as Miss World 2019 by singing versions of both *Never Enough* and *A Million Dreams* from *The Greatest Showman*. As she was in isolation and couldn't sing live in the venue I was going to conduct both songs without her and we would use video and commentary over the top. A great shame that she wasn't there – I was so looking forward to this possibility given that Toni-Ann is such a wonderfully natural and emotive singer. The orchestra was really very good and Angel and I had a fabulous rehearsal with them the day before in the Pablo Casals Symphony Hall. Anyway, notwithstanding all that, the orchestra obviously had to make sure that their remuneration was correct, and for the next hour and a half, there were discussions between various lawyers associated with both the orchestra and the sponsors paying them, all trying to make this work. Everyone was waiting. The contestants were ready, the professional dancers were ready, all the camera operators, sound operators and crew were ready – even the $20,000 dress was ready!

Finally, a deal was brokered and two and a half hours after we were supposed to start the dress rehearsal, we began. By this time we basically had thirty minutes left to record what we could, so we just went for it. Orchestra, Angel and me dressed in our 'civvies'. *Miss World* is not about the orchestra, obviously, and the most important thing is that some of the show with the contestants was indeed filmed.

I think it was around 11pm when we finished recording and everyone was sent home. There was then a further discussion about what we could do to salvage things. Our feeling was still that with so many girls missing and the possibility that the number would rise on the next morning, that we should abandon the show. The sponsors disagreed very strongly and we eventually went back to our hotel expecting that the next day we would make the live transmission and finish the show. Covid, of course, had other ideas and the next morning at 6am

Donna was phoned by Julia with the news that more girls and even Steve himself had tested positive. Steve, who had been with us the day before and who had been very close indeed in our crisis meeting; Steve, the show runner/producer who holds the show together with his voice-overs. With alarm bells ringing, Julia finally told Donna that the show would have to be stopped and that in a few hours there would be a major press release. What disappointment for everyone and especially the girls, but finally the inevitable was announced... Ye gods!

How Donna, Andrew and I dodged the Covid bullet is beyond me, but we did. Once the decision had been made, we managed to change our flights home and, armed with our negative PCR tests, we left Puerto Rico. We were extremely fortunate. Some of the team and some of the contestants had to isolate until past Christmas Day, but it could have been so much worse. I am sure that the resilience of *Miss World* will prevail and I wish them well, but this was too much of a close shave. It really was.

*

My musical journey has had so many twists and turns and when 2005 appeared, around a dark and murky corner after I had finished my regular MD commitment on *Rock You*, I had no idea that things would get even more complicated and full. Ah, the joy of looking back at it all!

Now, you may remember that I made note of an extraordinary young pianist when I was on my stint of auditions for *Star For a Night*, Chris Egan. Well, my next little theatre venture was where we formed a musical bond that lasted for a decade and which, even now, has happy repercussions. The director and choreographer, Kim Gavin, who had worked on the *Shane*

Richie Experience, with Donna Derby as his assistant, called me about a musical theatre show based on the song, *Love Shack* by the B-52s, and incorporating some original material by Gary Barlow and a whole raft of other contemporary songs. I loved the idea and met up with Kim to talk through everything and he asked me if I would mind working with a young and exciting arranger that he had come across. A certain Chris Egan. Well, of course I remembered him and I was more than happy to work with him on the show.

Love Shack was not a piece of Musical Theatre that changed the world but it did bring together a beautiful cast of people, including Faye Tozer from *Steps*, John Lee from *S Club* and Noel Sullivan from *Hear'Say*. It was a very pleasant and jolly piece that was most notable for the fact that half way through the tour we had to cut our title song from the opening of the show and replace it with another tune because the rights to use it had not been secured. So the show *Love Shack* couldn't use the song but it could still be called *Love Shack The Musical*. It was farcical! The cast and band somehow continued to make the show work – all credit to them.

Chris, though, proved his worth and I knew that here was a major young musical talent with boundless enthusiasm and an almost superhuman ability. Over the next few years we worked together on many musicals including, *Footloose* with Derek Hough, Steve McGann and Cheryl Baker, *Never Forget,* which was the *Take That* musical that ran both on tour and in the West End but was not supported by the band, and much later *Bodyguard* which did become a smash hit at the Adelphi Theatre and on tour around the world. However it was my next extraordinary collaboration that would really bind us together.

I had made the decision to leave Tim Hancock and join a new agency run by my friend from *Doctor Dolittle* days, Bronia

Buchanan. Tall, smart and elegant Lady B, as I call her, suggested that I make new contact with some of my previous colleagues in TV, people with whom I had lost touch, I suppose. I called the Head of Music at ITV, Rachel Williams, and asked if there were any shows coming up that I may be suitable for. Rachel had been at LWT back when I first worked on the *Royals*, *Comedy Awards* and the *Brian Conley Series*, and though she had been a great campaigner for me back then I was still expecting her to gently fob me off, but no, she told me that a certain Dame Shirley Bassey was about to be asked to make a second *Audience With* programme, that DSB didn't currently have a Musical Director and if I did the show with her then the *Royal Variety Show* would again be mine. Phew! Well this was pretty big news. I went for a meeting with the producer of the *Audience With* show, Glen Middleham, where he took me through his ideas for the Dame and officially asked me if I would be involved. Of course, I agreed.

Another fascinating chapter in my Musical life was about to begin.

TWELVE

DSB AND THE EPIC

On my very first meeting with Dame Shirley I had to convince her to do something that she had never done before. DSB is not known for her gentle acquiescence so I was fairly sure that this would be tough. Basically, Glen Middleham had suggested that we put all three of her James Bond songs together as a medley, for the first time. Everybody knows *Goldfinger* and *Diamonds are Forever* but to add *Moonraker* – which she hadn't really performed since she recorded it in 1979 – was the difficult ask.

All three songs had music composed by John Barry. Leslie Bricusse and Anthony Newley wrote the lyrics for *Goldfinger*, *Diamonds* had lyrics by Don Black and *Moonraker*, lyrics by Hal David. I made sure that I had sketched out a musical routine that would give the best bits of each song before I sat at the piano, so that when I started playing the medley for her it sounded pretty reasonable. To my surprise, and relief, once she joined in singing it through, she really rather liked it.

All three songs were over and done with in just over four minutes which she loved. It started with those evocative and mammoth opening chords of *Goldfinger*, went into the dreamy *Moonraker* and finished with the end section of *Diamonds* – basically from '*I don't need love*,' to that famous long '*E-ver————!*' at the end. I had gained her trust, and she was very happy.

The second hurdle took a little more time. For the end of the show Glen wanted to string another medley together, to end with *I Am What I Am*. The other songs incorporated were: *Maybe This Time*; *Never, Never, Never*; *As I Love You*; and *Kiss Me, Honey Honey, Kiss Me*. All was going well, I had, again, prepared a guide routine to work through, but getting into *I Am What I Am* was proving problematic. In the end, the best way to segue from one to the other was to let the penultimate line of *Honey, Honey* pause on the end of the word *Honey*, basically just hang in mid air, and that note just happened to be an octave higher than the beginning of *I Am What I Am*. Bingo, the transition was done. DSB actually got that totally instinctively, brilliant!

Once we had decided on all the songs and the routines of the songs I then handed the dots over to Chris for him to weave his orchestral magic. We had a pretty big orchestra, in television terms, of thirty players. Basically it was a 'Big Band' with strings, French horn and harp. Chris's orchestrations were simply fantastic and in the rehearsal room the day before the show, when we played through everything, first just the orchestra and then in the afternoon with the Lady herself, the clarity and power of them was absolutely second to none. These orchestrations became the bedrock of the next few years with DSB, they were so good.

In that rehearsal room, when we finally got to the end sequence and DSB sang *I Am What I Am* right beside me, with the orchestra in full flow, I got to experience just how much weight, power and emotion her voice carries. I swear that she was as loud, if not louder, than the orchestra, and she could have done it without a microphone, she really could.

The show was finally called *Another Audience With... Dame Shirley Bassey* and, as is normal with the format, a few of the celebrity audience were armed with questions for the star guest. All went incredibly well. There was one hiatus where an ear-ring decided that it preferred the floor but in the end the decision was made to keep the moment as if it were live, so Shirley's "Bloody ear-ring!" as she picked it up remained in the show, it actually made her look real and the audience loved it.

Alasdair Macmillan directed impeccably and a couple of weeks before the show aired in March 2006, the entire creative team was summoned to ITV headquarters on the South Bank by Mark Wells who was Head of Entertainment. He treated us to a viewing of the show in the VIP lounge at the top of the building plus dinner but most importantly of all he said that in his opinion the end result was simply the most perfect show he had ever worked on in his whole career and he thanked us, with sincerity and honesty. It was actually quite moving, really. Glen Middleham's original vision of how the show could be, really did work and I am honoured to be able to say that this was my introduction to working with Dame Shirley Bassey.

A week after we had recorded the DSB show I was back in the same studio with a rather different kind of talent. I was Musical Director, with a small four piece band, for *Another Audience With...Joan Rivers*. No songs, just a couple of play-ons, the band with a mirror behind us to make us look twice the size and plenty of time to laugh and giggle at her mastery with an audience. Just before we went live the director of the show, Peter Orton, asked that Joan be very careful with her swearing. "Please, no F-words until at least thirty minutes in and, remember, no C-words at all!" he said. Well, the first F-word came after about a minute and naturally, it was not very long before the C-word followed. So much for that request then.

Just after that show I was in Cardiff for a benefit concert on behalf of Kidney Wales. It was a show put on by the lovely Kate Jones, from the *BBC Voice of Musical Theatre* and her long time friend and associate, Lucy Morgan, a beautiful viola player who also was the first call if you needed to find any musicians in Wales. One of the good contractors, actually. It was in the new Wales Millennium Centre and proved to be a happy diversion before my second visit there a few weeks later.

Rachel Williams had mentioned those magical words, *Royal Variety Performance* when we initially spoke about Dame Shirley and the 2005 *Royal* was my first at the helm since 1993. A truly amazing array of talent on show, including the winner of *BBC Young Musician 2004* Nicola Benedetti – who incidentally was a complete joy to work with, and one of the most talented, too – and Bradley Walsh opening the show with a huge version of *Seventy-Six Trombones*, incorporating the Royal Welsh Regiment Band and some Hip Hop kids called Parkour Urban Freeflow. That routine was quite complicated to put together, but everything recedes into the distance when compared to our very own DSB headlining at the end of the show.

The first section of her set was quite straightforward, starting with *Goldfinger* then *The Living Tree* which featured Pete Callard playing a stunning guitar solo. After that the big curtain came down with *The Royal Variety Performance* emblazoned on it and DSB talked to the illustrious audience. As that curtain came in, the huge stage truck, with our forty piece orchestra on it, trundled unseen and unheard to the back of the stage and while it was moving we began the final song, *Music* by John Miles. I had truncated the verses of the song with a key change to add variety and give it a lift which all worked really well. As the fast section of the song started Dame Shirley walked off stage right to make her way underneath the stage for a quick change, while the *Royal Variety Dancers* gyrated their way through the first thirty-two bars of the familiar pulsating music.

As the music developed into the second fast section the entire company of performers gradually started to fill the stage and take their bows. Myself and the orchestra were now miles away, safely parked with the handbrake on and I knew that under the stage DSB had enough time to make that quick change, place herself on the stage lift and magically appear in time to sing the glorious final verse. So all was going swimmingly. The Treorchy Male Voice Choir were singing all the backing vocals beautifully and the orchestra was sounding fabulous with Chris Egan's orchestration fizzing with energy.

However, the performers sort of forgot to leave the right amount of space for the trap door and there was a slight moment of mayhem as the turns realised and gently pushed and shoved outwards to make the space. I could see all of this in the tiny TV monitor in front of me which was, incidentally, my only way of seeing the stage, but I also knew that the amount of music I had to play before Shirley's appearance was finite and we were getting very close, very close indeed. I could hear the director, Russell Norman, in the talkback in my ear, and realised that this problem was holding her reappearance up so I slowed everything down and the rallentando that I had rehearsed with the orchestra became extraordinarily elongated until I could hold it no more.

The camera zoomed into the place where DSB should have been, just as she finished singing the first line of the last section – *"Music was my first love"* – under the stage and as it zoomed in closer, suddenly up she popped, as if from a bazooka, in her incredible red dress with the biggest look of relief on her face and to rapturous applause. Of course I had put another key change in this last section and the reaction from both the stage and the crowd at the end of the song verged on the adulatory. Quite rightly – this was *their* Dame Shirley Bassey, from Tiger Bay literally just outside the theatre, owning this moment of *Royal Variety* history. A magnificent end to the show.

At the after show party Bryn Terfel, who had sung a special arrangement I had written of *The National Anthem* with the boys from the Treorchy Choir, came up to me, shook my hand, and said, "Well held, Mike, that was close!" I was most grateful that the orchestra followed me, almost to the point of no return, but honestly, they were magnificent.

Meeting the Queen was again an absolute honour and I was particularly proud that year of the *Royal Variety Theme* that I had written. It seemed to fit the occasion perfectly. Plus the Dame and I seemed to have found a good working relationship and there was more fun and frolic to come.

A gentle start to 2006 with a very interesting concept at Greenwich Theatre. *The Ten Minute Musical Challenge*. Put a lyricist and a composer together for a day, with two actors, a brilliant director, Fiona Laird, and me, and then at 7.00pm we perform a ten minute musical for the punters in the foyer before they go and watch the show in the main house. It was a bold initiative and we did it for a week, culminating in a competition with all six mini musicals on the Saturday. It was really challenging and the basic concept has been taken and extended by various theatres since. We repeated the event in 2007 as well.

I was also able to work with Mike Reed again on a benefit concert directed by Dougie Squires for dear Dan Crawford, who had died suddenly aged 62 in July 2005. It was at the Novello Theatre and we revisited *Mr Cinders, Bless the Bride* and a host of other shows from the King's Head's history and I was especially happy to work again with my gals from Dressing Room No.6, Janthea Brigden, Julie Ann Blythen and Stephanie Lunn, twenty years after we had first worked together on *Cinders*. One of the versions of *Footloose,* another of my collaborations with Chris Egan, also opened in Cardiff before going to the Novello Theatre (again!) in the West End but after that it became the start of the really epic stuff.

First of all a TV appearance for the Dame in a show called *All Time Greatest Movie Songs* and then it was *The Prince's Trust 30th Anniversary Concert* at The Tower of London.

When I had the initial call about *The Prince's Trust* gig, Rachel from ITV told me it was just a few acts. The performers included: Lionel Richie, Annie Lennox, The Bee Gees, Will Young, Ronan Keating, Kate Rusby, with Ant and Dec plus Cat Deeley presenting. Actually it was a really uplifting event. All the turns were fantastic to work with and, of course, Chris wrote some beautiful orchestrations. He also made sure that he got to feature playing the 'keytar' solo at the beginning of Lionel Richie's *Dancing on the Ceiling,* quite a feat of keyboard dexterity, may I say! (The instrument is the keyboard that you wear around your neck like a guitar hence it is called a 'keytar'.)

Annie Skates and her gang were singing backing vocals throughout and the quite substantial band of twenty-one plus one itinerant baton waver were on a raised platform at the back of the specially designed stage in the moat at the Tower. Meeting Princes Charles, William and Harry afterwards was also a bit of a thrill.

The only person who couldn't be at either of the rehearsals, at Music Bank, Bermondsey the day before the show, or on the day itself on stage, was a certain Mr Lionel Richie. Now, that is not to say that he is in any way difficult, because he isn't. It may even have been a bit of a test for me, who knows. However

Lionel has a brilliant right hand man/Musical Director called Chuckii Booker who understands how he performs down to the last semiquaver or sixteenth note and basically he stood in for Lionel at ALL the rehearsals. We were playing *Dancing on the Ceiling* and *All Night Long* with *Hello* sandwiched in the middle.

Even though Chuckii was so good and put us completely at our ease there was still a sense of trepidation because our first run through with the man himself would be LIVE on TV. There was no room for manoeuvre or doubt, it just had to work. For *Dancing on the Ceiling* and *All Night Long* which are straight down the line constant tempo songs, that wasn't so much of an issue. We knew the tempo would be exact as we had his click in our ears, however when he sat at the piano to start *Hello* it really did dawn on me that this was a bit of a first. I looked down at him, he looked up from his extraordinarily high seating position at the piano, which was at a forty-five degree angle to the stage, and off we went together. Everything gelled perfectly and as the first bars of the famous guitar solo started, which Pete Callard played exceptionally well, Lionel just looked up to me and gave me the biggest smile and nod of approval. The nod of mutual musical respect, if you like. It was very special.

Over the next few years whenever Lionel needed a British band I got the call. We did spots on *Parkinson*, *The Paul O'Grady Show*, Ken Bruce's *BBC Radio 2 Live in the Morning* from Maida Vale Studios MV3, *Totally Saturday* with Graham Norton, *GMTV*, *Jonathan Ross*, *This Morning* and *X Factor*, we even did the Capital Radio *Summertime Ball* at the Emirates stadium in 2009, but my two favourite gigs were when he guested on *Proms in the Park*, which I was already conducting for the BBC and *An Audience with... Lionel Richie, Live!* which was only the second time in the *Audience With...* format's history that the show went out in real time, actually live.

2006 With Lionel Richie – Proms in the Park

Incidentally, Lionel has great natural charm, is a really cool musician and one of the nicest people to work with. The last show we did together was in 2012, again for ITV, it was a mix of two formats, really. Some 'as live' performances and some interview footage filmed at his home in L.A. It was called *This Is Lionel Richie* and had guest appearances from Pixie Lott and Rebecca Ferguson. It was a good swansong for me as MD for Lionel as well.

Back to 2006 and a certain lady was gearing up for a tour and a couple more big television appearances. I was essentially now Dame Shirley's personal Musical Director, though there was never any formal agreement, and it was time to don the hard hat and get properly working on *The Dame is Back!* with her. Putting together a full tour with DSB is always going to be fraught with interesting twists and turns but after a lot of histrionics, giggling and cajoling we put together a really good set of songs. A good mix of the old and new.

On that short tour I learnt a lot. Everyone knows that the two words Diva and Bassey are forever entwined, but having been there, in that theatre of war, if you like, I can perhaps explain a little of what really happens and offer my perspective.

I learnt back in my *Joseph* days that going into the *top turn's* dressing room and having those last words of encouragement before every show was vitally important. On tour with DSB I did the same and offered happy thoughts to try to allay the fear, instil confidence and prepare for the performance. Once that meeting was done and giggles were had I would go to my position on stage, behind the curtain, just stage left of centre with the orchestra on platforms in front of me, and a walkway in the middle for The Dame to walk down. Because the curtain to the auditorium was behind me, none of this could be seen by the audience.

Then I would wait until The Dame was in position, in my eye line, dead centre at the back of the stage and ready to walk down to her position centre stage. A fascinating and extraordinary thing would happen. The small, nervous lady would be just plain Shirley back there, then suddenly, as I bring the orchestra in with the glorious chords and the heraldic trumpets of the opening of *Goldfinger*, the curtain would rise and right before my eyes little Shirley Bassey would become DAME SHIRLEY BASSEY, like a tropical butterfly metamorphosing right there and then, or a fantabulous balloon filling with fairy dust and tinsel. The audience only saw the glorious end result, of course, but I have been lucky enough to witness this phenomenon on a number of occasions in very close proximity.

As an aside, there is one job that I would never recommend anyone for. It is up there with running the United Nations or explaining to a certain ex Head of State that his Twitter account has been deleted. The job is looking after the on stage monitor mix. It is always difficult balancing the singer's microphone level with the orchestra but in this situation, with DSB nervous and still finding her way with the set of songs, no matter what you do it will always be wrong. Only when the audience first unleashes its affirmation will all suddenly settle and peace reign.

Rehearsals and gentle learning sessions are different, though. The process of learning a song and then delivering it is often talked about and many different performers have processes that vary wildly. Sitting at the piano and working one to one is very intimate and demanding and with DSB always educational. The song, whether it is old or new, has to be thoroughly learnt and in her muscle memory before she can get close to performing it. It is the one defining thing about the way that she performs, it can only come from the heart if it is fully IN the heart and soul and if a song doesn't go in quickly then it can be discarded, quite harshly. My job, on a few occasions, was to metaphorically pick the song out of the waste bin and help her to make sense of a difficult bit of melody, or tricky lyric, and gently cajole her into appreciating that the song could indeed work for her and that we should persevere just a little bit longer. Sometimes this worked and sometimes it didn't, but generally we got there in the end.

When I am working in Musical Theatre it is acting through song that is the modus operandi, and frequently there is a lot of soul searching to be done to find that journey, a lot of analysis before a really truthful performance can happen. All that is totally instinctive with Dame Shirley. Any analysis that happens is done entirely subconsciously and though the meaning is sometimes discussed, it is not that discussion that enables the performance to live, rather it is the act of learning and getting those lyrics and that tune into the muscle memory which lets the song rise above and become a *Bassey* song.

This whole process really came to the fore when we were working on her album *The Performance* in 2009. Film composer and thoroughly good guy, and the man with the driest wit I know, David Arnold, was producing, with me looking after the vocals production, and it would be fair to say that David's idea of getting a lot of contemporary pop acts to create new songs for DSB did meet a certain amount of resistance to begin with. Patience was tried on all sides as we sifted and worked slowly through all the songs that we had to choose from. Most of them were given a demo treatment by David but when it came to Gary Barlow's song, *This Time*, Gary actually came to meet us in Air Lyndhurst studios one Sunday to play it through for her. It was a really good idea as she was able to see the passion and commitment in him as he sang it sitting at the piano.

During the creation of the album Alan Yentob made a BBC documentary and witnessed us in the rehearsal room, the orchestral recording sessions (brilliantly conducted and orchestrated by Nick Dodds, by the way) and at Grouse Lodge Studios in Ireland where we stayed for a week recording DSB's vocals. There was only one time at Grouse when it all got too much and she kicked the music stand over. To be honest I didn't blame her, one section was just not working and after the music stand had been replaced and David and I, DSB, her assistant Jenny Kern, and executive producer Paul Carey had drunk a couple of pints of Guinness in the private bar and had a good night's sleep, the following day in the studio the same moment was recorded in the blink of an eye.

The Girl From Tiger Bay was the name of the programme that was aired on the BBC, from the title of the song written by the Manic Street Preachers, and it ended up being a pretty true representation of the album's creation. Yentob showed his true professionalism quite early on because he had asked to come in to some rehearsals to witness events and then to interview DSB. That basically was fine. The lovely Jenny and myself were in the Warehouse in Waterloo (where the year before all the rehearsals had taken place for *Another Audience With...Dame Shirley Bassey*) and it was just a very calm piano rehearsal with me playing. Alan's producer/director Dione Newton and one camera crew were also there with us.

After we had finished the rehearsal there was a camera set-up for the one on one interview between Alan and DSB. Jenny and I were on the other side of the room, out of shot but close at hand in case we were needed. All was going well until Alan started to ask more probing personal questions and we both noticed an unease in her body language. Her hands gave the game away, she was most definitely not comfortable so we very carefully and gently interrupted the interview and asked if she was feeling alright. Dame Shirley has had some major tragedies in her life and she made it very plain that she would prefer that the whole interview was terminated. Alan was brilliant. He apologised profusely, sympathised with Shirley and then agreed that the interview should stop but to keep momentum going he also suggested that it continue in DSB's apartment in Monte Carlo whenever she felt was the right time and with whomsoever she wanted as back up. It was actually filmed exactly as suggested around two months later, and the edited version is in the programme. I think because Alan was so diligent and witnessed all aspects of the creation of the album it has ended up as a really fine documentary and I'm really happy to have contributed.

After the album was released the BBC decided to feature Dame Shirley in their *Electric Proms* season for that year of 2009 so off to the Roundhouse we went for a bit of a hybrid concert featuring a mix of the established old favourite songs like *Diamonds are Forever, Goldfinger, Big Spender* and *Light My Fire* plus *Apartment, The Performance of My Life, Almost There, After the Rain,* and *The Girl From Tiger Bay* all from the new album *The Performance* and featuring David Arnold, James Dean Bradfield from Manic Street Preachers, Tom Baxter and Richard Hawley. Out of all the concerts that I conducted for Dame Shirley that was probably the most difficult because of the percentage of new songs. The fact that she included so many was actually very brave and, though in rehearsal there were a few tears and some histrionics, by the time jolly Dame Audience made her presence felt DSB was comfortable and really went for it. The BBC Concert Orchestra and our hand picked rhythm section of Andy Vinter (Piano), Jeff Leach (Synthesiser), Dave Holmes (Guitar), Steve McManus (Bass guitar) and Ian Thomas (Drums) played their hearts out and ultimately it is one of the best concerts that we did together.

Back in 2006 we were finishing the tour with a concert at the Salle des Etoiles in the Monte-Carlo Sporting Club, with one of the most breathtaking views out across Monaco. The concert itself went brilliantly – it was getting there that was the problem! We were all supposed to be flying to Monaco from Heathrow on the morning of August 10th when the airport was suddenly shut down because of a terrorist plot to blow up planes with liquid explosives. After frantic phoning around and pulling a few strings our Executive Producer and Tour Manager, Phil Bowdery, managed to get a private jet to land at Biggin Hill and take us all – orchestra, hair stylist, make-up artist, stage management and me – to Monte Carlo just in time to rehearse with the house band string section and all the technicians that evening. The concert itself was on the next day, fortunately, and naturally it was a barnstorming success.

We also filmed another concert in 2006 – *Dame Shirley Bassey at Faenol*. Sadly it has never been shown nationwide on the BBC as it was a BBC Wales only production but it was a cracker. Bryn Terfel hosted his own festival in Faenol near Bangor, Wales in the early 2000s and on August 27th 2006 Dame Shirley was the headliner. As it came straight after the end of the tour we pretty much did a carbon copy show. The brilliant addition was a duet at the end with DSB and Bryn singing *We'll Keep a Welcome* which brought the house down. That evening the audience really showed their allegiance – it was pouring down and they were completely drenched and yet they screamed and hollered for our DSB. The fact that it was raining actually makes some of the TV shots rather special and DSB looks and sounds her absolute best.

We had a *Get The Party Started* moment for Marks and Spencer's Christmas campaign that year. Steve Sidwell did the orchestration and we recorded it at Angel Studios and then filmed it in Acton. The success of that campaign became the inspiration for what was probably the most extraordinary and epic moment of my time with The Dame – Glastonbury 2007.

Early in 2007 The Dame worked with Nikki Lamborn and Catherine Feeney of *Never the Bride* on an album which featured a full version of *Get the Party Started* and their own song, *The Living Tree*. The album was quite successful and then later in the year, when the Dame's appearance at Glastonbury was confirmed, we included the songs in the set, with Nikki and Catherine on stage as well.

I think I am one of the few people who can say that he drove himself to Pyramid Stage to perform at Glastonbury and the whole event remains one of those '*did I really do that?*' moments for me. We rehearsed a couple of days before at John Henry's rehearsal rooms in Camden and then the whole set up, including microphones, music stands, sound desk and musical instruments, was taken down to Glastonbury, put back together again exactly as it had been so that we could perform without any sound check. I believe this is the norm for the festival but it was certainly a first for us. It meant that we had to trust completely that everything would sound exactly as it had done in that rehearsal room. The one thing that no rehearsal room can factor in, though, is what it feels like to suddenly find yourself on stage, with seventy-thousand screaming fans in the audience.

Dame Shirley arrived by helicopter in wellington boots encrusted with diamanté DSBs, the band was taken by coach from London and Natalie and I drove into the venue, down through the mud and the crowds and parked right outside my dressing room, which was in between Dame Shirley's and The Who's! We had also taken wellingtons but with no diamanté DSBs on ours. The forty minute set began with *Get the Party Started* and continued with all the old favourites including the *Bond Medley* and *Big Spender* and ended with *I Am What I Am*. Standing beside Dame Shirley when she was at her very best was such an absolute thrill and the whole experience was amplified by that enormous crowd. You can feel an almost visceral power directed to the stage, in fact all of us responded to it. I can remember Simon Morgan, who is hugely experienced and a fabulous horn player, just beaming from ear to ear as we proceeded with the set – even while he was playing his heart out. That one gig will be the experience that I metaphorically take to my desert island as my luxury, it was truly epic.

2007 Dame Shirley – Glastonbury

*

Before I got to the end of 2006 there were two other pieces of musical theatre and a couple of TV shows that kept me busy. The theatre shows were diametrically opposed on so many levels; *Daddy Cool* which opened at the Shaftesbury Theatre, and Bernstein's *Peter Pan* which opened for the Christmas season at the dear old King's Head.

My first comment about *Daddy Cool* is that it is one of a small handful of shows that felt like the wrong fit for me. This was a celebration of the works of Boney M., Milli Vanilli and their German producer, Frank Farian. I had never been a fan but Bronia thought it would be a very good show for me to be do so I reluctantly agreed. I managed to get Steve Sidwell in as orchestrator and Chris Egan was my Associate Musical Supervisor. The Musical Director was another great musician and keyboard player, John G. Smith, who had been Assistant Musical Director for me on *Superstar* back in 1996. I created and crafted some interesting vocal arrangements and dance breaks; the work with the rest of the creative team and the cast was really very pleasant and the show itself ended up being rather good.

The problem that I had was, well... Frank Farian. Obviously he is a hugely successful music producer but his knowledge of the workings of Musical Theatre are pretty much null. All was going swimmingly and we got to the first preview without too much incident, except that Frank was completely wedded to some ridiculous parrot idea – a three metre high puppet that was flown in from the auditorium roof – anyway, notwithstanding that, all was going well. On this first preview I was sitting on the end of the centre of the back row, beside the Director, Andy Goldberg, and the Sound Designer, Richard Brooker. About twenty minutes into the show there was some noise behind me at the sound desk. Frank had decided that the show didn't sound right and was berating the sound operator and hissing instructions at him. On the first preview everyone is in a mild state of panic and I felt that Frank's behaviour was completely wrong and out of order; so I left my seat and quietly walked up to him, gently moved him away from the desk with a, "Not now, Frank. Wait until after the show to give notes." Public previews in major Musical Theatre are a fantastic luxury for technicians and creatives. The time when teething troubles are carefully soothed away and when the show starts to gain its momentum, however, to achieve that requires a certain trust and patience which Frank didn't have. His undue haste in rebuking the sound operator could have derailed the show – and it was the very first time with an audience. Sound Designer Richard would have said and done the same, but I was closer than him to the disturbance. Anyway, reluctantly Farian went away, left the sound operator to get on with his job and I went back to my seat with a feeling in my stomach that this episode was not yet over.

Well, as the final song ended and the audience started to make its way out of the theatre via the brightly lit green exit signs, out of an anteroom came Frank in high dudgeon. He was gesticulating, pointing his finger at me and shouting, "Zong Killah, you are Zong Killah!" Though, when written down, that looks like yet another title of one of his songs it was most definitely not. He came closer to me, right up to my face and continued his screaming. I stayed completely still and tried to put my case to him but he just ranted and raved at me and the more I tried to explain myself the more he shouted.

In the end, with my heart racing but my pride very much intact, I turned away from him and walked down to the pit where, as calmly as I could, I gave Musical Director John G. Smith my notes from the preview. I also very carefully told John that I probably would not be around for rehearsals the next day so I asked him to give my notes to the cast and my apologies.

I left the theatre and immediately phoned my agent, Bronia, to relay what had happened, by then I was very nearly hyperventilating because I so hate confrontation, particularly when it is completely unjust and could be interpreted as bullying. The next morning there was a meeting in her office with theatre producer Robert Mackintosh, where I basically said that I was too long in the tooth to be shouted at like that and that I felt it would be better for both my well-being and ultimately for the show if I took a step back. Reluctantly he agreed and, though I kept my title as Musical Supervisor and Vocal Arranger, I stayed away until the show had opened and Frank had gone back to Germany. It wasn't the most enjoyable few weeks but I did survive, just!

Fortunately the other show was a considerably different experience.

It was such a great loss when Dan Crawford died so suddenly and unexpectedly in 2005. The King's Head WAS Dan and he had been one of the major driving forces in what is now known as Off West End, but I still like to call it The Fringe. Dan's widow, Stephanie Sinclaire, who tragically died in 2021, had taken over the reins of running the place and she asked me if I would like to work with her on a piece that had never been performed in its entirety before, Bernstein's *Peter Pan*. She had the theatrical rights but the full orchestral version that was licensed by the Bernstein estate was rather too large for this little one hundred and two seat theatre. Could I make it work?

It proved to be a real labour of love and after I had contacted the estate and explained what I wanted to do they rather surprisingly agreed and sent me the full score in digital form, all I had to do was send them my orchestral reduction at the end. There was a caveat that no keys were to be changed and no restructuring of the score would be allowed. Hmm! A rather unrealistic request given that every single show that I know has morphed into a different version by the time the audience has been allowed in. Well, I ended up making two versions. The first was what we used, songs reworked, order slightly changed and keys singable; then the second one, which I sent back to the estate, had everything exactly as the original.

I made the new orchestration quite minimalist for just cello, woodwind and piano. A proper chamber version. It was delightful. With Stephanie directing, Marc Urquhart choreographing and Alexander Bermange as Musical Director; a joyous immersive piece of theatre, with the Lost Boys, Pirates and mermaids all running through the little theatre trying to avoid our Captain Hook, brilliantly played to excess by Peter Land or supporting Peter Pan, also brilliantly played by Stephanie's daughter, Katey Kastin. Tinkerbell was to be played by two young girls who alternated the role and I suggested that my younger daughter, Meg, should audition. Altruistic, I know, but she got the part completely on her own merit and was dead right for it. Meg also had her tenth birthday while she was working on the show. She was spoilt rotten by the cast. Perfect. I was immensely proud of her, not only was she really professional but she was utterly real as Tinkerbell, a quality that many actors strive for, with Meg it was and is instinctive.

There was some interest in the piece as it was the first ever complete performance of a Bernstein work and we must be one of the only musical theatre shows to have featured on BBC Radio 3's *In Tune* programme hosted by Sean Rafferty. A live interview and performance at Broadcasting House. Very good reviews followed the opening night, the show completed its season successfully and with full houses.

The TV shows were also quite interestingly different. The first was working with David Cassidy as a guest on *Children in Need* for BBC and on *GMTV* for ITV and the other was a fascinating first attempt at a show which very nearly became an interesting series. *Duet Impossible* was made for the BBC and recorded at Pinewood but, sadly, the ratings were not high enough after transmission and it became a one off. The concept was ground breaking; current singing stars placed in a virtual duet with someone from the past, using technological wizardry.

Roy Orbison with Westlife, Dusty Springfield with the Sugababes, fifteen year old Lulu with McFly, Boy George with a younger version of himself and Eva Cassidy singing *Somewhere Over the Rainbow* with Katie Melua. Chris Egan worked with me on this and I still don't know how he managed to make the guitar track for *Somewhere Over the Rainbow* sound exactly like the original so that Katie Melua could actually sing with her inspiration, Eva Cassidy. That section really was the highlight of the show. This was another of the TV shows where all the tracks were recorded beforehand and played in for the singer as the show was filmed. Personally I much prefer it when the orchestra is live with the singer but in this case, as we were adapting original old tracks and fusing new with them, it absolutely had to be pre-recorded. It was called *Duet Impossible*, after all.

*

If 2006 seemed busy then 2007 was mildly ridiculous and probably the most exciting and varied work year that I will ever have. This was the year when Chris Egan and I had to book a helicopter to enable us to finish a *sitzprobe* in London before a Technical Rehearsal in Cardiff, the year when within one week I was waving my arms around on stage at Glastonbury, Windsor and the new Wembley Stadium, plus it was the year when I wrote and conducted the music for the Royal Opening of St. Pancras Station (HS1 and Eurostar). Bonkers!

After the joy of *Peter Pan,* which ran into the New Year, theatre continued to take prominence with another version of *Footloose* which opened at the Lowry Centre in Salford before setting off on tour. Matt Smith was our brilliant Musical Director this time, another of the bright young MDs, who has gone on to become one of the most sought after chaps in the West End. Once our involvement in *Footloose* was done I embarked on a TV series for Channel 4 called *Musicool.*

Fiona Laird, Director, Sean Cheesman, Choreographer and me on a boot camp with a motley crew of young emerging talent. MCs, singers, rappers – and one death metal artist – with the aim of creating a brand new theatrical piece at the end of the ten week series which they perform at the Bloomsbury Theatre live on Channel 4! We had special mentors each week who were also from very varied backgrounds; including Kwame Kwei-Armah, Jermaine Jackson, Gary Kemp and Tamzin Outhwaite. In the process there were tears and tantrums but we moved things along to a pretty clean performance. Our erstwhile rappers, death metal screamer and emerging talent actually came out of it all with some new skills and a proper appreciation of just how difficult Musical Theatre is, so it was really worth it.

Whilst in the process of working on all these events I had already started having meetings about the huge ceremony to celebrate the re-opening of St. Pancras with the new HS1 link to the Channel Tunnel. Jon Teeman was in charge of delivering the end product, code named *Purple Haze,* and Mark Fisher, designer of *We Will Rock You* et al, was creating an auditorium to seat one thousand five hundred dignitaries and making the inside of St. Pancras, all newly refurbished, the star of the show.

Although the event itself wasn't until November the lead time for our preparation was, of course, most of the year and given that the HS1 project had taken ten years to build that wasn't bad in comparison.

Mark's design incorporated a set of screens that could slide across the whole building so that specially commissioned films could be shown. The screens were some one hundred metres wide, it was a big event! Whilst the films were playing I conducted the Royal Philharmonic Concert Orchestra playing live on a huge raised platform right beside the specially commissioned sculpture by Paul Day of a nine metre tall couple embracing called The Meeting Place Statue.

2007 Royal Opening of St Pancras and HS1

David Coulthard starred in one of the mini films so this was the closest I ever got to my childhood dream of being a racing driver because I wrote the music to accompany it! Sadly I never got to meet him nor did I get to meet his co stars, Kristin Scott Thomas, Terence Stamp (though as previously documented I did once play piano for his singing lesson) and Tom Hollander but I did get to work with Katherine Jenkins and Lemar who sang a Beatles medley and also with Timothy West who played the part of William Henry Barlow, the original engineering genius who had designed the 139-year-old station for the Midland Railway, and who, in full Victorian costume, took the audience through a visual and vocal tour of the great terminal.

The highlight of the event was the arrival into the station of two Eurostar trains, one of which was the new Hitachi train, and I had written music to herald their entrance. In the rehearsal I had warned the orchestra that we may need to repeat a section of the piece, if the trains were for any reason delayed. On the Royal event itself, lo and behold, the drivers didn't hear their cue to set off at the prerequisite time and, yes, they arrived late! I was so glad that I had the foresight to have the option to extend the music and I thank fantastic Stage Manager Sam Hunter for the heads up to make that call. It ended up being seamless and not a soul in the audience would have known.

In preparation for the gig I had rehearsals in both of my favourite studios. First a full run through in Abbey Road Studio 1 with the full orchestra, choir and rhythm section and then the next day a similar set up in Angel Studios. The difference between both days was that because the studios at Angel are much smaller we had to link two studios together with a video relay. Myself and the orchestra in 1 and the rhythm section in 2. Complicated but, because I had learnt so much when I conducted the *Royal Variety Shows*, the separation of the two was actually easy to run.

A few weeks before the November 6th performance it became apparent that one presentation was not going to be enough so two more shows were added. Unfortunately Katherine Jenkins and Lemar were unavailable for the extra performances so I asked Annie Skates and Tommy Blaize if they could make them instead. The two of them were available, ultra professional and performed flawlessly on November 7th and 8th. Although the Queen was only there for the first showing there was still a great sense of occasion for the other two – and the trains were on time for both extra shows!

Chris Egan again looked after most of the orchestration but our mutual woodwind playing genius, Martin Williams, assisted and ended up creating the most gorgeous Ravel-like orchestration of one of the pieces I had written which was used for the part of the show where lighting designer Durham Marenghi highlighted the spectacular refurbished roof with a mesmerising light show.

Before we launched into our opening orchestral piece, Walton's *Crown Imperial*, I had asked Chris and our other keyboard player the peerless Andy Vinter, if they would mind filling in while we were waiting for the Royal party to enter the building by playing together on the one piano. I had suggested Erik Satie's *Trois Gymnopédies* to give us a little European balance and, though they played them with elan and panache, if I could have videoed the joy and schoolboy mirth of the two of them as they passed the melodic lines completely spontaneously between them it could easily have gone viral. Two of my favourite musicians having a really good time!

Back in April I was with Dame Shirley on a special Dame Edna Everage show called *The Dame Edna Everage Treatment* and then it was auditions and pre-production for the Take That musical *Never Forget* which was to open in late July but then at the end of June came the utterly mind blowing week.

It started with the Dame Shirley Glastonbury performance on June 24th. Four days later I was conducting at Elton John's *White Tie and Tiara Ball* in Windsor and three days after that it was *The Concert for Diana* in Wembley Stadium where I conducted the Andrew Lloyd Webber section.

I think some explanation is necessary.

Just before Glastonbury I had a phone call from The Really Useful Group asking if I could be available to wave the special segment for Andrew Lloyd Webber in the Diana Concert. I was thrilled to be asked but there was a problem. The rehearsals in central London clashed with rehearsals at Bray Studios with Dame Shirley. The solution was a Taxi bike which meant that I could effectively be in two places at once. Genius!

Dame Shirley had been asked to perform for Elton's Ball a few months earlier so that was firmly in the diary, but a couple of days before that rehearsal Elton asked if he could sing a Sinatra song with our Dame Shirley Orchestra. (Well, actually, in this instance the orchestra was a mix of Tom Jones' and DSB's as there was not room at the venue for both sets of musicians.) I was completely happy to organise an arrangement of *Moon River* and, Elton being Elton, on the night of the gig he also joined in with Tom Jones singing *Delilah* and The Dame singing *Big Spender*! The marquee in the grounds of Elton's house was filled to excess with star names and the performances matched. Everyone wanted to see Dame Shirley and her Glastonbury diamanté Wellington boots but sadly they were not available, even for hire…

The Princess Diana concert was also full of excess and the performers stellar. The Wembley stage was huge and I was working with the English National Ballet Orchestra along with the Wix Wiggins house band. Our list of performers was Andrea Bocelli, Sarah Brightman, Josh Groban, Connie Fisher, Lee Mead, Jason Donovan, Donny Osmond and Anastacia for the twenty minute segment. All hugely experienced performers and quite a few that I had worked with before, fortunately. On the Sunday morning I met Andrea in the rehearsal room at The Really Useful Group offices in Tower Street because Andrew wanted me to work on *The Music of the Night* from *Phantom of the Opera* with him; it was to be one of the central parts of the musical segment and Andrew was a little anxious.

Andrea was truly delightful to work with one on one and his phrasing of the song was impeccable. However his pronunciation did leave a little to be desired so I suggested that he record me singing, well half singing, so that he could practice over the next few hours before the concert which was later in the day. Veronica, his fiancée, now his wife, was there with us and she made the recording and then she relayed my pronunciation to him through his in ear monitors as we performed. All went well, I'm pleased to say, and there was a veritable feast of ALW served up in those twenty minutes. One of the absolute highlights for me was having three Josephs on stage all at the same time, Jason Donovan, Donny Osmond and Lee Mead. It was a great shame that Phillip Schofield wasn't there to make it a full house.

Prior to this extraordinary week rehearsals for *Never Forget* had started so there was already a large amount of careful time juggling or plate spinning to manage. My long term commitment to *Grease* was also current and a revamped version was about to start a new season at the Piccadilly Theatre plus on top of all that *Footloose* was opening in Bromley. To say that things were complicated would be somewhat of an understatement! All was going well until the producers of *Grease* and *Never Forget* seemed to have forged a conspiracy against Chris and me by informing us that the *Sitzprobe* for *Grease* was going to be on the same day that *Never Forget* was to start technical rehearsals. The fly in the ointment was that those technical rehearsals were in Cardiff, at the Millennium Theatre, and the band calls for *Grease* were at the Union Chapel in Islington. What could we do? Well, we looked at train, taxi, taxi bike, 'beam me up Scottie' matter transference and sling shot but the only way that we could finish at 5pm in Islington and be in Cardiff for seven was to fly by helicopter from Vanguard Heliport, a short taxi ride from Islington, to Cardiff Helipad, a short taxi ride from the Millennium Theatre. This was only two weeks after the Glastonbury/Windsor/Wembley week, it was indeed a completely bonkers time!

The whole escapade worked a treat and Chris and I arrived safely and in full working order after a thoroughly heartening *Sitzprobe* ready to launch into the joys of Tech in Cardiff. There were quite large grins on our faces which took a few days to fade away but it was most definitely worth it.

Never Forget was a fun show, produced by Tristan Baker and by my agent, Bronia. The original idea was Kim Gavin's, who is Take That's creative director, and Gary Barlow had given the OK for us to use the early oeuvre of Take That songs which were mostly written by Gary. Unfortunately the rest of the band didn't green light it and Kim pulled out. The result was that we had permission to use the songs for five years and Ed Curtis directed with Karen Bruce choreographing and the piece was written by Ed, Guy Jones and Danny Brocklehurst.

The basic premise for the show was that a disparate group of chaps would be put together by a slightly roguish manager and they would create a boy band similar to Take That and compete in a 'Battle of the Tribute Bands'. Along the way they would meet various tricky characters who would try to derail them and also cause problems with the relationship of the lead character, Ash Sherwood and his fiancée Chloè Turner.

It was a simple story and ended up being quite a good jukebox musical with the lead characters played by Dean Chisnell, Graig Els, Stephane Anelli, Tim Dreisen, Eaton James, Sophia Ragavelas, Joanne Farrell with Teddy Kempner playing the manager, Ron Freeman. It previewed in Cardiff then moved to Manchester Opera House where it opened to pretty good reviews. It was even filmed for a DVD release. In 2008 it opened at the Savoy Theatre, again to mostly good reviews, where it ran from May to November. I would say that it was one of the better jukebox musicals and it should have had more of a life. The trouble was that Take That had decided to make a comeback, so who in their right mind would want to watch a bunch of actors feigning at being a tribute Take That when you could watch the real thing? No matter that our boys were hugely talented and all of them could sing, dance and act superbly well. People naturally flocked to the stadium tour while our little show gradually faded away. There was a little flicker of a tour in 2009 but that was also snuffed out pretty quickly.

2007 continued to deliver though and just before the St. Pancras opening there was a demo recording of a new idea from Leslie Bricusse. It was a Peter Sellers musical called *It's All in the Mind Folks* which I recorded at Olympic Studios in Barnes with Chris, Pete Callard, Andy McGlasson and Andy Pask in the band; Lance Ellington, Annie Skates, Lee Gibson and John Antrobus taking the lead parts.

There were a couple of gigs with Dame Shirley, one at Grosvenor House for Michael Heseltine and the other in the Royal Albert Hall for *Fashion Rocks* which was transmitted on Channel 4; an ITV special called *Saturday Night Divas* where we played for Myleene Klass, Chaka Khan and Jamelia and a special Andrew Lloyd Webber *Friday Night is Music Night* for BBC Radio 2 which featured a host of stars which I will expand upon in the next chapter.

Then after St. Pancras came the 2007 *Royal Variety Performance*. The timing of the event meant that I couldn't go to *Miss World* that year so I prepared the tracks at home and sent them to

China, thereby keeping my association with the show alive. The *Royal* was to be at the Empire Theatre in Liverpool as it was the European Capital of Culture for 2007 and the producers wanted to open the show with an homage to the Fab Four. I put a routine together based on *Lucy in the Sky With Diamonds* for Seal to take the lead vocal and stage director Brian Rogers and choreographer Ashley Wallen created a dance routine to go with the arrangement that was in the finest tradition of *Royal Variety* excess. There were trapeze artists, ice skaters, stilt walking showgirls, a fifty piece choir, ballet dancers and even a young opera singer, Natasha Day, singing a soprano descant that I had written for her. Quite normal for a *Royal Variety Show*, really! At the end of the show Jon Bon Jovi sang a version of *Let It Be* which closed the whole evening with a neat Beatles bookend. All orchestrated with great deference and originality by Chris Egan. Amongst the star names performing that year were Katherine Jenkins, Darcey Bussell, Lang Lang, Jimmy Tarbuck, Michael Ball, Russell Brand, Dame Kiri Te Kanawa, Joan Rivers, James Blunt, Paul Potts and Enrique Iglesias; hosted impeccably by Phillip Schofield and Kate Thornton. So many of them I had worked with before but my personal highlight was working with Dame Kiri again. She sang my arrangement of *The National Anthem* at the beginning of the show but later she performed *O Mio Babbino Caro*, from Puccini's opera *Gianni Schicchi* which once again showed the great skilfulness of the musicians contracted by Rachel Williams for ITV after initial discussions with me. It's a bit like creating a special orchestra for three days, that's how long we have together, but it's an orchestra that has to sound as if it has been playing together for years. It's an art form all of its own being a commercial music session player and versatility is key.

There was one item that didn't make the show but which, had it happened, would have been the moment that would have been used in all the 'Best Of' shows for years to come. Kanye West and Lang Lang in duet. Let that sentence sink in and I will explain. Glen Middleham, our producer from *Another Audience With... Dame Shirley Bassey* had a crazy idea to put them together and we came up with a plan of a fusion of Lang Lang playing Liszt's *Hungarian Rhapsody No. 2* around Kanye performing *Stronger*. I asked Simon Hale to work his magic on the orchestration after I gave him the musical parameters and about a week before the Royal we rehearsed with Lang Lang and our *Royal Variety* rhythm section in London to make sure that the musical juxtaposition would work.

It was a dream rehearsal and Lang Lang proved his utter mastery, so much so that he was positively bubbling with excitement about the whole collaboration. Very unfortunately Kanye had to pull out because of a family tragedy leaving us to fill the void with Lang Lang playing the whole of Liszt's *Hungarian Rhapsody* solo for the show. Obviously he played it with virtuosic brilliance but it was such a shame that it wasn't our newly forged 'boyband' in their duet together and I do remember in the bows at the end of the whole show Lang Lang and I had a little moment of simpatico from stage to pit which I took to be a little tinge of regret that we had been unable to make that little bit of musical history.

2007 ended musically for me with a Broadway Concert with the Hallé Orchestra in Manchester's Bridgewater Hall. Another of the great orchestras and though rehearsals were a little fraught because time was short, they proved their worth when it came to the performance and my year of years was done.

*

Zorro: how about being Musical Supervisor on a musical based on the story of the masked, swashbuckling Mexican Robin

Hood, then? John Cameron, orchestrator of *Joseph*, and Chris Renshaw, original director of *Rock You*, asked me if I would like to be involved while I was in the mayhem of 2007. Of course I said yes and in early 2008 we embarked on putting the show through its paces, first on tour and then at the Garrick Theatre in July. The late Stephen Clark wrote a brilliant script – when I say wrote I mean rewrote and rewrote, I think there were something like twenty five drafts before we got to the West End – and the music was a mixture of some of the Gipsy Kings greatest hits adapted and built upon by John. Ultimately I wrote a couple of small parts of the show too but that was only after being cajoled into it by Chris much later in the process.

John is a fastidious writer and his orchestrations were always detailed and smart. After all, he created the sound of *Les Misérables* for Claude-Michel Schönberg and Alan Boublil as the original Musical Supervisor and Orchestrator back in 1980 and he and I had first worked together when he orchestrated *Joseph* brilliantly in 1991. He really does have form, in a good way! The initial band rehearsals and sitzprobe for the original tryout of *Zorro* in Eastbourne were somewhat marred by what could perhaps be referred to as too much detail. The players, all of whom were fine, strong musicians found themselves caught up in the notes on the page rather than the sound in the ears and, bearing in mind that most of the songs were based on the Gipsy Kings guitar led, very free improvisatory style, that meant that for some considerable time the music sounded somewhat stilted and didn't have life, breath or heart. I gently suggested that everyone relax away from being so caught up in all those notes and gradually the penny dropped and the music started to live. Dean Austin was our Musical Director and amongst the band were my trumpet playing friend, Stuart Brooks, from *Grease*, who was a dab hand at playing cod Spanish Trumpet, and a very fine young flamenco guitar specialist called David Buckingham.

With a fabulous cast and some authentic fiery flamenco dancing choreographed by Rafael Amargo the show stood a real chance of becoming a success. Matt Rawle as Zorro, firstly Aimie Atkinson (BBC Voice of Musical Theatre 2006), on tour, and then Emma Williams as Luisa in the West End, Adam Levy as Ramon and Broadway's Lesli Margherita as feisty Inez, led the company with real style. In fact Lesli won the Olivier Award for *Best Performance in a Supporting Role in a Musical* that year. On top of the musical theatre aspect, the fights, the magic and the stunts all combined to make it a thoroughly enjoyable show. It even received almost entirely favourable reviews but sadly the West End version lasted for only nine months. Maybe if we had a star name playing Zorro, who knows, but whatever it was the audience dwindled even with Charles Spencer of The Daily Telegraph referring to the show as, "An insanely enjoyable musical." Sometimes that Dame Audience is too tricky to entice.

Zorro has had more life since then and one iteration I am particularly fond of is the version that we did in Paris at the *Folies Bergère* in 2009. I stripped away a lot of the fiddly aspect of the orchestration and made it much more guitar led; our French cast headed by Laurent Ban, Liza Pastor and Geraldine Larossa, as Zorro, Luisa and Inez, also had a great deal of latin fire and energy and made the show their own. We had already made a London Cast Recording of the show but our French producers wanted their own version so I produced one with a fabulous French producer called Volodia.

One of the great things about my personal musical journey is that I have visited so many grand and glorious places in the world. Here I was on *Zorro* in 2009 and I was to live for three months in a beautiful apartment opposite the Tuileries Gardens and have the honour of working in one of the foremost international Cathedrals of Theatre. The *Folies Bergère* is not dissimilar to *The London Palladium* in that respect.

One of the rooms in the building did hold a surprise though. After a particularly long day of technical rehearsals director Chris Renshaw and I went exploring front of house. At the back of the stalls was a little staircase down to an unused and closed up room. We gingerly opened the door to a chamber that felt very cold, very damp and full of detritus from the years since the Second World War. It just felt wrong to be there and later we discovered that it had been used in the war by the Nazis as their 'special entertainment' space whenever they came to the theatre. Rumours abound as to what actually went on there but for me one thing is for certain; I will never walk through that door ever again. It chilled me to the bone.

Work continued to be as varied through the rest of 2008. One minute I was conducting a show called *Guilty Pleasures* for ITV where the performers were Magic Numbers and Kelly Osborne and the next I was writing music for the launch of the P&O Grand-class cruise ship MV Ventura in Southampton Docks. In October I also had a few days in Toronto with Dame Shirley where she was performing for an AIDS Benefit Concert at The Metro Toronto Convention Centre transmitted on Canadian TV called *Fashion sCares*. Spooky!

In amongst this broadly varied musical life I was also working on a project for London 2012 called *Welcoming the World*. Through designer Mark Fisher I had been introduced to a wonderfully elfin girl called Robyn Simpson. She is one of the top aerialists in the world and we had worked together on the naming ceremony of the P&O cruise ship MV Arcadia back in 2005 where she had performed and choreographed an extraordinary routine on a vast specially built frame at the back of a massive clear screen through which, when the kabuki curtain dropped, the whole ship was illuminated and effectively became centre stage.

This project for 2012, though, was organised by LOCOG (London Organising Committee of the Olympic Games) with Robyn managing it under the auspices of a company called *A New Direction*. Over a period of four months I visited sixteen primary and secondary schools in and around the east of London and worked with their music teachers and musical pupils to create sixteen original pieces of music that illustrated what they felt about having the Olympics so close to them. At the same time there was also a photography project by D Fie Foe and a film made by Kali Films called *Diversity in Motion* for which I wrote the soundtrack. Remember this was four years before 2012 so it was very much part of the effort to get the Olympics and the positive prospect of the Games in the minds of as many young people as possible.

The schools were completely diverse and it was a real education for me to see how the value of music teaching was so drastically different in each establishment. There was one school in Walthamstow with a fantastic computer set up, a full on state of the art keyboard studio and a very earnest and committed teacher. Sadly there were only about two pupils who had any interest whatsoever and at one point the rest of the class flew over to the classroom windows because a police car with siren blazing had zoomed into the school car park, deposited its fully 'tooled up' police officers who ran full pelt into the main entrance of the school obviously searching for person or persons unknown. Though I had a suspicion from the reaction of the class I was in that the 'unknown' was very well known to them.

Whatever the standard of the equipment that was available for the pupils, in all schools the commitment of the music teachers to make some sense of music education was really moving and their inspiration was evident. I kept thinking about my young self with Mr Parish and Tref Farrow and how I was so lucky to have had my talent recognised and nurtured by them. In every school there was potential and even though the results varied drastically I think that we made something special happen in all of them and the culmination of the project was a day in June when everyone got together to perform and view their finished work. A very joyous celebration of just how diverse we now are.

I conducted my first concert at the Cheltenham Jazz Festival with my good friend Guy Barker and also *Andrew Lloyd Webber's 60th Birthday Concert* in Hyde Park. ALW's concert was a month after I had conducted his collaborator *Don Black's 70th Birthday Concert* at The London Palladium and they were both for BBC Radio 2. As you can imagine they were star studded affairs with an array of great performers including, Idina Menzel, Elaine Paige, Marti Webb, Mica Paris, Maria Friedman, Michael Ball, Gary Barlow, Steve Balsamo and Joss Stone. My favourite little nugget of memory, though, is that for Don's concert I shared a dressing room with Michael Parkinson and Michel Legrand. Three Michaels all together in one room with two famous and one still occasionally pinching himself to make sure all this extraordinary stuff really was happening!

There were two other TV shows in 2008 and the first was ITV's *For One Night Only*, a series of duets essentially, where I worked again with Jimmy Tarbuck but this time on a song and dance routine with Emma Bunton; they sang *Let's Face the Music and Dance*. The late Steven Gately, Ronan Keating, Denise Van Outen and Michael Bublé also featured in duets. At the end of the year *We Are Most Amused* was a *Royal Variety* sort of show which was transmitted with the Prince of Wales in attendance to celebrate his 60th birthday. Musically I didn't have a lot to do, apart from overseeing the singing performance of *Star For a Night* winner Celestine Walcott-Gordon and playing cod piano for a little skit with John Cleese, but witnessing the huge comedic talents of John, Robin Williams, Rowan Atkinson, Joan Rivers and Bill Bailey up close and personal was pretty amazing.

The end of 2008 brought life and work firmly together again because my dear Dad, now eighty-three, was taken seriously ill. Natalie and I were on holiday in Kenya when we were called with the news. We arrived home to find him not quite at death's door but pretty damn close. There was no specific reason, it was a combination of heart disease and bronchitis and just getting older, I suppose. It was devastating to see my strong and seemingly indestructible Dad like this and to watch his gradual demise over the next two months was tough in the extreme. A couple of days before he died, when he was flitting in and out of consciousness, his older brother Fred came to see Mum, Jackie and I in Plymouth's Mount Gould Hospital, he brought with him his little whisky flask and silently with due reverence we toasted Dad's life. It was particularly poignant to witness this as Uncle Fred had seen his two younger sisters, Betty and Louie, die a couple of years before and here he was saying goodbye to his beloved younger brother. Uncle Fred, himself full of vigour and seemingly even more indestructible than Tom, held himself together as he and I raised that 'tot' to Thomas Patrick. Dad held on until just after midnight as the firework celebrations of New Year 2009 cascaded all over the sky and, as happens so often, he waited until we had all left the room before he gently and peacefully slipped away. On New Year's Eve he had received communion and briefly regained consciousness to say, "Amen" as he took the bread and wine. A fitting final word for a man who was the embodiment of simple, unfailing and unquestioning Christian faith.

THIRTEEN

CONCERTS & FRIDAY NIGHT

The start of 2009, which of course was full of memories of my dear Dad, was interspersed with prep for an extraordinary concert in Abbey Road Studio 1. It was a live performance of the whole of Elbow's album *The Seldom Seen Kid* with Elbow themselves, Richard Hawley plus the BBC Concert Orchestra and winners of the BBC Choir of the Year 2006, Chantage. A live radio and TV broadcast with specially commissioned new orchestrations from Nick Ingman and, unusually, with a small audience in the studio itself. Nick's charts were entirely perfect and completely matched Elbow's performance so that the two days that we spent all together rehearsing and then performing were a real joy.

Initially there was some trepidation and a little resistance from the band because this was entirely new territory. They hadn't worked with a sixty-five piece orchestra, thirty piece choir or a conductor before so the process had to be digested and understood. Of course in the creation of the original album there had been some small instrumental overdub sessions but that was after the tracks had all been recorded by the band, here we were all in it together and I was in front of them all on the conductor's podium.

Guy Garvey, Craig Potter, Mark Potter, Pete Turner and Richard Jupp proved that they are really rather remarkable musicians. They ascended the steep learning curve extremely quickly and with great positive energy. In rehearsal and during the gig they even turned around to applaud the orchestra and choir a couple of times so it was obvious that they really got into the process. It is fair to say that they really appreciated the work that Nick had done with his orchestrations and then the great way that the orchestra and choir made almost immediate musical sense of those hieroglyphics by sight reading them all, nearly perfectly, first time through. I think, in fact, that the sight reading ability of all the great orchestras is probably the most astonishing 'smoke and mirrors' moment when witnessed for the first time, particularly by pop and rock musicians who have such a different work process.

Guy and the band even appreciated and cottoned on very quickly to me waving my arms around, keeping everything together and trying to create the right feel for the whole piece. There was one particularly special moment in rehearsals when Guy took the choir and their Musical Director, James Davey, into Studio 2 to coach them. It wasn't that they were doing anything wrong but he wanted to to get them to sound a little more like Elbow with more 'rock and roll' edge and less regimentation. It was done with such generosity of spirit that by the end of the ad hoc rehearsal the choir were all absolutely eating out of his hand and they responded with complete and unstinting commitment.

2009 Elbow, BBCCO & Chantage at Abbey Road
Ben Yacobi with permission – benyacobi.com

Our BBC sound engineer, Rupert Flindt, was in his absolute element live mixing the concert for radio in that hallowed control room with the huge 72 channel Neve mixing desk. He was grinning from ear to ear every time I went in to discuss musical matters or to have a listen to how it was sounding. The only problems that were unresolvable were that Nick had written some huge bass drum hits on a super large six foot Gran Cassa in the fortissimo moments plus some very high piccolo lines that both sounded absolutely brilliant live in the studio but sadly in the control room they were the loudest thing on every single one of the hundred and sixty or so microphones, thereby obliterating everything else, and we had to cut them for the gig.

It was one of those dream concerts and I have such fond memories of those two days. One memory, in particular, does still make me chuckle:

Studio 1 has two separation booths, one usually used for vocal recording and the other for piano. About half an hour before the live recording I was in the piano room getting changed when 'Whispering Bob' Harris suddenly walked in en route to the VIP area of the studio, we exchanged pleasantries and after he had gone I realised that I had greeted the legendary DJ practically with my trousers around my ankles!

Later in the year there were more of the interesting collaborations starting with working on *Ant and Dec's Saturday Night Takeaway* as vocal coach for the boys, Brian Conley, Liz McLarnon and Jonny Wilkes. Then Lionel Richie for the *Capital Radio Summertime Ball* at The Emirates Stadium followed by a DSB Concert for the Prince of Wales at St James's Palace and a concert at The Queen Elizabeth Hall for Helena Kennedy, Baroness Kennedy of The Shaws, called *Helena Kennedy - 10 out of 10*, where my small band of five, Andy McGlasson on drums, Phil Mulford on bass, Pete Callard on guitar, Nick Moss on saxophone and me on piano, had a great time playing for theatrical luminaries like Sharon D. Clarke, Hal Fowler and Sophie-Louise Dann with Jon Snow making the introductions. I had an extremely fruitful afternoon with Don Black on a retrospective for Sky Arts where I finally got to play for Marti Webb - the first of many times - and that was followed by all the work with DSB on her album *The Performance* with David Arnold and then *The Electric Proms* and that great concert at The Roundhouse.

But then things went a little weird with Dame Shirley asked to take part in *Children In Need Rocks The Royal Albert Hall*, which had Steve Sidwell at the musical helm - the Dame was asked to duet with Dizzee Rascal. We did a hybrid version of *Diamonds Are Forever* with an extra space for Dizzee to rap and then he duetted with DSB at the end of the song. Gary Barlow had also previously joined us on piano for his song from *The Performance* album, *This Time,* so it was both fun and strange jumping in and conducting Steve's band for the couple of songs that we did. Being around the Dame always brought surprises and just before our segment on the show I went into her dressing room to do my usual, "you'll be fabulous," gee up and pep talk when Paul McCartney gently popped his head around the door to also wish her well so my *Five Handshakes of Separation* again went through the roof!

Lady Gaga singing *Speechless*, playing live piano and our *Royal Variety Orchestra* accompanying her sounds pretty reasonable when written down like that, but, once you add that she was playing a grand piano with Dali-esque legs that were three metres high and that she was lifted up on her piano stool by a flying chain hoist, dressed in a red latex dress inspired by the fashion of Queen Elizabeth I, with two red eye patches, then it starts to sound more like the normal excess of a proper Royal Command Performance!

The show was recorded in Blackpool at the Opera House. It was hosted by Peter Kay who first appeared rising up with the Mighty Wurlitzer on stage right, miming of course, but making quite a good job of watching me to finish 'playing' at the end of the sequence; with Anastacia, Lulu and Chaka Khan opening the show, Diversity dancing, a host of other stars performing including Katherine Jenkins, André Rieu, Alexandra Burke, Miley Cyrus, Michael Bublé and then Bette Midler closing the show, oh, and not forgetting that there was an excerpt from the show Sister Act with Whoopi Goldberg introducing them, it truly was just a run of the mill *Royal Variety*. Simon Staffurth directed and Anthony Van Laast choreographed with his usual flair.

The rehearsal with Lady Gaga did show just what a world class performer she really is. The piano didn't have its Dali legs attached so she was seated at a normal height. I had already met with her 'people' by telephone to make sure that all would be right musically and the chart for *Speechless* had been carefully written by Chris Egan, so we were as prepared as we could be. Hence it was a remarkable surprise when at the beginning of the rehearsal she came over to me on my podium in the orchestra pit and asked to see the score. I duly gave her my copy, she went off to the piano, not yet on its three metre legs, and proceeded to read it through as we all played it together – me, now minus the score. She came back to me afterwards and sat on her haunches to get down to my level and we talked through a couple of teeny changes before we did it again. It was another of those magical 'pinch myself' moments!

Early in 2010 I started work on an extraordinary version of *Hair* that was to be imported lock stock and barrel from the Al Hirschfeld Theater, Broadway to the Gielgud Theatre, London. It was for producer Cameron Mackintosh and the show, directed by Diane Paulus, had been an absolute smash on Broadway. The plan was to bring the American cast over to the West End, use a British band and also use British performers as understudies and swings (ensemble understudies) with a view to creating a UK company to eventually take over. I was to be Musical Supervisor and I had suggested one of the young breed of wunderkind Musical Directors, Richard Beadle, who had been MD on the tour of *Grease* for a couple of years, to lead the band. It meant a few weeks on Broadway getting to know the show and then some auditions back in the UK to find the understudies, put the band together, rehearse them, run the obligatory *Sitzprobe* and then keep everything musically shipshape.

To be honest it all went unbelievably smoothly. Cameron, who has been known to be a little on the tricky side, was completely knocked out at the *Sitz* and through all the Tech rehearsals. The American company, which included Will Swenson who I had worked with in Vegas on *We Will Rock You*, was stellar and, though the show was heralded with huge positivity and lauded once it was open, it unfortunately only lasted five months. The audiences also loved it, they exuberantly took to the stage at the end of every show, but sadly Cameron had to take the decision to close it before we had the chance to see and hear our fabulous UK cast taking over. However, there was one conversation that is worth recounting – and one that you would not hear in any other business meeting except a 'show business' meeting, nor would it have been heard in a meeting about the original show or even the 1980 version that I did.

It was in Tech week and a post rehearsal HOD get together at the back of the stalls. Everyone airs their grievances and the Production Manager gets on with working out how best to problem solve. Generally very tedious but necessary. On this particular day we had got to the end of Act I and the nude scene, which I hasten to add, in this production was utterly beautiful and very tastefully and respectfully done, beautiful lighting, the nudity almost ending up in silhouette form; but there was a major concern that our cast may have overdone their, ahem, personal grooming. There was even talk of, in some cases, having to provide merkins (pubic wigs) to make sure that everyone looked suitably hippy-like and just as they would have back in the late sixties. After a short discussion the decision was made to leave things as they were, but to gently ask some of the male and female cast to keep away from their razors for a little while. A delicate conversation with a very subtle result in this age of #MeToo!

In 2010 around the middle of April I had a very surprising call from the BBC. They were filming the live shows in their *Over The Rainbow* series where Andrew Lloyd Webber headed the judges and the search was on for the new Dorothy in the West End. Nigel Wright was Musical Director – he had produced the

Joseph and *Grease* albums and the music for the Evita movie so I knew him pretty well – but in week three, when there were still nine girls left Nigel got stranded in Malaga by the great volcanic dust cloud that had come from the Eyjafjallajökull volcano in Iceland and apparently Andrew had said to producer Suzy Lamb that the replacement should be either Dave Arch or me.

I was supposed to be at a family reunion that weekend so when the call came on the Thursday I very carefully said that I would be only too happy to help out BUT if Dave Arch was available then I would be equally happy to leave it to him. Thereby, very respectfully, getting out of it, or so I thought. I had a second call on that Thursday saying that Dave was stuck too, so please could I do it. Heigh ho – as I have said before, always say yes and work out the logistics later!

So the next evening I was in Fountain Studios, Wembley for the camera rehearsals, first with the band and then with all the girls. I knew just about all the musicians, they were a dream to work with and, even though all the contestants were very young and inexperienced, they all behaved totally professionally so that it actually became a bit of a magical weekend. On the live Saturday evening show Andrew made a point of mentioning me and referencing that the fact I was there showed that it was a totally 'live' show. Host Graham Norton was his usual ebullient self for both the Saturday and Sunday programmes, he really is a natural. I must say that it did feel pretty strange jumping in at the last moment but all my previous TV work stood me in good stead in understanding exactly how everything worked and I think I 'got away with it', as we always say. Danielle Hope eventually won the competition but my experience of that weekend was that all the girls had great potential and any one of them could have clinched it. I was very happy and honoured to jump in and keep the curtain up, so to speak.

My association with those talent shows also brought me into contact with Helena Blackman, who was runner-up in the *How Do You Solve a Problem Like Maria?* BBC show from 2006. I was asked at the end of 2010 to be Musical Director and Producer for an album of Rodgers and Hammerstein songs reimagined for Helena to sing. The result was a lovely album with orchestrations from Simon Hale, Tom Kelly, Michael Bruce and Chris Walker and a particularly productive two days in Angel Studios with the legendary Steve Price working his engineering magic. I had a twenty-eight piece orchestra and Helena was truly a star in the recording process and in the development of the album.

Speculation, run by Neil Eckersley, financially produced the album and oversaw the creative process. If those two names look familiar then you may have seen them in the list of businesses on the Musicians Union's 'ASK US FIRST' list, so beware! I am very proud of all of our work on this album and, even though in the end it was really rushed after Eckersley insisted we mix straight after finishing recording – a process that took Steve Price and me until 5 am the next morning – it really does sound quite good but I will never work with *Speculation* ever again. I always prefer honour and honesty, don't you? I knew it was a labour of love from the start and I was happy to make the album for Helena, but once a deal is agreed then it should be adhered to. Enough said.

*

During my time as a regular conductor of BBC Radio 2's *Friday Night is Music Night* I have worked with some of the finest BBC radio producers, presenters and script writers. (Special mention to Anthony Cherry, Ken Bruce and Colin Edmonds in each of those categories.) I have been able to suggest ideas for shows. Here's an example: for producer Jodie Keane we put together a special Cornish *FNIMN* recorded in March 2010 with soloists Adrian Clarke and Sarah Pring (fabulous opera singers and friends from Treyarnon) and I even had an original thirteen minute suite performed. It was called *The Coast* and was a musical homage to the environs of Treyarnon. I have also been able to suggest performers, orchestrators and repertoire. But the single most important aspect of the whole twenty or so years is that I have been able to work with one of the finest orchestras in the world, *The BBC Concert Orchestra*.

To say that they are a versatile orchestra only just touches the surface of how good they actually are. Their ability to read, inwardly digest and then produce emotionally driven performances is quite something to behold and in the past fifty or so concerts that I have conducted with them the sheer variety of music is breathtaking. In one special for BBC Radio2 Day in 2013 which was filmed for TV as well as transmitted on radio we went from *The Festival Overture* by Shostakovich to *That's How Strong My Love Is* sung by Mick Hucknall and from *The Theme from Superman* by John Williams to Tony Blackburn, generously assisted by leading percussionist Alasdair Molloy, playing everything but the kitchen sink in *The Sabre Dance* by Khachaturian. Not only that but we also had Jamie Cullum, Sinéad O'Connor, Gary Barlow, Clare Teal and Elaine Paige performing; the orchestra played Bernstein's *Candide Overture* plus Elgar's *Pomp and Circumstance March No. 1* and this huge variety of music was featured in just one concert. When written down it looks extraordinary but the orchestra essentially does similar in every concert it performs, and with style and great musicianship.

In a concert early in the 2000s we were performing Khachaturian's *Theme from The Onedin Line*, which is actually the *Adagio* from the ballet *Spartacus*, and in the middle of the piece there is a pronounced rallentando (gradual slowing down) which leads to a massive statement of the *'famous bit'* of the theme and in the middle of the slow down I got lost, I kept waving away but basically I got to the *'famous bit'* one bar earlier than I should have. Half the orchestra went with what my pronounced gesticulations were signalling and the other half went with what was written down in front of them. Within the space of half a bar all of them had jumped to the glorious tune and the audience would have noticed a small hiatus but that is all. However, though all this took place in the blink of an eye, to me it lasted a lifetime and I felt gut-wrenchingly awful having made the most excruciating mistake. All I could do at the time was indicate to them all that it was my fault and gesture my apologies – it was live and I had to get on with it – and that is exactly what happened, we all just got on with the concert and what seemed to me to be *The Great Cock Up* fortunately disappeared into the ether. I still get that awful kick in the stomach feeling when I think about it though.

Through my twenty years the personnel has changed quite considerably and I have worked with four different Leaders (Concertmasters) and associate Leaders: Cynthia Fleming (another Trinity College of Music alumni), Rebecca Turner, Charles Mutter and the current Leader, Nathaniel Anderson-Frank. The relationship between conductor and leader is so very important as this is where the communicating of ideas and a great deal of the liaising with the orchestra happens. Rehearsal time is always very short and sometimes the pace has to be pretty relentless so trust between you is paramount; the trust that musical nuances have been noted and comprehended and the trust that you as conductor will give the same tempos and musical signals in performance as you do in those frenetic rehearsals. I always say to any young conductor who asks my advice, "Remember, the baton doesn't make any noise!" and it is always a truth worth remembering when you stand there – the orchestra makes that beautiful noise so trust and respect them to do so!

Since 2007 and that Andrew Lloyd Webber special *Friday Night is Music Night* concert the producer that I have worked with most is Anthony Cherry. He is a study of brilliance; dapper, witty and steeped in radio and the history of all forms of music. A man who has worked with all the great broadcasters of our time and who has made a career out of creating iconic radio events that are not just ephemeral but have some real heart and soul.

It was with Anthony that I got to work with all sorts of amazing people. A whole concert with Idina Menzel – astonishing – how about Henry Mancini's daughter Monica – and then *Elvis Forever*, in Hyde Park, hosted by Chris Evans with Elvis's TCB band actually there and for a few of the numbers replacing our rhythm section; famed guitarist James Burton, bass player Jerry Scheff and iconic drummer Ron Tutt there with me on stage – and, incidentally, we had a great time!

2010 Elvis Forever at Hyde Park:
he TCB Band, James Burton, Jerry Scheff & Ron Tutt

A celebration of the work of Leslie Bricusse with John Owen Jones, Michael Jibson and Hannah Waddingham introduced by Parky and with some specially commissioned orchestrations by my longtime friend and collaborator Roy Moore.

Andrew Lloyd Webber's 60th Birthday Concert – again from Hyde Park – where the list of performers included Idina Menzel, John Barrowman, Elaine Paige, Ruthie Henshall, Maria Friedman, Ramin Karimloo, Philip Achille, Lee Mead, Jodie Prenger, Jason Donovan, Daniel Boys, Jonathan Ansell, Hayley Westenra, Duncan James, Denise Van Outen, Rhydian, Joss Stone, Steve Balsamo and some of the finalists from the *I'd Do Anything* BBC TV search for Nancy: Jessie Buckley, Niamh Perry, Keisha Amposa Banson and Rachel Tucker.

Concerts where we featured film music and where I got to conduct *Star Trek*, *Star Wars*, *Mission Impossible*, *Harry Potter* and *Jurassic Park*. I have to say that seeing my daughters, Lillie and Meg, straight after that particular concert was one of the most emotional moments of any of the gigs. You see Lillie had always said to me, "If you're ever going to conduct the music from *Jurassic Park* or *Star Wars* then we HAVE to be there!" So I made sure that they were and that performance was just for them.

The Cheltenham Jazz Festival, with the ever talented Guy Barker playing trumpet and orchestrating in such an original and quite mesmerising way. We did *The Billie Holiday Story* where Anthony had to work hard on the powers that be at the BBC to enable his brilliant script to retain its authenticity of language – in other words get permission to use the F-word live on BBC Radio 2 – and the *Billy Strayhorn Story* which had some equally gritty moments. There were also concerts where we celebrated the life of David Jacobs, where we broke a Guinness

World Record – well, strictly speaking Ken Bruce did – and where we celebrated Jazz Royalty with Georgie Fame, Madeline Bell, Martin Taylor and Charlie Wood.

With Anthony I also worked on two concerts which gave young performers of the future an extraordinary opportunity to sing with the orchestra. The first was with the Brit School in 2011 and the second was with ArtsEd in 2014. For both concerts we treated the students as if they were professional. We went through an audition process which was followed by coaching sessions and then on the stage in front of the orchestra they had to deliver the goods which, by and large, they did in style. Those that didn't get to sing solo formed the choir or ensemble so everyone got to experience what it is like singing with that remarkable orchestra backing them.

In 2018 a special concert from the Palladium with Michael Parkinson being interviewed by his son and with the chat interspersed by *My Kind of Music* – performed by Joe Stilgoe, Alison Jiear, Gwynn Jay Allen and Hailey Tuck, and the orchestra joined by the BBC Big Band making a stonking sound. It was particularly exciting to see Parky in rehearsals at Maida Vale Studio MV1 having the time of his life listening to the band in swing mode at point-blank range playing the famous Buddy Rich version of *Love For Sale* at full pelt, utterly exhilarating! Most recently early in 2020 we did a 50th anniversary concert of *Bridge Over Troubled Water* with poet Lemn Sissay presenting and Will Young headlining, again a special *Friday Night is Music Night* offering that Anthony cleverly dreamed up.

2018 With Parky and Anthony Cherry at Maida Vale MV1

With the other producers, Alan Boyd, Jodie Keane and Bridget Apps, I also conducted some pretty original concerts. From the Cornish show, already mentioned, to a special Old Time Music Hall show entitled *They Played the 'Alls*, with Dame Barbara Windsor introducing Roy Hudd, Anita Harris plus ukulele virtuoso and George Formby impersonator, Mark Walsh; *Proms in the Park* with Lionel Richie; a Coronation Street special featuring a show written by Trisha Ward (more of that later!); a show with Judy Garland's daughter, Lorna Luft, where we actually got them to sing *Somewhere Over the Rainbow* together – virtually – and Frances Ruffelle, Linzi Hateley and John Barrowman were on the show as well; Helena Blackman singing most of the Rodgers and Hammerstein album that we had recorded; a Leading Men special with Tamzin Outhwaite introducing John Owen Jones, Matt Rawle, Ricardo Afonso, Paul Spicer and Alex Gaumond – that particular concert was with the BBC Philharmonic led by Yuri Torchinsky, recorded at their base in Salford and Ricardo's performance singing Queen's *The Show Must Go On* still sends tingles down my spine just thinking about it – and, of course, Christmas Specials with masses of tinsel and even an illuminated baton!

A lot of these concerts had scripts written by Colin Edmonds who I knew from the long distant days of the Brian Conley series where my love of comedy and his interest in what Musical Directors do seemed to very gently and successfully collide. Actually Colin and I had worked together before that as he was script associate on my first *Royal Variety Show* back in 1989, but at that time our paths didn't actually cross. Colin's *FNIMN* scripts always made me chuckle and he also seemed to be able to work my name into the show far too frequently, though I did marvel at how he always seemed to write the script in the 'voice' of whoever was actually hosting the show. That in itself is an art form!

Through Colin I was introduced to a young man called Josh Barry who was researching one of his books about the entertainment industry. He wanted to interview me about the *Royal Variety Shows* and we ended up talking for hours about the whole industry. He is extraordinary. He has quite severe cerebral palsy and writes onto his iPad with his nose. In 2016 Colin and I went to the Isle of Wight to support him in the launch of his documentary series called *Following the Money, The Story of the British Theatrical Agent*. Since then he has continued to grow and he has interviewed just about everyone there is to know in British Entertainment. *Beyond the Title* is his long term project and I applaud his ambition.

There were also three very special concerts from The Royal Festival Hall celebrating the work of Tim Rice, Don Black and Tony Hatch. Both the Tim Rice and Don Black concerts were also transmitted on BBC TV and had very starry guest artists including Rufus Wainwright, Laura Mvula, Gemma Arterton, Tim Minchin, Alexander Armstrong, Julian Ovenden, Petula Clark, Tom Chaplin, Rick Wakeman, Sophie Ellis-Bextor, Frances Ruffelle, Roger Daltrey, Cynthia Erivo, Eliza Doolittle, Gregory Porter, Michael Ball, Maria Friedman, Laura Wright, Marc Almond and Marti Webb. Michael Grade introduced each of the concerts and over on the side of the stage there was a little enclave where Don, Tim and Tony were interviewed in between songs. These were all exciting concerts to conduct with such a varied bunch of songs and musical illustrations and, because, as ever, the rehearsal time was so short, all my musical diplomacy skills gleaned over the years, and inherently from my Dad, were put to the test in a good way. Actually that kind of high pressure scenario is almost beyond exciting and I do seem to thrive on it.

2014 With Sir Tim Rice Rehearsing at Maida Vale MV1

In 2015 the other co-producer on these concerts, Ollie Rosenblat, asked me to conduct a one-off performance of *How To Succeed in Business Without Really Trying* again at the Royal Festival Hall. It was a sensational one-off gig directed by Jonathan Butterell and starring Jonathan Groff, Cynthia Erivo and Clarke Peters with a selection of 'marvy-old-pros' in the supporting roles. Barney Ashworth was my assistant and though we had a great time the event itself was somewhat marred by the fact that when we came to rehearse with the RPCO half of the rehearsal time was taken up with correcting mistakes in the score. A hazard of music hire where Vocal Scores and Full Scores have not been proofread properly by the hire company and somewhat frustrating when rehearsal time is so short!

The Don Black concert was the last time I worked with brilliant bass player Steve McManus. We had worked together so many times, including a lot of the Dame Shirley concerts and *Royal Variety Shows*, but in early 2014 the cancer that he had been stricken with a few years before finally took him from us. His sunny disposition and 'nothing is too much trouble' attitude will be missed. He died far too young.

Allied to *Friday Night is Music Night* were a set of concerts and events which were joint productions with TBI Media run by Phil Critchlow. Some were known as the *Minute by Minute* series but essentially the format was the same. Special anniversaries of world changing events were selected; Jonathan Mayo would write a script incorporating live recordings made at the time which would be performed by a group of actors and presenters and Phil, Jonathan, Anthony Cherry and I would select musical offerings that would be played live and sometimes underneath all the action. All of this was interspersed with songs of the era or new songs either interpreting or putting a new spin on the event.

The first that we did was on the centennial anniversary of the loss of the Titanic. This set the standard with Jeremy Vine and Dermot O'Leary taking the lion's share of the commentary and discussions with experts. I had recently been introduced to a new young orchestrator, a 'jolly hockey sticks' lady with an extraordinary musical ability called Jen Green and on the Macmillan Centenary Gala that I conducted at the Palladium in 2011 I needed an orchestration of *One* from Marvin Hamlisch's *A Chorus Line*. Jen created the arrangement from scratch in the twinkling of an eye and from that moment on at any opportunity that I have I ask her to work with me. So when these *Minute by Minute* shows came along she was my first choice to orchestrate and she made light work of all the music needed, some of which, for quite a few episodes, was my original stuff. It was also where one of the finest spinning round of a song idea happened with Billy Bragg performing a song from the point of view of the oft misunderstood iceberg naturally called *The Song of the Iceberg*.

This show in 2012 was also my first time with Jacqui Dankworth and her husband the jazz piano player Charlie Wood. They were tasked with creating an arrangement of *Alexander's Rag Time Band* by Irving Berlin. It was utterly beautiful and took the song to a very different place musically. My quite small ensemble of six string players, with Charles Mutter leading and Steve McManus on bass, had moments where, rather than accompanying, they were emulating the sound of the ship, creaking and moaning under the strain of the collision. It was a mesmerising performance and since then I have worked with Jacqui and Charlie at concerts in the Cadogan Hall in London with players from the Royal Philharmonic Orchestra, in the National Concert Hall, Dublin with the RTE Concert Orchestra and in the Philharmonic Hall, Liverpool with the Liverpool Philharmonic Orchestra.

In November 2013 it was the 50th anniversary of the assassination of President John F. Kennedy that was the subject and we recorded this one in Maida Vale MV3 – that's the studio with the plaque informing you that Bing Crosby made his last recording in this studio on 11th October 1977, by the way. Broadcaster and writer Bonnie Greer joined Jeremy Vine, Dermot O'Leary and Louise Minchin for this one and amongst the musical performers were Paul Carrack, Eliza Doolittle and Alfie Boe singing with a slightly wayward bagpipe player.

We also did what proved to be one of my favourite days in studio, ever. It was on 11th February 2013 in Abbey Road Studio 2 and the basic premise of the day was to record new versions of the Beatles' *Please, Please Me* album at the same time that the Beatles had recorded them fifty years earlier back in 1963. The twist for us was that as we recorded each song it was transmitted live on BBC Radio 2 – no second takes, and a BBC TV programme called *12 Hours to Please Me* was also made out of all the footage.

Here is a list of performers and tracks:

> Gabrielle Aplin – *There's A Place*
> Stereophonics – *I Saw Her Standing There*
> Joss Stone – *A Taste of Honey*
> Ian Broudie – *Do You Want to Know a Secret*
> Paul Carrack – *Misery*
> The Merseybeats & Friends – *Boys*
> Chris Difford, Glen Tilbrook, Paul Jones – *Please, Please Me*
> Mick Hucknall – *Anna (Go To Him)*
> I Am Kloot – *Chains*
> Graham Coxon – *Baby It's You*
> Beverley Knight – *Twist and Shout*

My band for the day was:

Ralph Salmins – Drums
Huw Davies – Guitar
Dave Holmes – Guitar
Phil Mulford – Bass Guitar
Neil Angilley – Keyboards
Mike Dixon – Piano/MD
Nina Foster – Violin 1
Sarah Tuke – Violin 2
Fiona Leggat – Viola
Llinos Richards – Cello

Jen Green again looked after the charts and Stuart Maconie, Chris Evans and Jo Whiley were the presenters with my percussion friend Steve Socci contracting the band.

I think the three highlights for me were Gabrielle Aplin so gently singing *There's A Place* while playing guitar with our gorgeous string quartet, Joss Stone (who I had worked with when she was only 14 on *Star For a Night*) singing *A Taste of Honey* and learning the song just before transmission sitting beside me at the piano and Beverley Knight ripping the pants out of *Twist and Shout* at the end of the day (around 10.30pm), but really and truly the whole day was quite extraordinary. Studio 2 was full of music, also full of TV and sound equipment, and I certainly felt that four young men, raw and brand spanking new from fifty years before, were casting a warm shadow and embracing us all on that day.

2013 With Joss Stone 12 Hours to Please Me at Abbey Road Studio 2
TBI Media Ltd with permission

Along with these iconic anniversaries the *Minute by Minute* series also commemorated some of the devastating moments during World War II. Later in 2013 we did *Dambusters 70* from Biggin Hill where we not only had the BBC Concert Orchestra but also RAF Central Band and the Portsmouth Military Wives Choir, with Jacqui Dankworth and Gabrielle Aplin our soloists.

During the course of the day a Lancaster from The Battle of Britain Memorial Flight, with Chris Evans on board, landed just outside the Rizon Hangar where we were rehearsing. The sound of those four Rolls Royce Merlin engines up close like that is simply astonishing and so very heart stirring. I had a chat with Flight Lieutenant Roger Nichols who was piloting the craft and who was also the Squadron Leader of Battle of Britain Memorial Flight for that year and I mentioned to him the fact that Natalie's uncle, Alexander Durward, had been a Lancaster pilot towards the end of the war. His response was brilliant, "Bring him to our base in Coningsby and we will give him the royal treatment," he said, "and maybe we can get him on the flight deck of the 'Lanc' while he is there!"

So not only were Natalie's Uncle Sandy and Auntie Jennifer our guests of honour for this show, and we were able to get them backstage and to meet the performers, but a couple of months later Roger was true to his word and we took them to Coningsby for the day where we were all treated to a full VIP experience – lunch in the Officer's Mess with a few of the other pilots, a guided tour of the whole facility with the Spitfires, Hurricanes and Dakota and then some very special time getting Sandy into the belly of the Lanc. His face as he climbed onboard was a picture and it was as clear as day that this was a big deal for him. Unfortunately he was a little too frail to get up to the flight deck but, while he was chatting to one of the other Squadron Leaders in the hold, Roger, Auntie Jen and I went on up and we sat in the seats while Roger made a video for him as a reminder of what it was like to be in the hot seat and a walk through all the controls. The day was very special, Roger and the BBMF made a great fuss of Sandy and I was so happy that I had been able to engineer it all because I had conducted the concert.

In 2014 it was *D-Day 70* from The Royal Albert Hall where I remember a surreal moment when I had to cue the actor playing Winston Churchill early on in the opening music, Malcolm Arnold's *Anniversary Overture* Op.99. It wasn't the fact that I had to cue him, rather it was the fact that the actor standing beside me was none other than Sir Patrick Stewart, who incidentally was utterly charming and full of bonhomie. A delight.

During that concert I conducted *We'll Meet Again* for Katherine Jenkins but it was also a virtual duet with Dame Vera Lynn on a huge screen hung above the stage. Beverley Knight sang an absolutely brilliant version of *Stormy Weather*, the ArtsEd Choir joined with the orchestra to perform John Williams' *Hymn to the Fallen* and Prince William read from Shakespeare's *Henry V*. However, it was none of these things that made this concert especially memorable, it was the fact that a remarkable man called Jim Radford, who was the youngest known participant in the landings and a galley boy on one of the D-Day ships building Mulberry Harbour on the morning of June 6th 1944, sang his version of the events in a song called *The Shores of Normandy*.

That song proved to be the moment of the concert but the process had started a couple of months before when I was asked to be Musical Director for the event. Phil Critchlow told me that he had discovered a folk singer who had written a song and would I have a listen. Incidentally it turns out that he was a peace activist and supporter of CND as well. I was sent a raw recording of Jim singing the song, which is based on an old Irish folk tune called *The Dawning of the Day (Fáinne Geal an Lae)*, and as I listened to it I could hear in my mind a string arrangement accompanying him.

So I set about creating a demo using his vocal recording but adding synth strings so that Phil could hear how it would work. Jen then set to taking my demo and cleverly making it work for the orchestra – and also adding a little brass at the end just to add military colour. Jim also heard it and was happy, though he did voice a little worry because he had never sung with an orchestra before. To help to alleviate this on the day in the Royal Albert Hall I took Jim to the little piano room backstage and we gently went through the arrangement before we rehearsed on stage with everyone.

I had arranged it in a very 'colla voce' way, in other words there was lots of space for him to have freedom of expression and so I told him to sing it as if we weren't there. I would carefully keep the orchestra together with him. The only thing he had to worry about was waiting for me to cue him after the little intro that I had written had finished. Anyway, that is exactly what we did, the strings of the BBC Concert Orchestra kept with me as we ducked and dived our way around, but when Jim finished the song all 5,000 people in the

RAH stood as one along with all the magnificent actors beside Sir Patrick who were reading Jonathan Mayo's script with truth and honesty and I could also see Jeremy, Dermot and Louise very much affected by the moment as well. In theatrical parlance it, "brought the house down!" completely and utterly.

In 2019 on the 75th Anniversary we made a recording of Jim singing the song in aid of the Normandy Memorial Trust (a beautiful memorial for all the 22,442 service people under British command who died on D-Day and the subsequent Battle of Normandy) and Jim and I went to Ver-Sur-Mer for the inauguration of the monument by British Prime Minister Teresa May and the French President Emmanuel Macron; later that day he sang the song in Arromanches with me on piano, a French violinist and a British soldier playing trumpet. Just to be a small part in all that was so very moving and humbling, it was another of *those* moments.

Jim very sadly died of COVID-19 in November 2020, so he never saw the completed memorial, such a great shame, but at least we have both the video and the recording as a lasting and honourable memory of him.

2019 Recording Shores of Normandy with Jim Radford

The largest of these special concerts was in 2015, like *Dambusters 70* at Biggin Hill, but this one had one very special musical addition. A real Spitfire! It was *The 75th Anniversary of the Battle of Britain* and I think that I am the only person to have conducted Walton's *Spitfire Prelude* with the Rolls Royce Merlin engine of a Supermarine Spitfire started up mid way through the piece. The pilot, when asked if it would fire up first time, said that it sometimes did, but that it would realistically be a fifty-fifty scenario. Well, as it happened he switched on and that engine fired up first time right on cue!

Sophie Raworth joined Jeremy Vine and Dermot O'Leary for this one and the actors were led by Simon Callow and Martin Shaw. Jeremy Isaacs very movingly read from *Henry V* while the Concert Orchestra and the RAF Squadronaires played *Evening Hymn, Last Post & Sunset* with German trumpeter Sgt Stephan Müller and British trumpeter SCA Andrew Lofthouse exchanging musical phrases in a hugely moving tribute. Pixie Lott, Niamh Perry, The Shires, The Puppini Sisters and Shaun Escoffery sang. These concerts were filmed and live in cinemas around the country as well as on radio and TV.

2015 Battle of Britain 75 Rehearsal with Jason Isaacs Maida Vale MV1
TBI Media Ltd with permission

2015 Battle of Britain 75 Biggin Hill
TBI Media Ltd with permission

There was one concert in the Royal Albert Hall that was for Classic FM rather than BBC Radio 2 and that was the *VE Day 70* celebration. John Suchet and Myleene Klass introduced and David Bradbury narrated utterly breathtakingly. For this concert Wynne Evans (the GoCompare man), Rebecca Ferguson and Katherine Jenkins sang and as well as the Royal Philharmonic Concert Orchestra playing beautifully I also conducted the English Chamber Choir.

The last one that I did with TBI was a celebration of the 50th anniversary of winning the World Cup back in 1966 called *World Cup '66 LIVE*. We performed at what used to be known as The Empire Pool Wembley, now The SSE Arena; Jeremy Vine and Dermot O'Leary were again joined by Louise Minchin with Martin Freeman and Kevin Bishop leading the actors and performances from Sophie Ellis Bextor, Lemar, Jesse Smith, The Shires, Kerry Ellis, Chris Farlowe (whose song *Out of Time* was No. 1 in 1966), Squeeze, Reef, The Troggs, the cast of the Kinks musical Sunny Afternoon and Shaun Escoffery. Tim Maple created some fun underscores on this one and the reduced orchestra was led by Charles Mutter.

2016 With Martin Freeman World Cup '66
TBI Media Ltd with permission

At the end of the show two of the surviving players from that 1966 squad, Sir Geoff Hurst and Sir Bobby Charlton, came onto the stage to be interviewed. When Sir Bobby arrived he made a point of shaking hands with all of us at the front of the stage. That was, of course, wonderful, except that as he came up to shake my hand he didn't see the stage light on the floor right beside me and he tripped on it. A national catastrophe was averted as I caught him, fortunately OFF camera. Funny how the boy who did music because it got him out of Games at school saved a sporting legend from disaster!

In 2017 with Anthony we made a special performance to celebrate LGBT50 in Hull City Hall for BBC TV and radio called *I Feel*

Love and amongst the people we played for were Alison Moyet, Bright Light x2, Noah Stewart and Tom Robinson. It was a real rainbow gig with Scott Mills and Ana Matronic introducing it all from within the audience in a sort of pen. Noah got the biggest cheer of the night at the climax of *Nessun Dorma* which he sang exquisitely with me beside him accompanying on solo piano.

After the gig I had a message to say that someone was at the stage door waiting to see me. It turned out that John Goldsmith, who had played Woof in the production of *Hair* that I did in 1980, had been in the audience, right next to the pen and standing beside Natalie for the whole evening! I said it was a rainbow concert and it was made all the more special by this happenstance meeting!

All these *Minute by Minute* shows and a lot of the *Friday Night is Music Night* concerts were filled with 'pinch yourself' moments but they were also filled with hugely professional people either performing onstage or working behind the scenes backstage making sure that all the elements of the shows came together smoothly and seamlessly. All my theatrical and TV nous came into play because they were full on theatrical spectaculars, with script, major underscores, sound effects, performances and the occasional unscripted ad lib or interview to deal with. When we did that *D-Day 70* show from the RAH the only time we performed it all the way through was in the evening – the live Radio, TV and Cinema performance. There simply hadn't been time in rehearsal to run it completely so we rehearsed out of order and topped and tailed a lot of the dialogue sections. Truthfully that was the case for most of the shows.

They were proper 'For One Night Only' gigs!

FOURTEEN

HERE, THERE &
EVERYWHERE

When I conducted the *Friday Night is Music Night Salutes the Soaps* concert, and waved a short excerpt from a new musical by Trisha Ward back in 2010, I had no idea that two years later I would be conducting *The Coronation Street Musical: Street of Dreams* at Manchester Arena with Paul O'Grady and a host of West End actors and actresses. Unfortunately it turned out to be an unmitigated disaster and, though musically and performance wise it was well done, everything was coloured by the fact that the management of Trisha and John Ward were sailing very close to the wind in all ways. The show collapsed after that one performance and sad to say everyone involved, actors, musicians and technicians were left out of pocket, some very severely indeed. Really appalling behaviour and unforgivable.

The whole experience was made palatable by the humour, talent and optimism of all those wonderful 'turns' and the bonding spirit that always seems to run rings around negativity when in adversity. There was one other little moment that now defines the entire production and which occurred towards the end of rehearsals in one of the huge rooms at 3 Mills Studios.

We were all feeling very suspicious and worried about how the show was being handled and suddenly from the other side of this dark cavernous room came a shout, then a scream and finally a tall man being chased by a diminutive woman appeared in front of us as if from a mist. It was Paul running away hell for leather from composer, writer and co-producer Trisha Ward. He was shouting, "Leave me a-f***ing-lone, will ya!" and screaming, "Get her off me!!" at the top of his voice. We found out that there had been some 'small' altercation about the dialogue and direction of the show and just for a minute all our anxieties evaporated away as we watched this real comedy soap opera play out right in front of us.

Paul is to be commended. Ultimately he defended everyone and, after the debacle of the opening in Manchester, was vociferous in his defence of all the performers involved and in his criticism of the mismanagement by the producers. The whole event caused a lot of pain, hardship and anxiety and I sincerely hope the Wards keep well away from the professional world in the future. Never again for me!

Through 2012 and onwards there were a few forays into TV but mostly now my TV work was with the big concerts. I did enjoy working on a show called *Get Your Act Together* where Michael Ball mentored James Bolam and they performed *Me and My Shadow* together with a big band backing them and I also worked on *Surprise, Surprise* and *Text Santa* but basically work was taking me into yet more new directions.

Gale Edwards, who had directed *Superstar*, called me up out of the blue in 2011 and said that she was directing a show which was to run in Sanya, China. Now, of course, I knew Sanya very well from *Miss World* so when she told me it was for Wanda Cultural Industry Group with an international creative team and that we would rehearse in Beijing, I jumped at the chance. The show was ultimately called *Spiral* and did indeed have a life in China but it had to travel quite a rocky road to get there.

I was simply not available the whole time so I put in place one of the young MDs who had recently come to my attention, an ex army musician with a passion for musical theatre and with almost inexhaustible energy, Barney Ashworth. Barney proved to be worth his weight in gold on this project and held the fort with great fortitude while I flitted back to the UK every couple of weeks. It was a baptism of fire for him as Gale can be quite formidable and dealing with our Chinese employers was proving to be quite an arduous task for her in most of the rehearsals and production meetings, in all honesty. They were hugely keen but it was a little like 'all the gear, no idea' a lot of the time.

Beijing rehearsals were going pretty well, nevertheless, as I jetted back home one day. Then, when I landed at Heathrow and turned my phone on, there was a message from a slightly shellshocked Barney. "Mike, make sure you are sitting down before you listen to the rest of this message," he panted. I am quite good at following orders, sometimes, so I duly found a place to sit. The show was being written by a Chinese composer and lyricist and then moulded by us, the international creative team, that was how it was working, and that was how I left things the day before. I had no clue as to what could be so serious.

"Just after you left for the airport the composer was arrested," he blurted out in the message. "Something to do with Taiwan," he continued. It turned out that he had produced an album for a Taiwanese artist and the powers that be found out. That was that as far as our producers were concerned and we had to find another composer pretty damn quickly.

I returned to Beijing a few days later to meet with a new composer. There was no mistaking the fact that the government indeed had something to do with his appointment – he was a young General in the army! Anyway we had to go through with it however good or bad he was and fortunately, as it turned out, he was a good man and a very good writer.

Pretty much as soon as I landed Barney and I had a meeting with Gale, the new composer, Aaron Wu (Producer from Wanda) and one of the team of interpreters who seemed to be ever-present.

Gale talked the composer through the opening of the show, "So, through a gauze we see firstly a rope appear from the ceiling of the stage as if being dropped down a hole. It meanders down and we see the Spiral shell or Conch that is the subject of the show in front of us. A man climbs down the rope to the shell and, as the gauze flies out, we are magically transported back in time to when the shell had mysteriously been put there and we discover our wonderful mythical cast singing the opening number."

Obviously the translation took some time and overall it took us the whole day to talk through the show at least in a very basic simple way. It was a great start, though. Our composer told us that he would aim to have the opening completed in a couple of days and then we could continue, if we were happy.

All good so far. We continued working with our cast and polishing the material that the previous composer had left us with. As promised two days later we went to hear the music that our new composer had written for the opening. All brilliantly realised with orchestral samples and sounds. We were very hushed as we listened to this beautiful haunting music and could easily visualise the rope dropping through the hole and the man descending down to the shell and then, suddenly all the beautiful music was drowned out by an awful caw-cawing, screeching and caterwauling. To say that we were shocked would be somewhat of an understatement and Gale spat out, "Stop!!! What the hell is that racket?" almost apoplectic with rage. Everything stopped for a second as the composer calmly said something to the translator. A minute later we were told, "Well that is where the goose flies out. Like you said…"

We looked towards each other and suddenly the penny dropped. The interpreter had mistakenly translated 'the gauze flies out' as 'the goose flies out'. You can imagine the relief and the mirth that followed. Obviously the lesson about clarity of translation and understanding stage terminology was very quickly learned as we all, including the composer, heaved a sigh of relief!

The show did eventually open in Sanya and some of it was actually pretty stylish but I am sure that Barney and I will think twice before embarking on something similar! There were many giggles and good times though and, as ever, much was learnt while we worked there.

So much so that when, in 2014, I was asked to work with Maria Friedman on a show with Don Black and about Don Black entitled *From Hackney to Hollywood*, Barney was my first choice to work with me as Assistant Musical Director and, of course, we had the effervescent Jen Green orchestrating as well. It was a short tour around the country with Ria Jones, Gary Wilmott, Martine McCutcheon, Jack McManus and Ricardo Afonso. Great fun.

Bodyguard The Musical had been talked about for a year or so and the initial idea, with Oscar winner Alexander Dinelaris writing the script based on Lawrence Kasdan's original screenplay but making it much less diegetic than the movie, in other words finding places where the story is propelled and developed by the songs as opposed to just there as performance within the narrative, really appealed to me. As we got further into pre-production and then to rehearsals it became apparent that there was apprehension about going in that direction.

Thea Sharrock, a hugely bright and able theatre director, who incidentally made the rehearsal time an absolute joy by allowing everyone to feel very safe to experiment in the room, didn't fully embrace the Musical Theatre ethos and ultimately decisions were made that, to my mind, simply made the show a play with music. Alex and I did manage to get a couple of moments of pure MT in, nevertheless, and the two songs that stood out for me were the duet in Act 1, *Run To You*, for Rachel and her sister Nicki, where we get to see a glimpse of really using the song to move the narrative along plus their hidden yearning for the new bodyguard and in Act 2, *All the Man That I Need*, where we use the song to express, first, Rachel's honest feelings just after her first night of passion with her bodyguard, The Bodyguard no less, and as the number develops we morph from the bedroom to a full on recording studio with gospel harmonies and very full orchestration as if it was the finished track.

The show has become hugely successful and was a major hit at the Adelphi Theatre in the West End and worldwide. This was the last of my collaborations with Chris Egan as I am pleased to say that his career has become stellar in both TV drama and film. I did the vocal arrangements and together we routined the songs with Chris orchestrating the final versions. Richard Beadle, ex *Grease* and *Hair*, was our Musical Director and now looks after the show as Musical Supervisor with me as Production Musical Supervisor.

The choice of actors to play the lead roles was never more critical and our original cast of Broadway legend Heather Headley as Rachel with Lloyd Owen as the Bodyguard and Debbie Kurup as sister Nicki really landed perfectly. Gloria Onitiri, Beverley

Knight and Alexandra Burke have subsequently played Rachel and all of them have found individual takes on the original. No-one is trying to ever emulate Whitney but there are always the inevitable comparisons. I am just so pleased that all of them proved that they can both act and act in song.

Somehow my next musical venture was the antithesis of *Bodyguard* but it was immensely satisfying and enjoyable. *The New London Chorale* has been a bit of a phenomenon in the Netherlands over many years – a group of four contemporary singers performing a mixture of classical songs given a pop treatment by their director, Tom Parker – a vocal *Hooked On Classics*, if you like. Since their creation in 1979 the four singers have included Madeline Bell, Vicki Brown, Gordon Neville and Janet Mooney. Unfortunately in 2013 Tom died and I was called by Janet, who I have known as one of the best of the session singers since the early 1990s, and she asked me if I could join them as piano player and MD for a little Christmas gig they were doing.

The four singers turned out to be Janet, Jenna Lee James (from *We Will Rock You*), Gordon Neville (who I knew from early days on *Grease* when we had session singers singing in the booth) and Lance Ellington (one of the most sought after session singers around and a regular singer on *Strictly Come Dancing*), so it was brilliant – I knew all of them! The little gig turned out to be a Christmas and New Year special TV show filmed live in Jaarbeurs Utrecht Hall 1 with the Dutch Metropole Orkest (the Dutch equivalent of the BBC Concert Orchestra), The Inspirational Community Gospel Choir with special guests The Three Degrees and Tavares in front of an audience of around 5,000 people!

There was a lot of sadness as this was the first gig without Tom and I completely respected that and did what I could to generally musically direct their performance without getting in the way. I was very aware that this was really HIS gig. During the TV show there was a little moment of 'in memoriam' for Tom then the orchestra started, conducted by Maurice Luttikhuis, I played the grand piano and the four of them sang their hearts out.

It worked so well that I was asked to be their permanent MD and whenever I could, over the next few years, I joined them for both this regular Christmas/New Year gig and some summer tours. At the subsequent Max Proms Christmas and New Year shows the star turns included Kool and the Gang, The Trampps and Jermaine Jackson, and the staging was expertly finessed by Brian Rogers who I had worked with on a couple of *Royal Variety Shows*.

The little tours were particularly fun as it was just the four of them singing with me on piano for most of the performance. There was occasional respite with orchestral tracks on some of the bigger numbers but we made sure that there was always an 'unplugged' section which gave a very different and intimate feel to the show. You will read about my last gigs with them in the next chapter – I'm still not sure how I did those two concerts!

*

When you hear the words Theatre Royal, Stratford East, I don't know about you but I am immediately taken to a time and place where invention and creativity was at its absolute zenith and an utterly unique woman called Joan Littlewood ruled the roost with the likes of Barbara Windsor, Victor Spinetti and Murray Melvin attached to her apron strings. So when I had a call in 2013 from director Terry Johnson (he of *Cleo, Camping, Emmanuelle and Dick* fame, the play about the off-screen love affair between that same Barbara Windsor and her *Carry On* partner Sid James) and producer Chris Malcolm (the original Brad in *The Rocky Horror Show*) about their plan to make a new production of *Oh, What A Lovely War!* fifty years after the original but on the same stage and exactly one hundred years after the start of the First World War you will not be surprised to learn that I jumped at the chance!

I think the whole process of putting this piece on and being Musical Director for its initial run in Stratford East is one of my all time favourite experiences. I also decided that I would take on writing both the new vocal arrangements and the orchestrations – with dear Jen Green booked as copyist this time – so I was right back to being fully immersed in the creation of a fantastic new vision of a piece of theatrical history.

Terry is very much a cerebral director but with a wicked sense of humour and, if you catch him right, he has an abundance of wild and filthy stories to tell. Truth be told we got on quite well, really. Can't think why...

The show retained its Pierrot roots and the cast assembled, Caroline Quentin, Shaun Prendergast, Ian Bartholomew, Alex Giannini, Michael Simkins, Zoe Rainey, Alice Bailey Johnson, Tom Lorcan, Rebecca Howell, Ciaran Owens, Oliver J Hembrough, Kyle Redmond-Jones, Leanne Harwood and Marcus Ellard, was a fabulous mixture of serious actors and musical theatre performers. All were great actors and all were there with the single aim of telling the narrative as truthfully and as honestly as possible. Input from them all was valued and frequently acted upon. It was almost as if the ghost of Joan had spread her wisdom into the ether within the theatre to be accessed as and when it was needed, but only by those worthy of its fluence.

I had a smaller band than the original, finances at the theatre only allowed for five players, so I decided on piano: me, double bass: Frazer Snell, drums (with some timps and glockenspiel):

Ryan Martin, with a front line of trumpet: Graham Justin and cello: Llinos Richards. Slightly unusual but I desperately wanted the broadest palette of sound and definitely no electronics, to the point that for the church service section in Act Two I searched on eBay while we were rehearsing for an authentic old harmonium which was duly delivered and used for the whole run and subsequent tour.

Having the cello with the trumpet gave me a glorious string sound for rhapsodic moments and depth and support in more aggressive rhythmic military moments. It is such a versatile instrument and when played by someone like Llinos (or Sarah Bowler in the tour the following year) it is worth its weight in gold. I remembered that Mike Reed had used the cello as second front line instrument to the soprano saxophone in *Mr Cinders* in 1983 and just how much musical juice he had squeezed out of it. My mentors still casting a positive shadow over me more than thirty years later!

The show was received hugely positively and it kept its edgy feel with the futility of war at its core. Every night I felt totally immersed in the tragic narrative and its gradual journey from comedic mockery to devastating human loss. The lampooning aspect of the piece as potent in 2014 as it was when first created in 1963.

When we put the tour together a year later the past caught up with me again because Chris Villiers, who had been in the production of *Godspell* that I did in Exeter and Nottingham at the end of 1980 into 1981, was asked to be in the show and play the controversial 'donkey leading the lions' Field Marshal Haig. It was a happy reunion.

One other interesting and little explored fact is that *Oh, What A Lovely War!* is, in effect, one of the first Jukebox Musicals. It uses songs of the time, from *Goodbye…ee*, to *Pack Up Your Troubles*, *Keep the Homefires Burning* and *It's A Long*

Way to Tipperary to push the narrative line forward and the songs used at the end, *La Chanson de Craonne* and *And When They Ask Us* which was actually a parody lyric by Cole Porter, after the original Jerome Kern song, *They Didn't Believe Me*, were used with devastating effect and never failed to move me to tears every night.

The title song, which was male impersonator Ella Shields' signature song *Oh! It's A Lovely War* written by J. P. Long and Maurice Scott in 1917, underpinned the production perfectly and though many of the other songs had lyric alterations to make them more pertinent to the show, this song's lyrics stayed the same and I still find it puzzling that 'It's' rather than 'What' remained. I suspect that there had been a publishing issue with changing that one simple word. Whatever the reason *Oh, What A Lovely War!* was never actually sung, except by accident...

Although the show wasn't filmed, BBC Radio 2 wanted to use it as part of their centenary season about the Great War, so consequently it was recorded and transmitted as a special *Friday Night Is Music Night*. For me a rather poignant fusion of two aspects of my career.

Kerry Michael was artistic director at Stratford East and while *Oh, What A Lovely War!* was running he asked me if I would like to be involved with another of their projects. This was a musical version of David Baddiel's hit film, *The Infidel*, with songs written by Baddiel and Erran Baron Cohen. I loved the juxtaposition of the seriousness of *War!* mixed with the profanity of *Infidel* so I agreed. It proved to be quite a challenge but the end result was one of the funniest, offensive and entertaining shows that I have been involved with.

With songs entitled *Sexy Burqa*, *Put a Fatwa On It*, and *My Name is Jihad* and with a basic storyline telling the tale of an ordinary British Muslim man, Mahmoud, who discovers that not only is he adopted, but that his birth parents were Jewish, what's not to like?

I worked with another of the new generation of great Musical Directors again, Matt Smith, who had been Musical Director on *Footloose, Never Forget* and *We Will Rock You* in Germany for me. He has such a calm assurance about him, nothing is ever too much trouble and he is a super talented musician to boot.

Kev Orkian played Mahmoud, with Mina Anwar as his wife Saamiyah, Andrew Paul as Lenny, Alexander Andreou as Arshad and Siobhan Athwal, Melanie Marshall, Melanie Masson, Gary Wood and Steven Serlin playing the multifarious other parts. A fabulously diverse cast and with great talent.

There have been a couple of attempts since 2014 to resurrect the piece and bring it to the West End but as yet it remains one of those 'what could have been' shows.

After *Oh, What A Lovely War!* Terry Johnson talked to me about another war related project that he was working on. This time he was writing the book and directing a new musical version of the film all about the celebrated Windmill Theatre entitled *Mrs Henderson Presents*. Don Black, who I knew well, of course, was writing the lyrics and George Fenton and Simon Chamberlain the music. Now George, celebrated film composer, I had never met but Simon I had worked with on a number of occasions as he is one of the absolute top session piano players in the country. He had played for me on at least two of the *Royal Variety Shows* and a few sessions over the years. George and Simon worked together a lot and had written the original music for the movie as well. A formidable duo.

We talked at great length about who should orchestrate the musical and I was hoping to get Jen Green on board. Larry Blank, a fellow *Friday Night* conductor and very experienced Broadway Musical Director and orchestrator, was eventually decided upon. Experience being the deciding factor. In a way I wish that I had pushed harder for Jen but Larry, in all fairness, did create some absolutely masterly charts that made our little eight piece band, obviously including cello, sound gorgeous.

Emma Williams had been approached to play the young Windmill girl Maureen. I knew Emma very well because she had played Luisa in *Zorro*, beautiful voice and proper musical theatre acting chops. The role of Mrs Henderson was eventually taken with great style and class by Tracie Bennett, who had recently played Judy Garland in *End of the Rainbow* directed by Terry, and Vivian Van Damm elegantly played by Ian Bartholomew who was Field Marshal Haig in the first production of *Oh, What A Lovely War!* at Stratford East in 2014. I had asked Barney Ashworth to work with me on this and he was initially Assistant Musical Director then, after we transferred to the Noel Coward Theatre in 2016, Barney took over conducting duties a few weeks after we opened.

This show also had the delicate job of delivering a quasi historical view of what happened at the Windmill through those years leading up to and including the Second World War. That necessitated some very carefully devised nude vignettes for some of the girls, a full frontal moment at the end of Act One for Maureen and a raucously funny scene in which some of the 'stage crew' and Vivian Van Damm get embroiled in an argument about said nude scenes with the ladies, which culminates in some of the chaps exposing themselves as well. So basically nearly everyone except Mrs Henderson and the Lord Chancellor have to 'get their kit off' in some way or another during the show.

Terry worked out a beautiful way of broaching this by making a very inclusive and safe environment for everyone to rehearse in. At the end of the Tuesday of the third week of rehearsals he announced that the following morning all the cast members who had agreed to be naked would go together to the upstairs room where there would be a closed rehearsal to empower and acclimatise everyone. He quietly explained to me that he would talk about the whole ethos of the Windmill, with the nude girls always static as if in a painting, which is how they managed to get through the strict censorship laws laid down by the Lord Chamberlain, and would I mind playing some gentle in period music as he took the class.

On the Wednesday morning Terry, the stage manager, most of the cast and I traipsed upstairs for the great exposé. There was some tittering and much anticipation. Nothing really changes, I was immediately transported back to my first foray into nudity on stage, *Hair* in 1980, and the anticipatory giggling seems to be a rite of passage! No-one else was allowed into the room and Terry started his spiel. He spoke beautifully about the relationship between nudity and art, the history of the Windmill Theatre itself and what he was proposing would happen. Everyone in the room was transfixed and eating out of his hand.

As he finished his speech he casually announced that he would give everyone a piece of paper with a style of pose written on it – elegant Greek statue, strongman, holding an urn, innocent, shocked, holding a bow and arrow – that sort of thing. Then he nodded to me to start playing and said he would gently go round the room and touch the head of each person in turn and following on from each other they should quickly undress and walk to the makeshift stage and make their pose. I should also say that he had suggested that everyone wear loose clothing so that undressing would be simple, quick and in no way embarrassing.

The next ten minutes were completely beguiling as everyone in turn calmly and quietly made their way to the front, composed themselves and created their pose. Rather than being titillating it was entirely charming and all nerves seemed to evaporate as everyone joined in. In the end Terry also made a nude pose and I could sit clothed at the piano no longer, so I too took off my clothes and walked to the front, made a pose and went back to playing, not like Terry Jones in Monty Python, I hasten to add, though it may have looked similar. Once that ice was broken there was some gentle walking around the room, looking only into people's eyes and then as quickly as it had started the class was over.

Laconic George Fenton is tall, very smiley with piercing eyes that seem to constantly question anything you say and the blend of his personality with Simon's sometimes gruff northern 'heart on your sleeve' brusqueness is complex at times but they wrote some truly beautiful songs in this piece. Some were very deliberately pastiche numbers, *He's Got Another Think Coming*, *Everybody Loves the Windmill*, and others, like *Innocent Soldier, Whatever Time I Have* and *If Mountains Were Easy to Climb*, were stream of consciousness contemporary music theatre songs that required genuine acting through song techniques to make them work. Our cast were quality performers singing with real understanding of the lyric, the journey and in the moment.

How to describe Tracie Bennett? She is Dangerous, Inventive, Versatile and Astonishing all bundled up in one constantly questioning small and powerful frame. As the capital letters suggest, she is a true DIVA. We had a few run-ins during rehearsals. They were mostly about how much space she needed to sing *Whatever Time I Have* and eventually we found an equilibrium and a way that was both musical and enabled her to really 'live' Don Black's wonderful lyrics.

She can also pretty much drink anyone under the table as I discovered one evening after rehearsals. Simon joined us in the little pub around the corner from our rehearsal venue, The Union Chapel in Islington, and we set to with a bottle of red wine and fiery discussion about the show. Very quickly we were on to our second bottle, then third, fourth, can't really remember. We were all three of us so absorbed by the conversation we didn't think about eating anything and eventually at around ten I decided to wend my way homeward. Simon and Tracie stayed for one more. Somehow I made my way to Pinner station on the underground but when I got off the train I suddenly couldn't remember how to walk home. I really had no clue. Help! A twenty minute walk that I had done an awful lot of times over the years. What to do? I couldn't even articulate enough to get a taxi. So I did the only thing that I could think of in my stupor, I phoned Natalie – at least I could remember how to do that. She wasn't home. Of course she wasn't, she was in Cornwall and out with some of our close friends at Treyarnon. Fortunately she realised very quickly that essentially I had been rendered completely insensible by drinking too much with Tracie and Simon. She gently and patiently 'talked me home', much to the mirth and merriment of our pals beside her, and after around thirty minutes or so I magically found myself outside our familiar little white cottage, unscathed. A sore head the next day, yes. Tracie bowled up to rehearsals completely ok. Sharp and on it. She howled when I told her my story. All power to her but the winner for me was Natalie!

Part of my job was to meld the show into a cohesive musical and that involved creating underscores and dance breaks as well as scene change music to move us from one place to another. Generally all that is pretty straightforward and simple discussions between composers, director and Musical Director sort them out but just occasionally you get to show some originality of thought and there was one place in *Mrs H* that I am particularly proud of and that was the transition between the end of the reprise of *Now Is Not The Time* into the underground scene that contains the song *Innocent Soldier*. It was only eleven bars long and I called it *Elegy into Underground Scene* (how original) but I managed to get three song quotes into those bars with a dark change of mood. The point is that, like so many other crafted moments in musicals, if you notice them then they are too intrusive or simply wrong, but, if you as audience are transported emotionally without noticing then they have served the drama and the moment and your job is done.

We made a cast album which was recorded in Air Lyndhurst and Angel Studios. All the promotional recordings, which were recorded with a much enhanced orchestra, were recorded in Abbey Road. In the show itself, I played piano and conducted, but for these recordings I conducted, George produced in the control room and Simon played piano, which was a luxury for me and meant that I could concentrate on simply waving.

When the show was remounted in Toronto in 2017 Tracie reprised her role as Mrs Henderson and she was joined by Evelyn Hoskins as Maureen and the absolute legend that is Peter Polycarpou as Vivian Van Damm. Barney wasn't available so Francis Goodhand, who I had known from *The Ten Minute Musical Challenge* in 2006, became Musical Director and a fine job of keeping the show in top musical order he did too.

Mrs Henderson Presents was one of those near misses in the end. It received mixed reviews, the audiences seemed to love it but it only survived its initial six month run and didn't extend. A great pity.

Three weeks after *Mrs Henderson* opened at the Noel Coward Theatre I had some meetings with two remarkable women about a project that became the single most complicated and weird in my career. That's not to say that I haven't done a few weird things before – I did a workshop/masterclass for some heads of NATO in 2015 and just recently I played for a Zoom meeting of the ITU section of the United Nations – but this one out 'weirds' all of them.

Catherine Ugwu and Kate Hinchliffe, under the auspices of Catherine's company, Betty Productions, asked me to be Music Director for the *Opening* and *Closing Ceremonies* of the *4th Islamic Solidarity Games* in Baku, Azerbaijan. I knew them both because I had previously worked on the *Launch Ceremony* of the *2015 European Games* in Baku and as Catherine was Executive Producer of Ceremonies for *London 2012* our paths had crossed when I did the *Welcoming the World* project heralding the London Olympics in 2008.

Kate had been Catherine's assistant for *London 2012* but for Baku, Kate was a producer in her own right with Catherine as executive producer. That being said, Catherine is one of the most hands on executive producers I have ever come across. She has leadership qualities in abundance and a clarity of vision and drive that is totally infectious. Kate has also followed in her mentor's footsteps and leads elegantly and persuasively but never with any hint of dominance or arrogance.

So in my first meeting with Kate about this project she introduced me to Australian Nathan M. Wright who was artistic director. Nathan is young, vibrant with an infectious smile and bags of positive energy and this was his first Artistic Director job, though he had a history of working as a choreographer on other ceremonies including *London 2012* and was steeped in musical theatre. We sat and chatted about the ramifications of the job. It ended up that we were going to work on the *Launch, Opening and Closing Ceremonies* together and he outlined his initial vision of what they would be. We were meeting around fourteen months before the *Opening Ceremony* so you can see that the lead time for these events is enormous.

The contract ended up being just over a year and I was able to assemble a really top notch music team around me. I asked Marc Tritschler and Malcolm Newton to be my two associates. Malcolm, an experienced Musical Director with a great tenacity for detail, would be in Baku for the final nine months leading up to the event, so in effect, he would be my Baku liaison. Marc, who had been Musical Director for one of the versions of *We Will Rock You* in Germany and who is the *ying* to Malcolm's *yang*, stayed in the UK until the last couple of months so he became my UK liaison. I had meetings in Baku every couple of weeks until the last three months when I also decamped to Baku.

I was so pleased that I was able to get Jen Green on board, without question, to look after all the orchestrations and then I spoke to Ian Maclay, who was then in charge of bookings for the Royal Philharmonic Orchestra to ask them to play for all the recording sessions. That in effect became two CDs worth of music. Naturally I asked to use Abbey Road to record all the orchestral stuff. One week with a seventy-five piece line up in Studio 1, a second week with a thirty piece line up in Studio 2 and then two further weeks to mix and finish off. I managed to secure the services of Steve Price, who I had worked with on a number of occasions, including the Rogers and Hammerstein sessions at Angel for Helena Blackman, as lead recording engineer so I knew that I would be in very safe hands. That was January 2017.

Every musical element of the three events came under my jurisdiction and as the preparations developed with Catherine, Kate and Nathan, so did the creative team. Ultimately it was the most internationally diverse group of people I have ever worked with. Well, here is an example. The first Production Meeting in Baku, which was in the middle of 2016, had around eight heads of department around the table. By the time we got to the final few Production Meetings there were twenty-two HODs and at least thirty associates and assistants in the back row. We had Brits, Australians, Greeks, Japanese, Italians, Canadians, Americans as well as a vast army of Azeri folk working with us.

The President and First Lady of Azerbaijan, Ilham Aliyev and Mehriban Aliyev were very hands on during the whole process. I had to source as much Azerbaijan music as possible and incorporate it into the shows. I also composed some of the music used and every time Nathan, Catherine and Kate approved a running order the music was either approved or rejected by the President and his wife. One of the pieces that I wrote was the *Fanfare* that was used to actually open the games once the President made his declaration. I wrote something that I thought was very bombastic and military and submitted it, fully expecting it to be rejected. It was one of the first pieces of music approved. Sometimes the most obvious is the best way to go. There were other places in the performance element of both the *Opening* and *Closing* where in the end we submitted well over six different musical ideas before the seal of approval came to us. It was a fascinating, if sometimes frustrating, experience.

Very early on in the process, Director Nathan had come round to my house to talk through the project and we threw some musical ideas back and forth. When I had been in Baku back in 2015 for the *European Games Launch Ceremony* I had been given a huge collection of recorded Azeri music ranging from classical through jazz to modern day, hours of it. One of the pieces that had stuck in my memory was a rhapsodic piano concerto written by a man called Farhad Badalbeyli. When Nathan explained that the performance section of the *Opening Ceremony* was to start with a young girl flying a kite with her grandfather in the park and that this girl and her kite would then take us on a journey through Azeri cultural history, I immediately thought of this piece. It is called *The Sea* and has wonderful soaring orchestral melodies with wild and flowing piano arpeggios.

He listened quietly as I played it to him and then suddenly he leapt up grinning from ear to ear and started dancing around the music room, whooping. We had found our first piece. Fortunately Badalbeyli is very well known in Azerbaijan and the seal of approval came from on high almost straight after it was submitted. Nathan and I heaved sighs of relief and knew that we would be able to add more glorious music to this piece over time but this was the way in. On our recording the RPO were joined by Ben Dawson on piano, he had just the right amount of 'bravura' about his playing and it truly soars.

In the process I learnt a huge amount about the great canon of music written by some frankly stunning Azeri composers. Composers whose works should be heard in all the concert halls around the world, not just over there. Names that we just don't know in the West, like Uzeyir Hajibayli, Gara Garayev, Eldar Mansurov, Vasif Adigozalov, Tofiq Zulfugarov, Arif Melikov, Maestro Niyazi and the unbelievable Fikret Amirov. It is a rich tradition and though some of it is steeped in Azerbaijan's Russian heritage there is so much music that has an individual sound. A fusion of Russian, Iranian and Turkish but sounding totally unique, as you would expect given Azerbaijan's geographical position.

So in January 2017 we set about recording everything brand new. We even recorded a new version of the Azeri *National Anthem*. Now it's not every country that has their *National Anthem* played by an orchestra of the calibre of the RPO, is it? The two weeks of recording were blissful. Jen had produced absolutely beautiful new orchestrations along with her assistant orchestrators Thomas Hewitt Jones and Callum Au and I had the arduous job (not!) of conducting the orchestra, with Marc and Malcolm there checking everything (and making sure the tight schedules were adhered to) and Steve Price just being his brilliant self recording it all.

The orchestra, led by their regular leader, Duncan Riddell, played with such passion and intensity. It was a complete joy standing in front of them and hearing this music as if for the first time. Some of it massive scale symphonic and some almost like chamber music. Of course the few pieces that I had penned were also pretty amazing to hear for the first time being played by one of the greatest orchestras in the world, I felt very humbled and honoured, another of those 'pinch myself' moments, really.

2017 My view of the RPO in Abbey Road Studio 1 BAKU Recording

2017 Steve Price, Marc Tritschler, Malcolm Newton & Jen Green
BAKU Recording Abbey Road

Once that was all finished we took all the master recordings to Azerbaijan and in March we overdubbed some Azeri musicians in the handful of places where we needed them. Meeting and auditioning the Azeris was an experience in itself. There are such rich veins of talent in Baku and our musicians were the very best.

We needed Balaban (a beautiful double reed woodwind instrument), Zurna and Tutek (double reed instruments, higher and with more edge to the sound), Tar and Oud (guitar like instruments), Kamancha (a bowed stringed instrument) and various Naghara players (types of drum). They were recorded at a little studio called Promix at the end of March. Our Azeri musical liaison was a very clever composer in his own right called Azad Valiyev and he became a great ally in the whole process. Very talented man.

There was one other musician that I worked with on this journey who should be mentioned. Natiq. An Azeri National Treasure with his fusion of folk rhythms and modern contemporary music rhythms and an absolute genius with his drum troupe. In 2015 I had met him as his troupe was used in the *Launch Ceremony* of the European Games and we found the ideal place for him for these Games in 2017. As the huge procession of athletes finished their walk around the stadium on came Natiq and the crowd went wild. Legend.

One of the most remarkable aspects of working on events of this magnitude is the sheer diversity of disciplines needed to bring the whole thing to fruition. Not just direction, choreography, music, set design, costume design, stage management, video content, sound, lights and volunteer performers, but also aerial performers, livestock wranglers, fire performers, pyro designers, military advisors, flag management, protocol advisors and government ministers.

As I have throughout my career, I wanted to know about

as many people as I could once we got into the Baku Olympic Stadium eight weeks before the *Opening Ceremony*. I got to know the aerialists led by Phil Hayes, the horse wranglers led by Steve Jefferys, stage management led by Sam Hunter, video content led by Richard Lindsay, project management by Piers Shepperd, lighting by Adam Bassett, as many of the content producers as I could but particularly Panos Adamopoulos, stadium sound led by Scott Wilsallen, the pyro specialists, props led by Pam Nichol, the designers, Joanna Scotcher and Thanassis Demiris, costume designers, Tim Chappel and Susan Kulkarni, casting (a huge department looking after all the volunteer performers) led by Lorenzo Gentile and logistics led by the ever considerate Valie Voutsa. I knew the TV director, Julia Knowles who had directed *The Shane Richie Experience* back in 1995/96 as well as a few of the camera operators and even head of health and safety, Conrad Schwartz who had been Master Carpenter at *Grease* at the Dominion Theatre back in 1993! A mass of people at the absolute top end of all their professions and all assembled by Catherine and Kate.

Everything was going amazingly well in the stadium. All the vast amounts of set were built and all the flying wires, sound equipment, lighting and cameras were untangled and hung. We had performed two full dress rehearsals and one of those was for the President and First Lady. All was approved.

In the late afternoon on the day of the one and only performance of the *Opening Ceremony* I was sitting with Marc, Malcolm and our music editor Max Trieder in the music room, tucked under the vast stadium on the ground floor, when a message was delivered. It read, 'Mike, can you come and meet Catherine and Kate in the VIP area, please. It is urgent.'

Well, I knew exactly where they were as the VIP area had been where we had assembled to watch all the major rehearsals, but now it was full of VIPs, VVIPs and security was as tight as the proverbial. I arrived five minutes later and was ushered into one of the plush ante rooms. I was introduced to the President's Head of Protocol and the highest ranking Imam in the country. Nathan and Kate were there and Catherine started speaking. She chose her words very carefully and explained that there was a 'problem' with the 'Belief' section of the performance.

Quick bit of background. The section referred to was nearly five minutes long, it had five hundred volunteer cast walking in a heightened choreographed pattern, the top Mugham singer in the world, Alim Qasimov, singing the *Call to Prayer* (actually miming to his own recording) atop one of the two twenty metre high minarets on the set and there was an end section where I arranged a beautiful version of the revered Azeri song *Sen Gelmuz Oldun* for balaban and the RPO strings. The whole five minutes, like most of the rest of the event, was completely linked with video content and lighting and was pre loaded into the extraordinary playback machine up in the control area at the very top of the stadium.

So, Catherine further explained that the version of the *Call To Prayer* that we had recorded with Alim was actually the wrong version. It was Sunni rather than Shi'a, and therefore contained some sentences that could have caused major offence to many of the competing nations. I asked if there was a compromise that could be brokered and the Imam told me that there were six of the sentences, sung amazingly by Alim, that we could use. I felt a little like a musical swan at this point, I was looking serene and calm but underneath my musical 'legs' were going five hundred to the dozen. I isolated which those sentences were, asked them to give me twenty minutes and hurried back to my music room.

Basically there were sixty seconds of the four minutes forty seconds that needed to be replaced, pronto! Marc, Malcolm and Max (you had to have a first name beginning with an M to be in the Music Dept in Baku, obviously) were primed and our guests, including Natalie, were alerted to the fact that we may be a little late meeting them before the ceremony began.

Now as you can imagine the journey from VIP section back to the subterranean music room was achieved in PDQ time and we worked out a modus operandi very quickly indeed. My suggestion was that I edit the incorrect sentences out and see if the string accompaniment used underneath the balaban playing the tune at the end could work just as the *Call To Prayer* ends and before the solo balaban plays *Sen Gelmuz Oldun.*

I set to on my computer while Marc and Malcolm alerted Alim that I would need to see him in a few minutes and that we had been told we had to make changes. Max was in charge of liaising with show control and getting the finished track into the playback machine. My idea was good and as if by a miracle the plan worked.

The strings on their own sounded beautiful in the middle of the piece and melded out of Alim's sung sentences as if we had intended it that way from the beginning. Then when the balaban played the tune it landed with even more resonance. I ran back to Catherine computer in hand, played the assembled dignitaries my proposal and got it approved.

The new track was an identical length: four minutes and forty seconds. All the time-coded lights and video could stay the same and essentially all the performers would be able to make their choreographic patterns in exactly the same sequence. I phoned Max and told him to leg it to show control and get the new track loaded.

Once that was done it was quite simple talking through the changes with Alim. He is a consummate professional and got it straight away. The choreographers were linked to the performers through 'in ear' technology the whole time, so they were able to talk the performers through the sequence but, the reality was that the entire team heard and saw the new version of the sequence only during the performance. 'For one night only' had special resonance for me in Baku! It was especially heartening when, as the solo balaban started playing *Sen Gelmuz Oldun,* the audience applauded and cheered for their familiar tune. International incident averted, quite literally!

The whole experience of being Music Director for these ceremonies really utilised everything I have learnt from my theatre, television, radio and live event musical career and taught me a whole lot more, so to say that I enjoyed it would be such an understatement – I bloody loved it!

One very sad note to my Baku experience. When we were in the final throws of rehearsals in early May 2017 I heard that Steve Price, recording engineer and friend, had been diagnosed with liver cancer. He died in September and the Baku recordings were some of his last. Everyone wanted to work with him, he was one of the very best.

In June of 2017, following on from working with them on the Baku recordings, the RPO asked me to conduct a concert of 'lollipops' for the Hampton Court Festival. *Fanfares and Fireworks.* It was certainly fun and, unlike all those *Friday Night is Music Night* concerts, I didn't have a compere so I had to do it myself. To be honest, I rather enjoyed it until I was introducing Elgar's *Nimrod* when I heard a little bit of heckling. In true 'live event' fashion I carried on regardless. The shouting got a little louder and I eventually stopped and it was only then that I realised that the 'heckling' was in fact a couple of people calling for a doctor. Apparently someone had fainted. Thank goodness it wasn't too serious and five minutes later we continued the concert. The joys of live music.

The rest of 2017 was filled with prep for the new version of *Doctor Dolittle*, which included a workshop, and prep for a concert with a singer/performance artist called Wrenne. Very distinctive and original and the show we developed was taken to the Edinburgh Fringe in 2018, called, *I Said Yes to Everything* and directed by one of my enthusiastic and inventive friends, Hugo Vereker.

FIFTEEN

THE CANCER FILES

The year 2018 had started amazingly well. Natalie and I had the trip of a lifetime – a month in South America, starting in Santiago and finishing in Rio de Janeiro with all points in between, including the Iguazu Falls and most importantly Estancia Cóndor in Patagonia, where Natalie's Mum and siblings spent their formative years. To call it a farm would not do it any justice whatsoever. Cóndor is nearly 542,000 acres and has 220,000 sheep. Basically it is the size of Herefordshire and when Natalie's grandfather was the manager back in the 40s and 50s it was a huge enterprise with a hundred plus 'Gauchos' working there, with those numbers at least doubling during sheep shearing time.

Witnessing Natalie realising her lifelong dream of standing on its somewhat hallowed ground is the third of my special life changing moments. Her face was an absolute picture as we turned the corner in our little Fiat Panda hire car, after negotiating a hundred miles or so of completely unmade road, to see the settlement with all the buildings and their red corrugated iron roofs. A picture! Almost as much of a picture as a couple of days later when we arrived at The British Club in Rio Gallegos where her grandfather had been president in 1958, for a cocktail party put on especially for us. They served never-ending Pisco Sours and proper deep fried empanadas made from lamb pino all evening and we were most honoured to be there, however, it would be true to say that we were more than a little tipsy when we repaired to our hotel!

The holiday finished with a couple of days in Rio on Copacabana Beach and we returned to London exhilarated and buoyed by how brilliant the four weeks had been.

Then I noticed a lump on the side of my neck, that's all it was, and my doctor thought I should have it checked out as it was more than five centimetres across. What follows is the trail of emails I sent out following the subsequent cancer diagnosis. Happy to report that I am continuing to be cancer free as of writing in 2021.

*

Email 1

27/3/18

Greets lovely chaps,

Sorry to say that I have been diagnosed with some cancer cells in a swollen lymph gland in my neck which I noticed back in mid Feb. Yesterday Natalie and I were given the results of a biopsy which I had two weeks ago. They think that whatever it is is curable, thankfully, but the next few weeks will be MRIs, PET/CTs and X-rays to determine exactly where the cancer is coming from – probably head or neck – and then consultations to work out treatment.

Yesterday was a bit of a surreal day but I remain positive and with Natalie at my side I will get through whatever the next few months deliver.

Sending lots of love to you all,
    Mike xxx

Email 2

9/4/18

Hi lovely peeps,

A good meeting with my Consultant this morning where I have discovered that the cancer is most likely only in my neck and tongue and can be treated (& probably cured) with radio therapy.

Next week I have to have an endoscopy and biopsy of the lump in the tongue under full anaesthetic. All being well the radiotherapy treatment should start soon after that. So Natalie and I are mighty relieved, today!

Onwards with *Dr Dolittle* Auditions today and the rest of the week and Parkinson special with BBC Concert Orchestra on Friday & Saturday!!

Much love & thanks,
    Mike & Natalie x

Email 3

19/4/18

Lovely peeps,

You have been so generous in your messages, thoughts and well wishes – thank you so very much. Natalie and I have embarked on a journey and having all of you there as well is a great comfort to us both.

Today I had a meeting about my forthcoming procedure and, briefly, this is what is now happening to me:

Wednesday 25th I will have the Pan-endoscopy of my neck and a biopsy of my tongue plus, to enable me to start radiotherapy in the near future, I also have to have a few of my lower teeth taken out. Best to get all this done in one General Anaesthetic so Thursday and Friday next I may be a bit woozy and gummy!

I don't yet have the full treatment plan but once this procedure is done I will meet with my Consultant, Mr Kumar – at No. 42 – to discuss the full results of all the scans I have had and the tongue biopsy.

Hopefully I will know more in a couple of weeks. Suffice to say that our dear old NHS is continuing to be brilliant and though some of what I will have to have done to me is slightly daunting, I am confident that I will muscle through with all of your wonderful support and, of course, Natalie at my side.

Family and friends – HUGE thanks and much love from us both,
Mike & Natalie xxx

Email 4

4/5/18

Lovely chaps – family and friends,

Your kind words over the last few weeks continue to reverberate with us both – you are so kind, one and all!

Another chapter today in my Cancer Adventure/Challenge:
I met this morning with both my Oncologist and his Registrar (Dr Chiu and Dr Anna Anosova) then with some of my Treatment Team. An amazing bunch of Medical Professionals at Mount Vernon Hospital Cancer Centre.

The result of the tongue biopsy from April 25th was passed on and, without getting too technical, my Primary cancer is in the back of my tongue, called *Base tongue squamous carcinoma in the oropharynx region caused by HPV16 virus*. In other words a virus driven cancer. It is Stage 2, so treatable and hopefully curable. Very good news is that a) the cancer is nowhere else in my body and b) as said before very treatable.

So onto the treatment – Dr Chiu has recommended Radiotherapy treatment only. No Chemo because the side effects would, for me, outweigh the benefits. I will be having six weeks of daily radiotherapy. Side effects range from loss of taste (Natalie says I never had any anyway…) to inability to swallow, with a fair mixture of fun and frolic in between! Suffice to say it will be quite intense and I am having a feeding tube, straight into my stomach, fitted the week before treatment starts. My Radiotherapy dates are 21st May – 28th June then a period of 8-12 weeks recuperation.

To enable all this to happen I had to have a special mask fitted. I did point out to my Radiographer friend that I'd worked on *Zorro* but not on *Phantom* so could it be that mask, please? No such luck! My lovely girls, Lillie & Meg, have offered to paint it to look like Marvin from *Hitchhiker's Guide to the Galaxy* but that will have to wait until the treatment is finished and I bring it home! I also had to have a teeny little tattoo on my chest which will help them line the machine up. After this is over I may expand that into "I Love Natalie" with a huge Cupid's arrow.....

This Sunday Natalie and I will go to the West Country – first to see my Mum, sister and family – and then the rest of the week in our favourite place in the world, Treyarnon Bay. A little bit of r'n'r before the 14th May when I have further appointments to prepare me for the 21st and that first Radiotherapy session.

I have also become 'clean shaven Dixon' today as bits of my beard may well get lost during the therapy – feels quite different but Natalie did still recognise me!

Much love to you all,
    Mike & Natalie xxx

Email 5

16/5/18

Lovely chaps – family and friends,

Thank you so much for all the messages you have sent in the last few weeks. It serves to remind how important friends & family are and we are so, so lucky to have you there.

Natalie and I managed to grab our week, seeing family and then spending time together, in Cornwall. No surfing – didn't want to catch a cold – instead walks, talks & fine lunches. If my sense of taste does go during the radiotherapy then at least I've got some good epicurean memories to fall back on!!

Since Monday afternoon I've been in Northwick Park Hospital having my tummy tube fitted. I won't go into the details but let's just say it's not an experience I would care to repeat quickly and it will take a couple of weeks to heal properly. As ever the NHS professionals have been brilliant though. The tube will enable me to feed once the radiotherapy is in full swing and my jolly old mouth becomes a 'no go area'! I was sent home this afternoon, a little tender but ok!

I start the radiotherapy on my tongue and neck with my fetching mask next Monday and every weekday until June 28th. The sessions should only be 15-20mins a day and we are so lucky to have Mount Vernon Cancer Centre only 2 miles away. Various other clinic visits in the meantime so never a dull moment!

Life changing events like this do make you think a bit. The first thing that really hit me was the fact that I am mortal. I had to get to 61 years of age before that simple truth hit home! Things like this only happen to 'other' people, until you find yourself being that 'other' person! Realising and *accepting* my own mortality brings me to my second thought....*Living with Cancer*. We all too often only see cancer as another word for 'dying', but it should not be, because while you have cancer you are 'living' with the disease. I find myself with cancer and I am in that particularly fortunate position of having a cancer that is probably curable, but if you find yourself with cancer, whatever type it is, you will be living with it, and somehow that definition must help in the day to day dealings with it.

Sending lots of love to all of you,
Mike & Natalie xxx

Email 6

26/5/18

Dear friends and family,

A heart felt thank you for your messages and all your kind thoughts aimed this way over the past ten days or so. They are much appreciated as this journey continues.

My tummy tube (or my 'second mouth' – as christened by Lillie & Meg last Sunday) has now pretty much healed and so far it is mostly there for decorative purposes! However I am pretty sure that in the coming two weeks I will be pressing it into service as swallowing becomes more and more difficult and number one mouth becomes a moisture only zone. I am getting used to the idea…

The Radiotherapy Treatment has now started and Week One is done – hoorah – only another five weeks to go!

I'm attaching a picture taken on Wednesday literally right after the session finished.

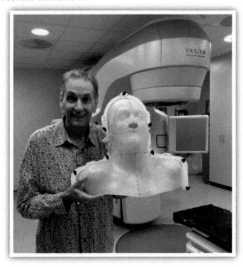

Briefly I am pinned onto the bed in that mask – very tightly so that there can be no movement – and for the fifteen minutes I lie there with my eyes closed. I hear clicks, buzzes, whirrs, whines & clunks as the machine does its stuff until finally there is a further 'kadunk' followed by the radiologist coming back into the room with a cheery 'All done for today'. I am pretty adept at recognising that 'kadunk' now, it has become my friend, actually, because seconds after it I regain my freedom and the mask is unclicked and removed. It is completely bearable, though, and how brilliantly quickly our minds and bodies get used to 'the strange' as it morphs into 'the norm'! Though my mouth feels a little different the only real side effect this week is nausea. My NHS team continues to be brilliant and I am now finding out which drugs will be most effective in relieving me of this 'feeling sick' nuisance. Yesterday Nurse Leah offered me Dom Pérignon.... when I asked her to repeat what she had said I realised it was Domperidone she was suggesting. Not quite the same but hopefully it will help!

Natalie is managing her patient extremely well and I have a full list of mouth exercises, mouth washes, pain relief etc etc all neatly put into Mike's Daily Cancer Schedule which keeps my day busy. We've included Piano Playing and Walks to the list to help keep our sanity, too.

So as my Cancer Adventure continues Natalie and I send love to you all,
    Mike & Natalie xxx

Email 7

8/6/18

Dear friends and family,

The adventure moves on and your kind messages continue to add to the resolve that Natalie and I have to beat this cancer, so thank you, one and all!

End of week 3 of Radiotherapy – HALFWAY!!!

Flowery shirts, flip flops, strange hats – yes, you have guessed it, I can finally acknowledge a distinct lack of taste. Joking apart, the side effects of being radiated daily in the narrow area of neck and back of tongue inevitably are discombobulating. Losing sense of taste and ulcers agogo are the principal ones, but the medications prescribed by my chief oncologist, Dr Lemon, are pretty much keeping me in check. First there was Mr Kumar (at No. 42), then Dr Chiu when I first couldn't swallow, and now a citrus fruit that would kill the back of my throat – ha! – don't you just love the names!!

This week I have started using my 'second mouth' to feed myself. Since last weekend I have mostly been eating/drinking the nutritional "feed" that they provide, given that my appetite has taken a leave of absence and my throat is almost too sore to swallow anything solid. These drinks are going to be my lifeline over the coming weeks so I will grow to love/hate them. 'Ensure' is the brand name and they will 'ensure' that I stay nourished AND don't lose too much weight so that my mask will still fit me, and I will still be able to continue the treatments.

The 'kadunk' at the end of each session of radiotherapy is becoming a hugely welcome sound, as you can imagine.

Thankfully as each day goes by, the end of the six weeks of treatment nudges a little closer!

I'll report back in a couple of weeks, dear chaps.

Much love,
   Mike & Natalie xxx

Email 8

21/6/18

Dear family & friends,

As I write this I have only seven more radiotherapy sessions left – finishing next Friday 29th – seven more mask wearing, whirring, kadunking sessions and the sense of relief that that date is so close is palpable! Obviously we will have to wait for a few weeks afterwards to find out whether those pesky cancer cells have been eradicated but fingers, toes etc will be firmly crossed.

As I reported in my last email I am feeding myself entirely through 'mouth number two' – the PEG tube – and mostly it is working well, 'mouth number one' is still being used for water and two or three cups of tea though everything ends up tasting like salt. Enjoying food and drink, regaining taste and being able to swallow proper food should all come back during my eight to twelve week recovery period.

This past week has had two major points to share with you.
   1: My wonderful girls, Lillie & Meg and their two boys,

Alex and David came over to us to celebrate Father's Day on Sunday. What I wasn't expecting was them bringing a flying shark with them! It was really quite bizarre and brilliant all at the same time. (Those of you who know Natalie's maternal family's connection with the Graf Zeppelin will be extra fascinated by this!!)

A real highlight!

2: A new side effect rather banjaxed me from Sunday evening through to Wednesday morning – major bunging up of the nether regions. Suffice to say, and sparing you the grisly details, a number of laxatives, suppositories and one enema later I am back to just dealing with the expected side effects of the radiotherapy. Oncology team at Mount Vernon continue to be amazing in their care, though…

Have to admit the last few days have not been the best, but having Natalie by my side has truly made the difference that keeps my spirits high.

I'll write again at the end of next week when that countdown to the end of treatment has got to the magic ZERO!!!

Your messages of support and love, cajoling and figuratively cuddling us do make all the difference. Dixon is going to get through this, dear chaps.

All love,
  Mike & Natalie xxx

Email 9
30/6/18

Dear Chaps,

So, rather emotionally, I have come to the end of my *Treatment* – a strange word, isn't it! I don't feel like I have had that many *treats* over the last six weeks but if the thirty radiotherapy sessions do what they say on the tin then my *treats* are yet to come! I will keep you posted as to progress on that front. Initially it is just weekly clinic sessions with my Oncologist but at some point I will be scanned etc and then I will know how well it has all worked.

Whilst I've been going through the last six weeks of the daily mask donning, the whirring machinations and finally the 'kadunk', my own brand of mindfulness has kicked in. I have had two very strong thoughts that I would focus on whilst trussed up. One musical and the other spatial.

The Musical Mike: A piece I discovered when I was about 13 by a little known French composer called Gabriel Grovlez. Written in 1911 and called *Petite Litanies de Jésus*. Simply a perfect piece. I think that if pressed I would have to say that this would go with me to that Desert Island on BBC Radio 4!!

The Spatial Mike: A walk with Natalie from the door of our caravan in Cornwall, out to the beautiful cliffs and sea at Fox Cove, and the view from the seat we put there in memory of my dear Dad. (If you look really carefully you may just see Captain Poldark and Demelza in the distance....)

These two things have got me through!

You have been so kind over these past months, dear chaps, a heartfelt thank you for all your kind words and thoughts from both of us.

Tomorrow I start my road to recovery and I will keep you posted.

All love,
    Mike & Natalie xxx

PS They did ask if I wanted to take home the mask, I am sure that you can understand that I declined…..

Email 10

6/7/18

Dearest family and friends,

Just a quick follow up to the last Kadunk…..

Sadly recovery is not instantaneous in this jolly journey and in all honesty, this week has been the most difficult of the whole 'living with and aiming to defeat cancer' adventure with all the side effects kicking in big time.

Today our lovely head and neck specialist nurse, Leah, who is incidentally about as teeny as anyone could be, had to look at the burning around my neck. Unfortunately some of it had opened up and I needed some pretty instant medication. She made me a choir boy ruff of special wound dressing. Oh, For The Wings of a Dove, anyone?

The tide should turn over the next week or so, however I should expect to be using the PEG tube (my second mouth) for the next few weeks as my throat very slowly heals.

Your messages of support and love are brilliant – a real tonic. Hoping to make it a proper Gin & Tonic in the not too distant future. Meanwhile, good luck to England on Saturday, & to Lewis Hamilton on Sunday!

All our love,
  Mike & Natalie xxx

Email 11

13/7/18

Dear friends & family,

End of week 2 post-treatment, and a positive corner has been turned. We saw one of my brilliant Oncology team earlier in the week and even though the side effects are strong and unpleasant he was extremely pleased with my progress. So much so that when Natalie and I mentioned that we were so looking forward to going to our Cara in Cornwall as soon as possible, he positively encouraged us to, and said the team wouldn't need to see me for another 2 weeks!

So yesterday Natalie drove us down and in the afternoon I did the little walk to my Dad's seat, the very walk that had sustained me during my treatment and yes, of course I had a little toot once I got there. It felt like a real step forward, though, and here is the proof!

My neck burns are very quickly getting better so, hopefully, gradually all the similar wounds inside my mouth and throat will follow suit.

Positive Mike is on the way back and these coming few days will be such a tonic that I won't even miss the gin!

The next significant hurdle will be attempting to eat instead of using my tummy tube but that is a few weeks off, I fear, but, you never know.

So much love and thanks to all of you.
      Mike & Natalie xxx

Email 12

20/7/18

Dear family and friends,

As I said in my last email – positive Mike is on the way back – and I am so pleased to be able to report to you that a HUGE hurdle has been leapt over. On Wednesday 16th I didn't use my PEG (Tummy) tube at all. I managed to eat almost normal food! Cottage Pie with lashings of gravy to make it wet enough for my dry mouth and so on. My Oncology team wanted me to eat Creme Caramels and Mousses this week but when I see them on Monday I will be able to say "Get thee gone, tummy tube, get thee gone!!". So I really hope that I see Doctor Chiu (Chew), can't think why?!? Not sure when they can take the tube out but I hope that it is soon as I continue this process of healing both inside and outside. The nasty burns on my neck are all healed and shaving is now very easy as I only have bristles on my sideburns, top lip and a few wisps of white in the centre of my chin – one side effect that is not horrible – yay!!! Swallowing is still difficult but with a little medication and determination it is possible, as I am now proving, and I can taste a little of what I eat. Nothing citrus or spicy to be attempted for a little while, though!

Our week in Cornwall has truly helped make this happen. The power of Trethias is a bit like having 'the force' with you and I feel a bit like Luke Skywalker. Obviously the young, vibrant one from the original Star Wars movies not the old one from the latest film! Here I am enjoying a Bacardi & Lucozade, light sabre safely tucked away!

Trethias is the name of the farm where our caravan sits, and when we had Dad's seat put in place, we wanted a fitting plaque to remember him by. My dear Dad had a favourite saying whenever it was cloudy, misty, drizzly or mizzly (which was and is generally a fair amount of the time) and that phrase was "It's liftin'!"

He was such a positive soul!

Obviously the resonance that the phrase has with me, particularly at the moment, is quite strong as I definitely feel that the fug of the last few weeks is indeed '*liftin*' for me! Slowly but surely.

Natalie and I aim to get back down there as soon as we are able. Hopefully we can go next week after the Oncologist Clinic, and, if the Tummy tube has been taken out, in a few days I will be able to get in the sea for a gentle surf. That would be fantabulosa! (I will be sensible, promise)

Thank you again and again for all your kind words and thoughts and we hope that all is as it should be in your many lives.

All our love,
 Mike & Natalie xxx

Email 13

24/7/18

Dear and lovely peeps,

I thought that you would like to know that Natalie and I had a simply amazing meeting with chief oncologist, Dr Lemon, on Monday. She was really pleased with my progress and I have now been given the sign off for 3/4 weeks! Yesterday morning my 2nd mouth, the PEG feeding tube, was removed and this morning we drove back down to Cornwall to continue the rest and recuperation in this most special of places! Also, from Saturday, I have been given the green light to go surfing again as the wound in my tummy should be sufficiently healed.

Here is a little picture – I have just eaten (admittedly with extra gravy to ease the dry mouth) a whole Barnecutt's Cornish Pasty – and you can see I'm nearly all the way through a pint of Doom Bar. I can't quite believe how well my recovery is going – it must be that all the positive thoughts from you wonderful friends and family are mixing up with the positivity of my dear Dad's '*It's liftin'!*' maxim to fix me in double quick time!

All I need now is my throat to fully recover, and the hair to grow back on my chin and at the back of head.

The scans to find out whether all of this treatment has been successful will be in early September so fingers crossed until then, dear chaps.

Thank you and lots of love,
 Mike & Natalie xx

Email 14

27/8/18

Dear family and friends,

I thought that you would like to know that I am back on the bike! I have just returned from Holland where over the last couple of days I have played two concerts with my dear friends, *The New London Chorale*. Lance Ellington, Jenna Lee James, Janet Mooney and Gordon Neville – classical crossover par excellence! It is my 5th year with them and we had a really good time!

Natalie became an honorary member as she was there with me, making sure I didn't overdo things as one of the remaining side effects is fatigue. Gradually I am getting stronger but I do have to be patient. I certainly couldn't stand in front of an orchestra, waving away for a three hour rehearsal and a two hour concert yet but working as I did at the weekend with four brilliant singers, a Gospel Choir and a mixture of backing tracks and me playing live piano was the best way possible to get me back in that jolly old saddle!

Henk v/d Reep with permission

My road to recovery is continuing well and though I've had a couple of dips basically the trajectory is very much upwards & onwards.

In a nutshell:

Taste – around 70% (No wine yet but Aperol Spritz has finally replaced Bacardi & Lucozade! Oh, and Elderflower Pimms is good – thank you, Phil White!)

Whiskers – still zero below my chin and still the comedy bald patches at the back of my head. Shaving is really easy so NOT a hardship.

Saliva glands – 10% so still very much 'dry mouth', continuing to need copious amounts of water to keep moist.

Back of throat & swallow – gradually much more like normal, which is brilliant. Finally not feeling like I'm sword swallowing!

Overall, eating is still a chore and I'm never quite sure if I am going to like the food in front of me. A Barnecutt's pasty and a pint of Doom Bar always hits the spot, though.

Late September I will meet with my surgeon – Mr Kumar (at No. 42) – and also have the PET scan. They like to wait for twelve weeks after the end of treatment, apparently, so not as soon as I thought, but then I should find out how well the radiotherapy worked and given that my saliva glands are still shot to bits I have high hopes that the cancer cells have been as well!

Thank you for all your so very kind thoughts and sending much love,

    Mike & Natalie xx

Email 15

14/9/18

Dear friends and family,

Your continued support and very kind messages are so much a part of my therapy on this journey. Thank you. Natalie and I take strength from so many kind words almost daily!

Most of the time on this journey my resolve has stayed firm and even when, early post treatment, I was at my physical worst, I stayed positive. Every so often, though, something happens to challenge that resolve and over the last few weeks I have had a bout of oral thrush which is proving to be a bit of a trial. I'm now on my third different set of drugs for it and though it is a small side effect of the radiotherapy it has completely knocked my appetite for six and I am having to rely on drinking my Ensure nutritional drinks (which I injected when I had the tummy tube) to get enough calories inside me. I have good and bad days with it and yesterday wasn't one of the better ones. Of course that followed a particularly brilliant day when I had a Production Meeting for the forthcoming *Miss World* and a meeting with composer, Mike Woolmans and director, Michael Strassen where we were plotting to take over the West End with Woolmans' new film noir musical that we hope to get produced some time next year. Not quite a 'taking small steps' sort of day, but it did my 'looking to the future' a power of good. Hopefully the thrush will be flying away very soon. I'm certainly fed up with it fluttering around at the back of my mouth!

I am going to have to be very careful over the next few months that I don't overdo things and though life/work is about to become busy, both of my forthcoming projects are headed up by people who understand and have big hearts. First of all I go into rehearsals for *Doctor Dolittle* (24th Sep – 7th Nov) which will be very exciting, with Mark Williams (*Father Brown* and Ron Weasley's dad in all the *Harry Potter* movies) as the Doctor, and then I fly to China for *Miss World* (8th Nov – 9th Dec). Julia Morley has very kindly enabled Natalie to come with me so I will have my own personal Miss World at my side! Then my dear friends, Nathan Wright and Andrew Bevis, are putting on a new version of *Aspects of Love* in Sydney (I passed on some of my knowledge of the show a few months ago) and so from 10th to 17th December Natalie and I will have a few days holiday there and support the show at the same time! Small steps…?

I had my big PET/CT scan last Friday – the joy of being radioactive for 10 hours – and I meet with Mr Kumar (at No 42) on 27th September to get the results and generally review progress and, to that end, everything remains crossed that can be!

I will let you know the results as soon as possible, in the meantime here's a picture from last weekend – Natalie and I dressed up for The Goodwood Revival Meeting!

Sending huge hugs to one and all and much love,
Mike & Natalie xxx

Email 16

27/9/18

Dear lovely family and friends,

So today I saw Mr Kumar for the results of the PET/CT Scan from 7th Sep.
As predicted by Dr Lemon (my Oncologist) there is still some activity in both the back of my tongue and the lymph node in my neck, so I am not quite clear of the cancer yet. I will have more tests mid December, when Natalie and I get back from China and Sydney, but in the meantime I will see Mr Kumar on 8th November for another regular check up.

Now, though this is not the best news, Mr Kumar and his team were really pleased with my recovery generally. He had a good poke around my mouth and neck and told me that he thought the thrush had ceased its warbling and had already migrated to pastures new. So I'm to stop the thrush treatment and hopefully my appetite will gradually resume, and I must now get myself to full steam ahead on the eating front.

They were also very pleased to hear that I had started work on *Doctor Dolittle* and *Miss World* with the proviso that I listen to my body and don't fall foul of the dreaded fatigue. Many of you have highlighted this to me, so I promise I will be careful and will rest when I need to!

Here's a little snap of me with Mark Williams – our *Doctor Dolittle* – when we had our first music call a couple of weeks ago. He is going to be brilliant!

Much love to all,
    M&N xx

Email 17

8/11/18

Greets to all friends and family,

My Cancer Adventure continues and in the past week I have had a further ultra sound guided biopsy of the lymph gland in my neck and today a catch up with my Consultant team at Northwick Park Hospital.

Nutritionists Hannah & Christine were very pleased with my progress – the loss of both appetite and the will to eat may last for up to two years – but overall I am doing well so I will take that and build on it!

Mr Kumar was very late – emergency surgery delayed him by 2 hours. So eventually we saw a Dr T Wildon (Registrar) who said that the result of the biopsy was inconclusive but was nothing to worry about. More scans and appointments to come.

So, though Natalie and I were hoping to be able to report more positive news at least we know that I am continuing in the right direction. My stamina and strength is improving every day and I think the whole process of rehearsals for *Doctor Dolittle* have been hugely good for me in making me feel human and normal again – though the word normal may be a bit of a misnomer in my case!!

Sunday evening Natalie and I fly to Sanya, China to join my *Miss World* family and I will post an update in two or three weeks of how things are going there. Natalie heaved a huge sigh of relief this afternoon when, after I had set off again for *Dolittle* rehearsals, she went back to the Chinese embassy to pick up her visa and all was well.

Huge thanks, again, to all of you for your continuing kindness and your positive thoughts which help us considerably.

Much love,
    Mike & Natalie xxx

At ITV a couple of weeks ago...Dolittle from 1998 (Phillip Schofield) and our 2018 incarnation!

Email 18

9/12/18

Dear Family and Friends,

Well, being on a Tropical Island with 118 Miss World Contestants – and Natalie, my very own Miss World – has proved to be a great tonic on my road to recovery! I am pleased to report that my energy levels, ability to eat and general wellbeing have all improved significantly over these last four weeks here on Hainan Island.

It is a tough schedule on *Miss World* but last night the culmination of our time here was a triumphant crowning of our new Miss World, Vanessa Ponce from Mexico, at the end of a three hour live TV Broadcast which was beamed to well over a hundred countries world-wide!

Tomorrow we fly to Sydney and we see the lovely new production of *Aspects of Love* – and have a little bit of a holiday – before returning to UK on 18th December.

The dark days of feeling the worse for wear during and after my treatment are now dim and distant memories. It is amazing how your mind has this filter to get rid of those difficult times and that you are able to gently forget, really quite quickly, how bad things were only five months ago! The power of positive thinking and great friends and family are also huge contributing factors in this – so thank you one and all!

Sending much love,
    Mike & Natalie xxx

Email 19

31/1/19

Dear chaps & chapesses,

Fantabulosa News!!!

Today Mr Kumar's registrar (called Mr Tun – but sounds like 'tongue') gave us the best possible news. The results of last week's biopsy in my neck show that there are NO remaining cancer cells. He also put a camera down through my nose to look at my tongue and completed his examination smiling, so I think it is now just carrying on getting over the treatment and side effects!

We were not expecting such a conclusive result nor could I possibly explain the mix of emotions that have filled us throughout the day. Suffice to say we are both mighty relieved and full of even more gratitude to our NHS and to you, dear friends & family, for your continued support & healing love.

Check ups will continue, to make sure I stay on the road to recovery but in the meantime here we are celebrating with a glass of very fine bubbly!

With all love,
    Mike & Natalie xx

SIXTEEN

AND THERE'S MORE...

My recovery from the cancer came in fits and starts and by the end of 2019 I was pretty much back to normal. I think it is usually the case that building back to full strength cannot be rushed, however psychologically I was probably always at least three months ahead of the physical.

Doctor Dolittle was not a success and early in 2019 the tour had to close. Yet again a lot of very fine young performers were suddenly without work eleven months short of their contract. I won't dwell on the reasons but it's enough to say it simply didn't work as well as it should have. Jen Green's orchestrations of my musical arrangements were magical and the company gave it their best shot. My Musical Director and Assistant Musical Director were Josh Sood and Katy Richardson – two young up and coming musical talents – and they are now both looked after by my agent, Bronia, destined for greatness.

Somehow there is always something lurking round the corner and this time it came from Irish theatrical producer Pat Moylan. She is a tour de force and particularly well known for producing the celebrated play by Marie Jones, *Stones in his Pockets*. She told me that she had been working on a new musical based on Frank McCourt's *Angela's Ashes*, which had been a hugely successful Alan Parker film. The musical had a run in 2017 but for 2019 they wanted to revamp the music hence the call to me. It was written by Adam Howell and Paul Hurt and was full of really very good songs.

With Thom Southerland directing and Ste Clough looking after the movement it was certainly a quality product. Thom is a director with huge potential, soft spoken, kind and yet with a very firm knowledge of what he wants. He also possesses an almost encyclopaedic memory of British musical theatre and Ste and he worked magnificently together. Angela was played by my friend from the 1993 version of *Aspects of Love*, Jacinta Whyte. Since that tour of *Aspects* we had also worked together on a couple of *Friday Night is Music Night* concerts and I therefore knew what a magnificent choice she was for the role. Eoin Cannon was Frank McCourt and it was as if the part had been created for him – sometime narrator and sometime young urchin growing up. Between the two of them and the brilliant Irish supporting cast it was such a great meld of comedic musical talent.

There was an unfortunate disconnect in the music team though and I was tasked with making that work. Pat told me that she had originally wanted a young Musical Director called David Hayes but in 2017 he hadn't been available. I interrupted her with a, "You mean David Hayes who looked after the music for *Riverdance* for years?" "Yes," she replied, quizzically. "He is brilliant," I replied, "please can we get him on board for this version?" Well, I am very pleased to say that he was able to be involved and on our first meeting in London, where I had assembled the music team together with Thom to try to undo some of the patently destructive disconnection that there was, David turned to me and said, "Mike, you probably don't remember but when you did *Eurovision* at The Point back in 1995 I was a young musical assistant on the show and I knew who you were and you were really kind to me when I spoke to you, and I've never forgotten that." I was taken aback, I did remember a young chap but I hadn't made the connection.

Now, of course, all was clear. He had wanted to work with me as much as I had wanted to work with him – a bromance was born! There followed a blissful few weeks of working; new arrangements and routines that we did together with David then orchestrating for a properly authentic band with great Irish musicians and a wunderkind Irish sound designer, Jason Fallon.

I loved the rehearsals in Dublin and though the tour was quite a short one there has been some gentle mumbling that the show will rise after the pandemic has subsided. It certainly deserves to – it is a rich tapestry of emotion and a truly worthy piece. David and I have kept very much in touch and just before lockdown in Feb 2020 I spent a few days working with him at CIT Cork School of Music where he is running a terrific Musical Theatre course and lectures in Popular Music, whatever that is...

After *Angela* there was a corporate event that was quite large in scale. The history of British pop music in one hour using a symphony orchestra, six singers and a video DJ! I put together the sequence of the greatest songs along with our Video DJ – Beat a Maxx – and then dear Jen orchestrated the lot. Throughout the project, which was curated by Brands at Work, I had Katy Richardson as my assistant and I was able to mine her knowledge of contemporary pop music to great effect. Annie Skates led the singers and in the course of the piece she was able to give us her absolutely amazing Kate Bush impersonation. We performed this mammoth piece in a one thousand seat marquee in the grounds of a country estate near Reading and we couldn't have had a better reaction! It was a huge success. Although this was a once only event we are talking about creating a concert series out of it and who knows, it may just work!

There have been a few pilot TV shows over the course of my career that have come and gone. All of them would have been interesting to do if they had been made into series but who knows?

Amongst them I did a version of *The Generation Game* with Paul O'Grady, *Name That Tune* with Bill Bailey and how about *Lost In Music* with Aled Jones, Bradley Walsh, Sheila Ferguson, Toyah Willcox and Barry McGuigan. The fun and frolic of the business!

*

I am proud to have been involved to a greater or lesser extent in three of the best orchestrators' careers. Steve Sidwell, Chris Egan and Jen Green have at various times worked alongside me and they have each written some amazingly inventive and stunning orchestrations for some of my projects. The fact that they all have forged ahead with stunning careers is not because of me, I hasten to add, it is simply because they are the best!

I am also very proud that I have been part of the burgeoning careers of Richard Beadle, Matt Smith, Barney Ashworth, Francis Goodhand, Stuart Morley, Josh Sood and Katy Richardson. Each one of them has musical talent in spades and I am pretty sure that if I were one of those jolly 'turns' on stage I would be only too happy to have any of them in the pit in front of me. Go Team MD!

I also hope that the little bit of work I have done with Paul Tomkinson, Nick Hutson and Alexander Bermange over the years bears fruit for them sometime soon. They each have an individual musical voice and they each have great potential with the material that they are writing.

As far as my writing is concerned, there have been a couple of forays into writing a musical. The second one, *The Rocky Crusades,* I wrote with John Theakston back in 2001. It was a *Joseph* like look at the story of the Crusades and was about to have a little try out in Chiswick in 2003 when the US and allies invaded Iraq. We felt it would be expedient to postpone it.

In 2016 we did make a recording of one of the songs to raise money for Médecins sans Frontières. The song was called *Lament for the Innocents* and I asked Siobhan Athwal and Melanie Marshall, who had just been working on *The Infidel* with me, to sing the song. I think it actually sounds and looks pretty good.

My *3 Love Songs for Choir (To Love and be Beloved, O Mistress Mine, Desire)* were recorded by Chantage in 2012 and released on the album *My Promise* in 2015. Chantage had been the choir we used on the Elbow concert in Abbey Road and it was so kind of their conductor, James Davey, to suggest that they record those songs for me.

In the first lockdown of 2020 I spent an hour every day recording some of my favourite piano pieces. I released 15 of them as *Mike at the Piano – The LOCKDOWN Recordings* and they might not have got into the top ten but I did get a mention from Ken Bruce on BBC Radio 2 and quite a few plays on Scala Radio. More importantly I proved to myself that after all these years I can still play the piano a bit!

Glory be! As of writing in December 2021, I have gradually started to resume working after the end of Lockdown regulations. Firstly, *Angela's Ashes* was gently resurrected in Dublin and in

August 2021 we filmed the show in the Olympia Theatre. To be in a room with all those wonderful musicians and actors making this happen, after what everyone had been through during the worst of the pandemic, was simply mesmerisingly gorgeous. The resulting film took a lot of time and effort from all involved but the results are stunning.

And secondly, another Anthony Cherry epic with the BBC Concert Orchestra, but this time in Malta at the Granaries Square, Valetta at the end of September 2021; with Tony Vincent, Carly Paoli, Tim Howar, Vanessa Haynes, Ashton Jones, Rachael Wooding, Annie Skates, Laura Tebbutt, David Combes and Steve Trowell singing and the legendary DJ Gary Davies presenting. The concert was called *It's A Kind Of Magic – The Queen Story* and along with a number of Queen hits we also played some of the music and songs that influenced Freddie, Brian, Roger and Deaky on their journey to mega-stardom: Liza Minelli's version of *Cabaret*, Hendrix's *All Along the Watchtower*, Led Zeppelin's *Rock and Roll* and even Prokofiev's *Dance of the Knights* from *Romeo and Juliet*! On a huge stage, with an uber rhythm section – Andy Jones and Dave Holmes on guitar, James Powell on drums, Andy Pask on bass and John G. Smith on keys – plus thousands of fireworks and a socially distanced crowd of 5,000, it was truly an event. An emotional reunion with Tony Vincent who had been our original Galileo in *We Will Rock You*, and also, as it was the first time for eighteen months that I had stood in front of the Concert Orchestra, I have to say that I felt more than apprehensive before the first rehearsal with them all. I needn't have worried, they all played with their usual panache and by the end of the concert the amount of joy coming back at me from them was utterly heart warming and humbling all at the same time. Back on the bike with a vengeance, if you like!

2021 It's A Kind Of Magic – The Queen Story – in Malta
Daniel Balzan with permission – Daniel Balzan/ Koala Media Malta

2021 With Tony Vincent and Anthony Cherry after the gig!

But what does the future hold? Well, future projects that are being talked about include:

Sammy, a new musical looking at the life of Sammy Davis Jnr by Leslie Bricusse. Directed by Clarke Peters and starring Giles Terera, it was one of the cancellations of 2020 and an early casualty of COVID. We did a workshop at the end of 2019 and had just finished the casting process in 2020 for a run at the Lyric Theatre Hammersmith when the first Lockdown hit. It may come back.

A Few Words With George, a project that was with Leslie from around 1999. After a question from Liza Minnelli where she asked whether she could ever sing the great tune from Gershwin's *American in Paris* – the movie directed by her father, Vincente Minnelli – Leslie's reply was something along the lines of, "Well, why don't I put a lyric on it?" and that was the start of him writing full lyrics to *Rhapsody in Blue, American in Paris, The Cuban Overture,* the *Concerto in F* and the *Prelude in C-sharp minor.* Leslie talked me through the project in 2010 and we did create a small workshop in 2011 but the whole project was never complete. Leslie's Musical Director, Ian Fraser, died in 2014 and so early in 2020 I worked with Jen Green to complete the arrangements that Ian had started. It now exists for Soloists, Choir and Two Pianos and we hope to get it off the ground in some way or other over the next couple of years. It will be a great legacy to dear Leslie if we do!

Man comma Woman. Mike Woolmans, composer of the theme music for the Jerry Springer chat show, Michael Strassen, director in the ascendancy, and I have been working gently on this piece written by Woolmans as a two hander. There is a lot of originality in it and maybe, just maybe we will get it produced. Woolmans' material is definitely worthy of production.

Craigberoch, a really innovative project set up by Gib Bulloch author of *The Intrapreneur: Confessions of a Corporate Insurgent.*

His vision with his Decelerator Labs is to enable people to meet, virtually or in person, to find ways to pull back from their hectic corporate lives and to then find new ways to create, empower and nurture a thriving global community of innovators and activists. Performance will play a big part in all this and we are currently exploring how we can make it work, as we all know music gets such amazing emotional responses, so let's see what we can do.

It could be a fascinating new future.

And then there is Dirk Maggs – we have nearly worked together a few times over the years and maybe, just maybe in the future there is a little project that isn't attached to a blanket and doesn't have the words 'don't panic' written on it that brings us together. I live in hope.

EPILOGUE

HAPPY WITH MY LOT

Music has been part of me for so long and in all its rich forms it has influenced, coloured and shaped my whole life in a wonderful way.

I've been excited, scared, intimidated, exhilarated, frozen, frustrated, proud, delirious, desperate, passionate, demonstrative, maddened, spiritual, hysterical, brave, cowardly, challenged, tearful, happy, adored and content through music.

I started life craving attention, happy to play the fool and gradually as my faith in music strengthened so did my faith in people.

To all the humungously talented musicians I have had the great fortune to work with over all these years – thank you.

To all the actors and performers, again – thank you, and the producers, directors, choreographers, writers, composers, orchestrators, sound designers, studio engineers and technical support. You are all amazing.

It sounds so sentimental to say this but it is heartfelt. My life so far has been a roller coaster ride, but one of those rides where you scream in utter disbelief as much as being scared. Where your heart is in your mouth and then in your stomach but it's always exhilarating and you never know what will happen around the next corner.

I also want to use this place in the book to say a special thank you to Natalie. Constant, loving, understanding, entertaining, supportive, challenging and funny. All in one gorgeous little package.

Lillie and Meg – you continually make me proud to be your Dad. You both have talent in abundance and you are two fine human beings. How could I not be proud!

Mike Dixon 2022

DISCOGRAPHY

1982 *Andy Capp - West End Cast Recording*
Piano
The Point Recording Studio, Victoria, London

1983 *Mr Cinders - Revival London Cast Recording*
Piano
Angel Studios, Islington, London

1984 *Bobby Crush - First Love*
Synthesiser
President Records

1989 *Mack the Knife - Original Soundtrack Recording*
Vocal Conductor and Assistant Musical Director
CTS Studios, Wembley, London

1989 *Aspects of Love - Original Cast Recording*
Synthesiser
Olympic Studios, Barnes, London

1989 *Tell Me On a Sunday - Julian Lloyd Webber, RPO, Barry Wordsworth*
Piano
CBS Studios, Whitfield Street, London
[On Julian Lloyd Webber Plays Andrew Lloyd Webber Album]

1991 *Joseph and the Amazing Technicolor Dreamcoat*
Conductor
Westfield Studios, London

1992 *Tierra!!! (Expo 1992) – RPO*
Conductor
Abbey Road Studios (Studio 1)

1992 *Flor de Nit – Dagoll Dagom – Wren Orchestra*
Conductor
Abbey Road Studios (Studio 2)

1993 *Grease – Original London Cast Recording*
Conductor
Whitfield Street Studios, London

1994 *Grease – Raimund Theater, Vienna*
Co-Producer and Conductor
MG Studios, Vienna

1995 *Grease – German Version*
Producer
Powerplay Studios, Switzerland

1996 *Jesus Christ Superstar*
Conductor
Whitfield Street, CTS, Metropolis, Olympic Studios

1996 *Evita – The Motion Picture Soundtrack*
Conductor
Abbey Road Studios (Studio 2)

1997 *Steven Houghton Album*
Conductor
Sony Studios, Whitfield Street, London

1997 *The Heart Is Slow To Learn – Kiri Te Kanawa*
Conductor
Abbey Road Studios (Studio 1)

1998 *Doctor Dolittle – World Premiere London Cast Recording*
Producer
The Pierce Rooms and Hammersmith Apollo Theatre

2002 *We Will Rock You – Original London Cast Recording*
Conductor/Piano
The Dominion Theatre

2002 *Party at the Palace – We Will Rock You Segment*
Conductor/Piano
Buckingham Palace

2002 *Seven – A Suite for Orchestra by Tony Banks*
Conductor
Air Lyndhurst, Lyndhurst Hall

2005 *Doo-be-doo – Vocal Warm-ups*
Producer & Composer
Jaspar's Studio, Rayners Lane

2006 *Daddy Cool – London Musical Cast*
Musical Supervisor
Metropolis Studios and The Shaftesbury Theatre

2008 *Act One – Songs from the Musicals of Alexander S. Bermange*
Co-Producer
Winterbrook Studios, London

2008 *Zorro The Musical – Original Cast Recording*
Musical Supervisor
The Garrick Theatre

2009 *Elbow & the BBC Concert Orchestra – The Seldom Seen Kid Live*
Conductor
Abbey Road Studios (Studio 1)

2009 *The Performance – Dame Shirley Bassey*
Vocal Producer
Air Lyndhurst, London and the Grouse Lodge, Ireland

2009 *Zorro The Musical – French Version*
Co-Producer
Folies Bergère and Apollo Studio, Paris

2011 *Helena Blackman – The Sound of Rodgers & Hammerstein*
Conductor and Producer
Angel Studios, Islington, London

2012 *Chantage – My Promise (3 Love Songs for Choir)*
Composer
St Jude's Church, Hampstead Garden Suburb, London

2013 *There's No Silent Night – Paul Tomkinson*
Producer
Ryan Martin's Studio

2014 *The Route To Happiness – Alexander S. Bermange*
Producer
Auburn Jam Studio

2016 *Mrs Henderson Presents – Original London Cast Recording*
Conductor
Angel Studios and Air Lyndhurst Studio 1

2016 *Lament For the Innocents – Siobhan Athwell & Melanie Marshall*
Composer and Producer
Resident Studios, London

2016 *Wit and Whimsy – Songs by Alexander S. Bermange*
Producer
Resident Studios, London

2019 *The Shores of Normandy – Jim Radford*
Piano/Co-Arranger
Tileyard Studios, London

2019 *La Bamba – Fernando & Adán Allende*
Vocal Producer
Abbey Road Studios, The Front Room

2020 *Mike at the Piano – The Lockdown Recordings*
Piano/Producer
Grange Cottage

2020 *Meg Rose-Dixon – Sunday Lockdown*
Producer/Piano
Grange Cottage

ABOUT THE AUTHOR

Photograph Daniel Balzan with permission –
Daniel Balzan / Koala Media Malta

Mike Dixon has been involved in the British music industry since late 1979 and has been Musical Director for more than twenty West End productions as well as a huge number of high profile television and radio concerts.

His career has taken him from London to China, via Los Angeles, Moscow and Azerbaijan, and he has worked with some of the most iconic artists of the 20th and 21st centuries, including Dame Shirley Bassey, Sir Elton John, Lionel Richie, Sir Tom Jones, Lady Gaga and Queen.

Born in Plymouth in 1957, he trained at Trinity College of Music in London and has become one of the most versatile and sought after Musical Directors in the music business.